Gas Price Arbitrations

A Practical Handbook

Consulting Editor **Mark Levy**

Consulting editor
Mark Levy

Managing director
Sian O'Neill

Editorial services director
Carolyn Boyle

Production manager
Paul Stoneham

Group publishing director
Tony Harriss

Gas Price Arbitrations: A Practical Handbook
is published by
Globe Law and Business
Globe Business Publishing Ltd
New Hibernia House
Winchester Walk
London SE1 9AG
United Kingdom
Tel +44 20 7234 0606
Fax +44 20 7234 0808
Web www.globelawandbusiness.com

Printed by Gomer Press

ISBN 9781905783779

Table of contents

Foreword

Professor Jonathan Stern
Oxford Institute for Energy Studies

These are interesting times for gas pricing and particularly for prices in long-term gas contracts. With the exception of North America (and to some extent the United Kingdom), long-term (15-30 year) contracts between domestic producers and exporters, and national or regional utilities provided the basis for the establishment and the initial decades of the gas industry's growth, particularly in continental European and Asian liquefied natural gas (LNG) importing countries. Prices in these contracts were wholly or mainly based on and indexed to crude oil and oil products. The price clauses in these contracts were complex and relatively rigid; adjustments to prices when market conditions changed were relatively slow (between three and nine months). Related to the pricing arrangements was the take-or-pay clause included in the majority of long-term contracts, which requires the buyer to pay for a specified minimum quantity of the annual contract quantity of gas at the contract price, whether or not that volume of gas was taken.

This contractual and price structure was designed for a world in which gas was being established in energy markets and its future was uncertain. Buyers had a monopoly (or at least a dominant) position in their markets which was supported either explicitly or implicitly by national, regional and local governments. Official prices of oil and gas were slow to be reported and had virtually no transparency. This is very different from the liberalised and competitive markets which are now either established or being pursued in many countries, and real time trading and pricing on spot markets and exchanges communicated worldwide on a continuous basis.

While this inflexibility caused some problems in the decades before the mid-2000s, over the past five years the situation has become substantially more difficult because of rapid changes in oil prices and the globalisation of gas markets, which increasingly means that movements in the supply, demand and prices of gas (and other energy commodities) in different regions have much more immediate impacts on gas prices than previously. Examples of such events between 2007and 2012 have been:

- the unexpectedly rapid development of unconventional (primarily shale) gas production in North America which caused Henry Hub prices to fall to much lower levels than had previously been thought possible, reducing US LNG imports to levels far below both expectations and existing import capacity, and raising the possibility of substantial US exports of LNG in the second half of the 2010s;
- the collapse in demand in the established LNG markets of Japan, Korea and Taiwan in 2009, followed by substantial recovery in the following year;

- the March 2011 Fukushima nuclear disaster in Japan, which significantly increased the demand for short-term LNG supplies in Japan on a sustained basis following the closure its nuclear power stations;
- the increase in crude oil prices to levels which, since the start of 2011, have been above $100 per barrel on a sustained basis;
- substantial fluctuations in international coal prices, which resulted in equivalent fluctuations in gas demand in the power generation sector;
- short-term power and carbon price movements that have led to changes in the 'spark spread' and 'dark spread' which have made gas-fired power generation relatively unattractive compared with coal-fired generation;[1]
- the emergence of significant new LNG markets in China, India, South East Asia, Latin America and the Middle East;
- the recession in Europe, which has been longer and deeper than expected, impacting on energy and gas demand, particularly when coupled with significant increases in renewable generating capacity; and
- political developments in (principally) North African countries (the 'Arab Spring') which curtailed gas exports from Libya for most of 2011.

These events have meant that, since 2008, the commercial environment for international gas trade has been subject to new (and increasingly difficult to predict) forces which have made it more difficult to comply with the relatively rigid oil-linked price formulae in long-term contracts. This resulted in significant financial difficulty for gas utilities in continental Europe and Japan due to a combination of high prices and competition from other gas supplies offered by new suppliers.

This has resulted in events never before seen in international gas commerce, with virtually all buyers seeking radical renegotiation of prices and a major increase in international arbitration, especially in continental Europe. By 2013 more than half of the gas sold in Europe was priced at hubs rather than based on oil products. In Asia, LNG importers began seeking alternatives to the Japan Crude Cocktail (JCC) price mechanism, with some new contracts being linked to US Henry Hub prices.

This book is extremely timely, as long-term gas contracts and prices are undergoing a fundamental change from the old world to a much more uncertain new world, and the issues in the chapters are becoming increasingly urgent for buyers and sellers to address.

Jonathan Stern is chairman and a senior research fellow at the Natural Gas Research Programme of the Oxford Institute for Energy Studies. He is also honorary professor at the Centre for Energy, Petroleum and Mineral Law and Policy, University of Dundee; visiting professor at Imperial College's Centre for Environmental Policy in London; part-time BP professor at the Moscow School of Management's Energy Centre at Skolkovo; and a fellow of the Energy Delta Institute. Since 2011 he has been the EU speaker for the EU-Russia Gas

---

1 The spark spread is the theoretical gross margin of a gas-fired power plant from selling a unit of electricity, having bought the fuel required to produce this unit of electricity. The dark spread refers to the similarly defined margin for coal-fired power plants.

Advisory Council. He is the author of several books and many shorter works on energy and natural gas issues in the United Kingdom, Europe (western and eastern), the former Soviet Union and Asia. His most recent edited book is The Pricing of Internationally Traded Gas, *published by Oxford University Press in 2012.*

Drafting an effective price review clause

Mark Levy
Allen & Overy LLP

The other chapters in this book identify a range of issues that can arise both before and during the course of a price review arbitration. This chapter draws together the various strands and considers why those issues arise, the extent to which they are often the product of imperfect drafting and how the uncertainties that these issues create might be avoided.

1. The nature of pricing disputes

The focus of this book is on gas price review disputes. Disputes are, by their nature, unpredictable. Usually, at the outset of the parties' contractual relationship, no one knows whether a dispute will arise, when it will arise or what it will be about. However, price review clauses are rare creatures in the context of commercial agreements, in that they provide a structure which actively encourages parties to identify, on a periodic basis, a dispute which can then be referred to arbitration.

Different laws place different emphasis on the primacy of the contractual language. However, whatever the governing law, the ultimate purpose of any arbitral tribunal should be to apply the bargain to the dispute. Even if the parties' entire bargain is not to be found in the agreement itself, the terms of the agreement will invariably be highly determinative to the outcome. How the price review clause is drafted will therefore usually play a significant part in shaping how a tribunal resolves any price review dispute.

In their chapter on the future of price reviews, Paul Griffin and Frances von Eupen quite rightly identify a growing user dissatisfaction with arbitral awards in this area. The most common complaint appears to be that tribunals arrive at decisions which are divorced from the commercial reality of what those in the industry could possibly have intended or wished for. The most frequently cited example is the *Atlantic LNG* decision, where the tribunal appeared to reach a decision that neither party sought or wanted.[1] Specifically, the tribunal amended the price formula in a way that neither party had proposed. (*Atlantic LNG* became public only because it was challenged before US federal courts.) While there is some sympathy with this view, the *Atlantic LNG* tribunal could 'rewrite' the sale and purchase agreement (SPA) only because the price review clause afforded the tribunal wide discretion. In fact, in its decision confirming the *Atlantic LNG* award, the US federal court in New York

1 *Atlantic LNG Company of Trinidad & Tobago v Gas Natural Aprovisionamientos SDG SA,* UNCITRAL, Final Award dated January 17 2008.

expressly noted that, in the absence of any restrictions in the price review clause, the arbitral tribunal could amend the formula the way it wanted to.[2] Thus, if the parties clearly tell a tribunal what it must do and how it must do it, the tribunal is compelled to do as it is told. Tribunals meander off course because they are given scope to do so in the agreement.

There are various ways in which the parties can prevent tribunals from reaching unpredictable results. They can add strict parameters which, for example, limit the extent to which the tribunal can amend the price formula. Just as importantly, however, parties should pay attention to the drafting of the clause and provide as clear guidance to the tribunal as possible. It is remarkable how many disputes in this area, involving hundred of millions or even billions of dollars, arise out of, or even because of, vague and ambiguous drafting. It is true that once a dispute arises, ambiguity can be a lawyer's friend. It is also the case that parties sometimes consciously choose to leave open how a provision is to be applied. As a general rule, however, commercial parties going into a dispute crave certainty as to the result. Effective drafting can go a considerable way towards providing such certainty.

Part of the problem is that many current long-term agreements contain price review clauses which belong to a bygone era. As Tristram Kennedy Harper explains in his chapter on price reviews from the client's perspective, price review clauses first emerged before the days of gas-to-gas competition, when European gas was commonly priced by reference to a basket of competing alternative fuels. However, while the pricing dynamics in markets have changed, the contractual wording in many price review clauses has not kept pace. There is remarkable homogeneity in the drafting and current clauses still bear a lot of resemblance to those clauses that commentators such as Brautaset were commenting on 15 years ago.[3] To the extent that experienced industry negotiators are relying on an assumption that everyone in the industry understands what these terms mean, this is dangerous. Absent compelling evidence, there can be no confidence that a tribunal will respect that assumption, even if it is factually correct.

The days when complex European gas pricing disputes were determined by panels steeped in industry knowledge, through an informal and non-adversarial procedure, have largely disappeared. Today, these disputes are usually presided over by experienced commercial arbitrators. These tribunals are adept at considering contested complex factual evidence and applying those facts to the law, but will often have very little direct, or even indirect, experience of gas pricing. While there are some experienced gas pricing specialists who sit as arbitrators, they are few and far between. It is rare to find one pricing specialist on a panel, let alone two or three. The effect of this is that general commercial arbitrators are often being asked to grapple with concepts with which they have no familiarity or experience. That can lead to unpredictable results. That problem is exacerbated if they are making this decision within the context of ambiguous drafting.

---

2 *Atlantic LNG Company of Trinidad & Tobago v Gas Natural Aprovisionamientos SDG, SA,* 2008 WL 4344525 (SDNY September 16 2008).

3 A Brautaset, E Høiby, RO Pedersen and CF Michelet *Norsk Gassavsetning, Rettslige Hovedelementer (Norwegian Gas Sales, Principal Juridical Foundations)*, Sjørettsfondet, Oslo (1998).

The rest of this chapter considers some common drafting issues and provides thoughts on what steps parties might take at the contractual, and pre-contractual, stage either to avoid disputes arising or to strengthen their position in case disputes do arise.

2. Pre-contractual negotiations

Long-term gas agreements often follow lengthy pre-contractual negotiations. During these negotiations, there will invariably be at least a discussion regarding the terms of the price review clause. When a dispute emerges as to what the parties intend the clause to mean, it is not uncommon for one party to rely on these discussions to support the construction that it urges the tribunal to adopt.

The extent to which pre-contractual negotiations are admissible will be a matter of the governing law. For example, under English law, such evidence is generally considered inadmissible as to interpretation. A contract under English law is to be interpreted objectively, in order to ascertain the meaning which the document would convey to a reasonable person having all of the knowledge which would reasonably have been available to the parties at the time of the contract.[4] The determination is therefore conducted by taking into account evidence as to the factual background to the contract, provided that such evidence was reasonably available to the parties. However, it is an established principle that evidence of the previous negotiations of the parties and their declarations of subjective intent is inadmissible.[5]

However, even under English law, the window is not entirely closed to using such evidence. It may be used to support a claim of rectification or estoppel by convention.[6] Evidence of pre-contractual negotiations may also be admissible where the communications between the parties, including their pre-contractual negotiations, demonstrate that they habitually used words in an unconventional sense. This 'private dictionary' principle applies only where the meaning alleged is unconventional and cannot operate to choose between conventional alternatives.[7] Although this principle is narrow in scope, one can see how it might apply in the context of a price review clause, where parties sometimes adopt language which has a particular meaning to them, based on usage in the gas business, which differs from its conventional meaning.

Other laws are less restrictive as to the extent to which evidence of pre-contractual negotiations might be used. For example, under Dutch law, contract terms are to be interpreted by determining the meaning that the parties in the given circumstances could reasonably have given to them and what they could reasonably have expected from each other in that respect.[8] This determination is conducted by taking into account all relevant circumstances of the case,[9] including the pre-

4 *Investors Compensation Scheme Ltd* v *West Bromwich Building Society* [1998] 1 All ER 98 at 114.
5 *Ibid*, at 114-115.
6 *Chartbrook Ltd v Persimmon Homes Ltd* [2009] UKHL 38 at 42.
7 *Ibid*, at 45.
8 Dutch Supreme Court, March 13 1981, NJ 1981/635 (*Haviltex*).
9 Dutch Supreme Court, February 20 2004, NJ 2005/493 (*DSM/Fox*).
10 Dutch Supreme Court, January 13 1978, NJ 1978/302 (*Swimming Pool/Diligentia*) and Dutch Supreme Court, July 1 1982, NJ 1983/682 (*Codicil*).

contractual negotiations.[10] Correspondence exchanged between the parties during the negotiation of the agreement (emails, drafts of the agreement and minutes of the negotiation meetings), as well as witness testimony on what was discussed during the negotiations, can be relevant to the interpretation of a contract term and as such will be admissible evidence in a dispute about the construction of a contract term.

Similarly, under French law, contractual construction is closely related to the concept of the common intention of the parties. Where the wording of the contract is clear and precise, every contractual term must strictly be applied. However, where the wording of the contract is ambiguous, the judge should use the rules of construction set out in Articles 1156 to 1164 of the Civil Code.[11] According to Article 1156 of the code, "one must in agreements seek what the common intention of the contracting parties was, rather than pay attention to the literal meaning of the terms". In order to establish the common intention of the parties, French courts can take into account "external factors" such as the parties' behaviour before and after they entered into the contract, pre-contractual negotiations (especially when set out in pre-contractual documents),[12] letters exchanged between the parties before they entered into the contract[13] or previous agreements between the parties.[14] Pre-contractual negotiations can therefore play an important role in contractual construction.[15]

The position under New York law is somewhere between the two extremes. When a contract is unambiguous, a court or tribunal cannot consider extrinsic evidence (including evidence of pre-contractual negotiations) to interpret the contract terms. However, if a court or tribunal determines that specific contract language is ambiguous, it can consider evidence of the parties' negotiations, minutes from meetings, prior drafts of the agreement or fact witness testimony to explain the ambiguous contract term.[16] If a court or tribunal determines that a term of a contract is ambiguous, the parties may offer extrinsic evidence to explain the ambiguous contract term to show the objective intent of the parties.[17]

The extent to which pre-contractual negotiations may be admissible thus varies markedly, depending on the governing law. However, as can be seen above, even in jurisdictions where pre-contractual negotiations are not generally admissible, the door is often not entirely closed. Further, international arbitration tribunals tend to apply rules of evidence less strictly than courts. It is therefore not unheard of for a party to adduce evidence of pre-contractual negotiations before the tribunal if it believes that such evidence supports its case, even if the strict laws of evidence do not permit it. While a party on the receiving end of such evidence may wish to apply to the tribunal for an order that it be struck out as inadmissible, such orders are relatively rare (as the tribunal can direct itself to ignore the evidence), and a party may be reluctant to draw even more attention to the evidence by making such an application. Indeed, even if such an application succeeds, the damage may already

11 P Malaurie, L Aynès and P Stoffel-Munck, *Les obligations*, Defrénois, Paris, 3rd ed, §772.
12 French Court of Cassation, Civ 1, February 18 1986, *Bull Civ I*, No 31.
13 French Court of Cassation, Com, December 8 1987, *Bull Civ IV*, No 262.
14 French Court of Cassation, Soc, February 21 1957, *Bull Civ IV*, No 205.
15 F Terré, P Simle and Y Lequette, *Les obligations*, Dalloz, Paris, 10th ed, §189 *in fine* and §450.
16 *Chapman v NY State Div for Youth*, 546 F 3d 230, 236 (2d Cir 2008).
17 *WWF Paper Corp v Quinlan*, 00 Civ 0512 (LAK), 2001 US Dist. LEXIS 3444, at *3 (SDNY March 29 2001).

be done in terms of the impression made before the tribunal. Far better, therefore, at least to have the option of presenting cogent evidence which contradicts that which has been adduced (even if it is presented on the basis that it is without prejudice to the position that such evidence should be given no weight).

Given the relatively high chance that a price review clause will be the subject of a dispute, and that different versions will be put forward by the parties in any dispute as to what their intentions were, thought should be given by in-house counsel at the negotiating stage to this issue. At the very least, counsel should ensure that someone on the negotiating team keeps a full and legible[18] record of discussions regarding the clause and its negotiation history (including full meeting notes). It may also to be prudent to produce an agreed form of minutes, although in the frenzy of a deal completion, this may not be realistic.

3. Common drafting ambiguities

The same interpretational issues arise again and again in price review disputes. As noted above, part of this is due to the fact that same imperfect clauses seem to be reused as standard in long-term supply contracts. It is also often the case that a phrase or concepts whose meaning may seem 'obvious' to parties at the time of the commercial discussions can be anything but to a panel of arbitrators, particularly when faced with diametrically opposed accounts from counsel as to what was intended.

The following is a list – by no means exhaustive – of words or phrases which are often central to pricing disputes. Despite their importance, many of these phrases are capable of meaning different things to different parties and different tribunals. It is worth considering at the drafting stage what different arguments can be raised in respect of what these clauses mean, and whether it is sensible to close down these ambiguities by specific drafting. As noted above, the parties might consciously decide to leave these issues deliberately open, so as to leave open the scope for maximum flexibility (and argument) down the line. But in those instances, there needs to be a proper understanding of what the implications might be.

3.1 Trigger event

Although there is no 'standard' price review clause, one common feature of price review mechanisms is their periodic application. Because long-term SPAs can last for upwards of 20 years, they often allow either party to serve a price review notice every so many years (often three years). In addition, it is common for long-term SPAs to provide either party with a fixed number of 'wildcard' reviews, which can be used outside of the usual cycle and in special circumstances.

Irrespective of the number of times that the price review mechanism can be applied, normally to reopen the price, the requesting party must first show that a trigger event has occurred. The definition of a 'trigger event' can vary markedly across price review clauses. At one end of the spectrum is the Sonatrach-Distrigas SPA, which

18 Relying on handwritten notes can cause problems. By the time that the dispute arises, the author of the note may well have left the company, meaning that it may be very difficult to locate his or her notes and decipher them, even if they can be found.

provides that the parties will meet "every four years" to discuss revisions to the contract price. In other words, the trigger event occurs automatically with the passage of time and neither party need show anything more to establish entitlement to a price review.

At the other end of the spectrum are those price review clauses which require the requesting party to show that certain qualitative changes have taken place in the relevant market (eg, changes in economic circumstances) before the price can be reopened. The Atlantic LNG SPA is a good example in this regard. That SPA provided that the requesting party must show that:

> *economic circumstances in Spain beyond the control of the Parties, while exercising due diligence, have substantially changed as compared to what it reasonably expected when entering into this Contract ... and the Contract Price ... does not reflect the value of Natural Gas in the Buyer's end-user market.*

The wording of the Atlantic LNG SPA, while by no means standard, is quite typical of the wording found in other SPAs in the Atlantic Basin. Despite the similarities, it is not uncommon to see different arbitral tribunals faced with different SPAs reaching different conclusions in respect of the same events, such as liberalisation in European gas markets or decrease in demand for gas in the power sector. Often these differences in tribunals' conclusions can be due to the differences in the trigger criteria.

Some interpretive issues that often arise in respect of such clauses are as follows:

- Significant changes in circumstances" – are the parties precluded from relying on certain changes, such as changes which are foreseeable?
- Beyond the control of the parties" – changes within the control of the parties are often expressly excluded as triggering events. However, does this mean that a party cannot rely on a trigger event if the other party has caused the event, or simply that a change must be beyond the control of the party that wishes to rely on it? This particular ambiguity can easily be resolved by clear drafting.
- Some clauses require an adjustment to "take into account" or "reflect" the change in value caused by the change in circumstances. Questions can arise as to whether this requires the tribunal to isolate the change in value caused by the change in circumstances and then reflect it in the revised formula. Evidentially, this can be a challenge. If "taking into account" is meant to mean something less specific than actually transposing a particular change in value into an adjustment, what precisely does it mean?

One way in which parties can avoid these interpretive difficulties, while at the same time not conferring an automatic right to reopen the price, is to provide a mechanical trigger criteria in their SPA. For example, the SPA in *Esso Exploration & Production UK Limited v Electricity Supply Board (Esso v ESB)* effectively required the contract price to deviate from the market price by a fixed percentage before the price could be reviewed.[19] The advantage of such clauses is that they provide greater certainty to the parties in respect of circumstances under which the price review mechanism will be triggered, and therefore reduce the possibility of uncertain

19 *Esso Exploration & Production UK Limited v Electricity Supply Board* [2004] EWHC 723 (Comm).

outcomes. However, the parties in *Esso v ESB* were able to draft their price review clause in the way that they did because the relevant market, the United Kingdom, has a liquid trading hub (the National Balancing Point), which market participants accept reflects the market price of gas in the United Kingdom. This is by no means true in every market, although it is becoming increasingly common in Europe. Over time, therefore, one might see price review clauses across Europe providing for more mechanical and objective trigger criteria as in *Esso v ESB*.

Aside from satisfying the definition of a 'trigger event', parties should also be careful about how they refer to the trigger events in their price review notices. Price review clauses typically require the party seeking a price review to serve a notice (commonly known as the 'price review notice') setting out the trigger event (or events) which it believes have given rise to a right to a price review. Once a price review notice has been validly served, the parties are usually required to enter into negotiations for a fixed period, at the end of which, if the parties have failed to reach an agreement, the dispute can be submitted to arbitration. One issue that can arise in the arbitration is whether the trigger events on which the requesting party is relying in the arbitration were properly identified in the price review notices. If not, it might be argued that the party's claims in respect of the unidentified trigger events are inadmissible and/or the tribunal lacks jurisdiction over those claims.

The tribunal in International Chamber of Commerce (ICC) Case 9812 had to consider a very similar issue.[20] The claimant's price review request specified the "impact of the forthcoming gas tax" on the price of natural gas as the only relevant economic change for seeking a price review.[21] However, in its notice of arbitration, the claimant mentioned several other circumstances, including changes in the border value of processed gas, changes in the movements in oil prices relative to oil prices in neighbouring countries, and the decline in the premium of natural gas.[22] In its award, the tribunal distinguished between:

new changes which do fall within the scope of the original price review request and therefore cannot be considered in the arbitration; and

"additional or different substantiation in support of the [price review] request" which form part of the arbitration.[23]

The tribunal also explained that any substantiation of a price review request which is not "specifically mentioned" in the original price review request must be:

"within the scope of the request for price review"; and

"sufficiently connected to the identified circumstance(s)".[24]

The changes alleged by the claimant, except for the introduction of a gas tax, were neither mentioned in the original price review request nor connected to the gas tax. As such, the tribunal held that those changes could not be considered in the arbitration.[25]

A similar issue has also been considered by the English courts. In *Esso v ESB*, the

20 ICC Case 9812 (*ICC International Court of Arbitration Bulletin*, Vol 20/2, 2009) Final Award, page 74.
21 *Ibid.*
22 *Ibid.*
23 *Ibid.*
24 *Ibid.*
25 *Ibid,* page 74.

Commercial Court had to consider whether an arbitral tribunal had jurisdiction to determine a gas price review dispute in circumstances where the seller had allegedly served an invalid price review request.[26] The SPA in *Esso v ESB* provided that either party could serve a price review request only when, among other things, it was "reasonably satisfied" in good faith that the contract price was below a certain comparator.[27] The court concluded that because the seller had committed an error in calculating the relevant comparator, its price review request was invalid. Consequently, no dispute had arisen that was capable of being referred to arbitration and the arbitrators lacked jurisdiction to determine the dispute.[28]

3.2 Price adjustment

As for trigger clauses, the extent to which a tribunal can revise the price formula varies significantly. As noted above, an immediate issue that a tribunal is likely to face is whether it should revise the price formula only to the extent necessary to reflect the proven change in circumstances, or whether it can effectively rewrite the formula. Both scenarios can prove challenging. In the former case, it may be difficult to isolate the effect of the proven change on the value of gas from other changes. Moreover, once that effect has been isolated, it may be difficult to transpose accurately into the revised price formula. In the latter case – that is, when the tribunal has the discretion to rewrite the price formula – it must consider what, if any, guidance the parties have provided in their contract. As noted above, in the absence of sufficient guidance, the tribunal can, like the *Atlantic LNG* tribunal, reach a conclusion that neither party requested.

Some interpretive issues that commonly arise in the context of price adjustment are outlined below.

(a) "In any case" clause

As discussed in the "Trigger phase" chapter, this is a common clause which takes its name from its standard opening words. The clause usually reads something like: "[Whatever adjustment is made] in any case the buyer should be entitled to market the gas economically". The question therefore arises as to whether this gives the buyer an independent right to market the gas economically, effectively giving rise to a self-standing ground for an adjustment in itself.

Even if this is not the case, a further dispute can arise as to whether the clause operates only a 'shield' – that is, it applies only in the case of an upward adjustment, acting as a ceiling on any increase that the seller might otherwise be entitled to – or whether it can also act as a 'sword' to increase the price reduction that a buyer might otherwise achieve to a level that enables it to sell the gas competitively.

There are arguments for and against all of these positions. Different tribunals will arrive at different positions, depending on the precise terms of the clause and the relevant circumstances of the case. However, this all gives rise to significant

---

26 [2004] EWHC 723 (Comm), para 2.
27 *Ibid*, para 6.
28 *Ibid*, para 27.

uncertainty. It is hard to see the benefit of deliberate ambiguity here – far better for the parties to address these uncertainties in the original drafting, rather than leave it in the hands of the tribunal to determine.

(b) ***"Market economically"***

What does this mean? Does it mean, for example, that the buyer should always be entitled to make a net profit on the gas that it sells so that the seller is effectively taking the price risk under the contract and guaranteeing the buyer a profit? If so, at what level should the profit be fixed? Is it fixed over the life time of the contract? Is the buyer entitled to sell the gas economically into all segments of the market – even the least profitable ones, where other sellers are losing money – or should it be aggregated across all segments?

(c) ***"Value"***

Common issues that arise include the following:

- Is value the same as price?
- Where is the value to be assessed – at the border, at the end-user level or across the entire spectrum of the market?
- When is value to be assessed? Is it at the date of delivery under a contract which may have been negotiated many months prior to delivery? Or is it at the date at which parties agree to buy and sell the gas, although delivery may be outside the review period (in which case, how is the actual price to be assessed)?

4. Other guidance which the parties might want to give the tribunal

As noted above, the scope for tribunals to stray off course is proportional to the extent to which the language of the provision permits them to. Generally speaking, the more prescriptive the clause, the more predictable the outcome should be. Of course, there is always a balance between aiming for certainty and crafting a clause that has sufficient flexibility to deal with unexpected changes in circumstances that may occur over the course of a long-term agreement. In addition to ironing out drafting ambiguities, thought should be given as to how prescriptive the parties want to be in directing the tribunal as to how it should make its decision. In this author's view, this is highly desirable. It takes discretion out of the tribunal's hands and puts it back in the hands of the parties. The objection to over-prescription is that the clause needs to be sufficiently flexible to deal with the uncertainties that may arise over the course of a 25-year agreement. This is true. However, the two aims are not mutually preclusive. One can direct the tribunal as to how it should (or should not) arrive at its decision without depriving it of the flexibility that it needs to deal with changes in the market that are unforeseen at the time that the agreement was concluded. To the extent that there is concern that over-prescription may make the clause unworkable, adding wording such as 'so far as practicable' will often ensure that the machinery continues to function in all scenarios.

Again, the list below is far from exhaustive. It sets out some examples where guidance might be given to tribunals:

- Comparators – if a tribunal is being asked to compare the value of gas in a market to the contract price, do the parties want to specify what the tribunal should be making the comparison with, so as to ensure an 'apples to apples' comparison? For example, should the tribunal compare the contract price only to the price of gas in "comparable contracts" – a phrase sometimes used in these provisions – although, again, what does 'comparable' mean? Should a tribunal considering a price review under, say, a long-term liquified natural gas (LNG) contract consider only the prices under other long-term LNG contracts, even if the supplies under that contract also compete with pipeline gas? How close must the contracts which are being cited as comparators be in duration to that under review? This issue is linked to what is said below about evidence of prices. The risk of providing a strict category of comparators (eg, other LNG contracts) is that there may not be much publicly available information from which to draw a representative body of evidence.

- Most price clauses require a comparison between two periods of time (at the beginning of the price review period and then at the end of the period) in order to assess whether there has been a change in circumstance and also, sometimes, whether there has been a change in value. On the face of it, this should be straightforward. However, it is not instructive to compare the value of gas on a day in the middle of summer to that in the middle of winter. Providing the tribunal with guidance on how to deal with seasonality can save a lot of argument.
- As noted above, an argument also sometimes arises as to whether value at a certain date should be assessed by reference to delivered prices at that date (which may reflect prices negotiated some time previously) or agreements struck during the relevant period (even if the gas is to be delivered outside the relevant period and assuming that the prices at which the agreements have been struck for future delivery are known or can be reliably ascertained).
- Prices delivered into the end-user market reflect many 'non-gas' costs, such as transportation, regasification and margins. There may be an argument as to how best to strip out these costs to ascertain the true market value of gas. Two of the most commonly used techniques are an assessment of border prices (so that the value of gas can be considered before the non-gas costs are added), or a so-called 'netback', where the costs are deducted from the end-user prices to determine the cost of gas at the border. Arguments can arise with regard to both approaches. A party may question the reliability of customs prices, which are often published by national authorities.[29] Similarly, to carry out a netback, one must know the various constituent elements, including the end-user prices, various costs and margins. However, there may not be publicly available and/or authoritative sources from which information can be gathered on these various elements. Moreover, while one might think that the value of gas that one calculates following either approach should be similar, for a variety of reasons this is often not the case.

29 The validity of the objection will of course depend on the specifics of the data in question and the terms of the relevant contract.

The value differential can be substantial, and so can give rise to significant disagreements between the parties and their respective experts. Thought should therefore be given as to whether the parties wish to provide guidance to the tribunal as to what is the preferred approach.

5. Evidence of prices

The issue of the price of gas unsurprisingly often features heavily in these disputes. This can be a contentious topic in itself. The problem is often exacerbated by a lack of certainty as to how one establishes what the price of gas is. In many markets, publicly available evidence of prices in certain sectors (eg, the power sector, where the gas is bought to produce electricity, rather than being sold directly to end-users) can be hard to come by – which leads to two questions:

- Is it satisfactory to rely on publicly available data, even if it is not necessarily reliable? Some jurisdictions capture prices in customs data. This has the advantages of being publicly available and having been put together objectively. However, arguments are sometimes put forward that this data has limitations which can undermine its veracity.
- To what extent is it permissible for parties to rely on their own prices in the market to establish value? It might be argued that these can be a more reliable source than publicly available data; however, such pricing information will usually be available only to the buyer which on sells to end-users in its home market. This can lead to an asymmetrical situation where the buyer can either choose to rely on its own prices (if they are helpful) or not disclose them if it does not consider them helpful, while at the same time criticising the publicly available sources – which are the only sources of information on which the seller can rely.

These problems may be resolved if the buyer is required to disclose its prices. However, some clauses limit expressly the scope of disclosure in price review disputes and it may be hard to compel disclosure if the buyer chooses not to rely on that information itself. In any event, disclosure is sometimes resisted in respect of commercially sensitive information such as prices. Although confidentiality in itself may not be a ground for refusing disclosure, it might influence the tribunal's decision. Furthermore, some tribunals take the view that in international arbitration, it is for each party to make its case and it is not permissible for a party to seek disclosure from the other party in order to substantiate its own case; rather, information can be sought only to test the other party's case. This can give rise to the potential asymmetry of information as described above.

These are difficult questions and it is unrealistic to expect them all to be resolved in the drafting of the clause, however desirable this might be. Nevertheless, thought should be given at the time that the clause is drafted as to whether:

- the parties do want to specify whether the tribunal should be entitled to base its decision on publicly available data' and/or
- a party which holds confidential pricing information should be required to disclose it.

6. Conclusion

While price review arbitrations share many characteristics of commercial arbitrations, they are in many respects quite different. They require the tribunal to invade a space that is normally the preserve of the parties – the negotiated price. This requires a commercial perception that is beyond the experience, if not the reach, of many tribunals. This can lead to disastrous and unexpected results. To some extent, that is an inescapable function of the process. However, the level of risk can be reduced by clear drafting and by giving the tribunal careful guidance.

The author would like to thank Rishab Gupta for his comments on the initial draft of this chapter.

Procedural issues arising in price review arbitrations

Michael Young
Allen & Overy LLP

1. Introduction

Procedural issues can arise in any form of dispute resolution. However, they are more common when the dispute resolution clause is complicated, multi-staged and (at times) subjective – more common and, often, more serious.

Price review provisions are a good example of this type of clause.

As other contributors to this book have noted, most price review clauses provide a staged approach for the resolution of any dispute. Normally, the first stage is the occurrence (and therefore the demonstration) of an initial 'trigger' event, entitling one (or possibly both) parties to start the process. That party (or those parties) will then deliver a review notice, relying on the trigger. In most cases, a period of negotiation follows. If that fails, ultimately the dispute will be determined by an arbitral tribunal. In reaching its decision, the tribunal is likely to apply prescribed criteria, mandated by the price review provision itself.

The risk of further procedural problems increases with each step – trigger, notice, negotiations, determination. This chapter considers each in turn, while also raising a number of additional points. However, in discussing these issues, the intention is not to suggest that price review arbitrations are inherently more prone to procedural difficulties. Their complexity – and their multifaceted nature – increases the risk of encountering procedural difficulties during the dispute resolution process. As always, the key point is to be aware of them from the outset.

2. Are these procedural issues specific to price review arbitrations?

A number of the procedural issues arising in price review arbitrations also occur in other arbitrations. For example:

- Should party-appointed experts be allowed, or should the tribunal appoint its own experts? Should there be a hearing, or can the issues be resolved on paper?
- Should the parties be able to provide factual witness testimony and, if so, from whom and in what form?
- What language should be adopted?
- Should there be partial awards on preliminary issues?

There are many such examples, and they could be applied to any form of arbitration.

As this chapter focuses on price review disputes, not the general procedure in arbitration, it does not address these issues, apart from where they overlap – such as on the admissibility of evidence.

Against that background (and tracking the chronology of most price review arbitrations), we begin by considering procedural and other issues that can arise with the initial trigger for a review.

3. Identifying the trigger event(s)

3.1 Different types of trigger clause

There is no standard trigger in a price review clause. However, there are broad categories of trigger (and accompanying trigger clause) which give rise to common procedural difficulties at this initial stage of the dispute resolution process.

Certain clauses trigger a price review solely on the occurrence of a scheduled event (typically, the passage of a defined period of time). In other words, the clause will provide for an automatic assessment of the contract price, rather than requiring a party to demonstrate that certain triggers have been satisfied before starting the process.

In itself, this is an acceptable approach. The difficulties arise where the tribunal's eventual mandate is made explicit later in the clause.

For example, the tribunal could be required to determine the dispute by reference to an assessment of specific changes in a particular market. In such a case, a potential jurisdictional and procedural issue arises. Can a tribunal – appointed to determine whether the contract price needs revision – be constituted properly if there are no changes in the relevant market? In other words, is the tribunal's mandate groundless if the reference point upon which it is based has not happened? On the strength of that argument, the receiving party might then seek to introduce the condition precedent of a detailed, complex trigger where none has been included expressly, raising it as a threshold procedural and jurisdictional issue.

However, in most cases such an approach is unlikely to be legitimate. While each occasion must be tested against the language of the relevant clause, the absence of an initial trigger requirement (other than, say, the simple passage of time) means that the arbitral tribunal will by definition have prospective jurisdiction the moment that the scheduled event occurs. Its appointment, and therefore its jurisdiction, requires no more than that. Of course, the legitimacy of its appointment should not be confused with the legitimacy of its performance as arbitrator: that is tested against the particular mandate set out in the clause. The presence of that performance mandate should not double as an additional bar to the tribunal's appointment in the first place.

However, these types of clause are rare. Most triggers are tied to the occurrence of one or more subjective events. Ordinarily – and as highlighted elsewhere in this book – this requires a 'material' or 'significant' impact on the 'value' of a particular element (described with varying degrees of clarity).

For example, the clause might require a party to demonstrate that there has been a material impact on the value of the liquefied natural gas (LNG) under the relevant sale and purchase agreement:

- in comparison with the value of LNG and/or competing fuels in the relevant market; and
- by reference to an earlier, prescribed date.

In well-drafted clauses, the impact is usually expressed to be outside either party's control, and an element of unforeseeability could also be imported (although this too can give rise to complexities – an event may be foreseen, but its effect on value may not be).

Thus, it is clear that many areas of disagreement and uncertainty exist within this single, threshold stage of most price review disputes. These, in turn, often give rise to procedural disputes in a subsequent arbitration.

However, where does the tribunal start? Since the trigger is a condition precedent to the entire process, its first task will probably be to assess the legitimacy of the trigger.

There is no 'one size fits all' answer to the question (or any of the related issues highlighted below): it is likely to be fact-dependent in each case, as tested against the terms of the relevant clause, and a definitive answer is not attempted here. Rather, the following paragraphs seek to identify (however briefly) a number of areas where disputes often arise, to provide a guide to potential pitfalls rather than a definitive list.

Against that caveat, the key issues for consideration by any tribunal are likely to include some or all of the following:

- There is often little guidance within the clause on what 'relevant market' means. That, in turn, could give considerable flexibility to the parties, their experts and (ultimately) the tribunal in framing the issues in different ways. This can be tested with a few simple questions. For example, is the clause referring to the end-user market, into which the seller sells, or to only certain segments of that market (eg, industrial users)? Or to the buyer's market? Or to both? Alternatively, does it refer to changes in the export market? In each of these cases, what geographical limits are relevant? What if (perhaps as a result of new regulations) the potential geographical limits are wider now than when the contract was executed?
- However, the correct definition of the relevant market is only the start of the analysis. When assessing the existence of a trigger event, many other issues are likely to arise. For example, a tribunal will need properly to analyse the relevant changes in the market, the effect on the LNG sold and purchased under the sale and purchase agreement, and the causal link between these two factors. Of these further issues, the latter – the causal link between those changes in the market and the effect on the LNG sold and purchased under the sale and purchase agreement – can often be the most difficult to establish, and is often overlooked.
- Whether there had been any control by the counterparty (or, rather, either party) over the changes in the relevant market must also be determined. Similar problems arise when the clause requires a party to demonstrate that the changes are, for example, significant or material. Such a requirement is

common, but it is much rarer to find any guidance elsewhere in the agreement on what is 'significant' or 'material'. This often leads to dispute between the parties. Indeed, the tribunal will need to assess whether the change has to be quantitatively significant (ie, having an effect which passes a certain threshold of significance on the contract price in comparison with the defined reference point), or qualitatively significant (eg, a structural change in the relevant market, leaving a permanent change in one or more of its key features), or perhaps a combination of the two.

- Other terms within the trigger (and the reference points for the tribunal's own deliberations) might also involve a degree of ambiguity. For example, what is meant by the word 'price'? It is not a term of art. Does it concern market prices (and, if so, which market, echoing some of the points raised above)? Is it net or gross? In particular, is it comparable to value – and what do we mean by 'value' in this context? The conflation between 'price' and 'value' can be one of the greatest problems in any price review arbitration.

Certain clauses also include a further, subjective element, along such lines as: "either party has a good faith basis for believing that [the trigger events] have occurred". The obvious risk is that this is all that is required. Arguably, if the only question is whether the change in circumstances (or other trigger event) had occurred, then that is all that the parties needed to provide for in their clause.

Ultimately, this will be a question of construction. In many cases, it would be expected to be an additional requirement, with the trigger events themselves (eg, the "change" in the relevant market) also having to be made out separately. The 'belief' requirement is more likely to serve as a safeguard against frivolous claims, allowing a tribunal to determine that a party attempting to trigger price review where it has no good-faith basis to do so has not validly triggered at all.

In short, tribunals are likely to have to face numerous issues when assessing the legitimacy of an initial trigger. The selection offered above merely provides examples of the potential arguments and areas of dispute. However, to what extent are they procedural issues? Realistically, they go to the substance of the dispute – in particular, at this stage, the substantive issue of the tribunal's jurisdiction to hear the dispute in the first place. If the trigger events have not been proven, there is nothing for the tribunal to go on to review. The claim fails at the first hurdle.

However, there are a number of issues which often arise in the context of these debates which can more properly be characterised as procedural (at least in part). Two merit mention here: the extent to which the parties' prior negotiating positions can be relevant in these exercises and the relevant time period for assessing the background facts.

3.2 The relevance of the parties' prior economic 'case'

To what extent can a tribunal assess the consistency of the claim (or defence) with a party's economic 'case' from the outset? This should be considered in context. Although there is almost always provision for a period of negotiation in any price review process (discussed in more detail below), the parties may have been discussing their position in meetings and presentations long before the trigger was invoked. Equally, PowerPoint presentations and documents are often created during the subsequent negotiating stage – leaving a user-friendly record of a party's (then) position. Moreover, a party is likely to have undertaken significant internal analysis in the months (sometimes years) before deciding whether to issue a trigger notice. That may also offer an insight into the perceived strengths and weaknesses of its case.

In the light of those earlier presentations and analyses, what (say) if the relevant market, or the alleged changes, or the economic impact, differ significantly in the trigger notice (and request for arbitration) from the parties' earlier negotiating positions? That might in itself be relevant (and potentially powerful) evidence. At the very least, the party might need to explain the difference.

Procedurally, this gives rise to a number of points. While the principles are not unique to price review arbitrations, they are felt here very acutely. There are few disputes which involve such a degree of lengthy, detailed and exhaustive forward planning and analysis before the dispute resolution process starts, or where a series of formal meetings takes place between the parties in which their respective positions are explained in some detail and candour.

The tribunal will need to assess whether such evidence is admissible at all. That, in turn, requires an assessment of whether any of this information has legal privilege. While those defences might be available to some or all of the internal documents (depending on their nature, the circumstances behind their creation and the applicable procedural law), it is more difficult to claim privilege over documents or information shared with a counterparty. Unless the parties had agreed to keep the information confidential (whether in the dispute resolution clause itself or, more likely, by subsequent agreement), there are unlikely to be any issues of privilege.

Arguments of confidentiality are also unlikely to succeed (to the extent that the tribunal considers that a justifiable excuse). The procedural issue is likely to fall on arguments of relevance. That, in turn, is usually regarded to be a matter to be determined by the tribunal, at its discretion.

Given the potential uncertainty from a procedural point of view, parties should approach this issue strategically – and do so from the beginning. There is an obvious advantage for a party to ensure that its position is consistent from the outset. Therefore, it is often advisable to involve external, independent experts early in the process. However, this must be tailored with the fact that the purpose of providing for a period of negotiation is to allow parties to exchange arguments with a view to seeking common ground. Therefore, it is understandable if a party shifts its position during these negotiations, or does not present its argument in a way which replicates exactly how it chooses to argue its case before a tribunal if those negotiations fail. There is also the related and important question of whether the earlier negotiations should be open or closed, with prejudice or without prejudice. We consider this further below.

3.3 Relevant time period for the assessment of available evidence

As noted earlier in this chapter (and elsewhere in this book), one of the essential purposes of a price review clause is to reflect a change in the relevant markets over time. Any assessment of change requires (at least two) reference points in time. There is much more likely to be a change in the ambient temperature of Paris between January 1 2012 and July 1 2012, than between January 1 2012 and January 1 2013. The temporal reference points are key.

Identical issues arise in the context of price review disputes. The various changes in the market – and increased instability overall – have driven the significant increase in price review disputes over the last five years. There are many examples. From the economic recession (particularly in Europe) to the growth of unconventional gas projects in the United States; from the deregulation of various markets to the development of certain gas hubs – there has been a considerable change in global gas markets and in the competition for the sale and supply of gas in many parts of the world. Given that instability and those changes, it is very important to ensure that the right temporal reference points are used. Expressing that procedurally, it is very important to ensure that evidence of the right time period and the relevant changes is presented to an arbitral tribunal.

A key procedural issue for any tribunal will be the cut-off dates for evidence presented by either party (whether internal or market-based) in support of its position.

The starting point is likely to be the relevant start and reference dates in the price review clause. However, the debate might not end there. For example, parties might try to argue that you can only assess change if you understand the true nature of a particular trend. Equally, it might be argued that the strict limits of the contractually prescribed dates provide a misleading picture, or fail properly to represent the nature of the changes requiring revision. As such, parties will often seek to identify the trends in the relevant market. Have things changed, whether over the explicit review period or beforehand? Are they likely to change in the future? What trends might there be for the period after the review period?

These questions are likely to depend heavily on the language of the relevant clause. If it is explicit enough, the only relevant data will be that within the review period – and perhaps just the two dates at the start and end of that period (along the lines of the January to January example above). Alternatively, the trigger might require the events under investigation "not to be short lived" or "which are likely to continue". If so, it may be easier for the parties to provide background information going beyond the review date to the tribunal. What is clear is that this is a very common area of dispute. Given that it concerns directly the range of data that is available to a tribunal to assess the market (and the changes to that market), the significance of these disputes is hardly surprising.

4. The delivery of the review notice

4.1 The content requirements of the review notice

In most cases, the right to start a review of the price formula will be conditional on a party complying with the notice requirements under the sale and purchase agreement.

For example, the contract might require a party to provide a reasonably detailed explanation of the basis of its claim. Indeed, many price review clauses require conditions such as:

- "the requesting party shall substantiate its reasons for considering that it is entitled to an adjustment of the Price Formula"; or
- "such notice to contain a proposed adjustment to the Contract Price together with reasonably detailed reasons therefore, including a description of reference to the trigger events".

The validity of these notices is sometimes challenged in price review disputes. However, in practice, two factors limit the potential to succeed. First, in assessing the extent of the trigger notice, many tribunals tend to approach the requirements commercially and reasonably: if the essence of the dispute is presented clearly, that should suffice. Second, however, (and, in practical terms, much more importantly), it is likely that lengthy negotiations, involving many meetings and presentations, and extensive correspondence, will have taken place before the notice is issued. Thus, in many cases it will be unrealistic for a counterparty to claim ignorance of a claimant's case, or that its only knowledge comes from the contents of the review notice.

Procedurally, it is rare (but not impossible) for a trigger notice to be rejected on these grounds. Nonetheless, if any party considers a counterparty trigger notice to be invalid, it should raise the objection immediately (as well as ensuring that any notice it might serve is compliant to the letter). Often, parties will act initially as if the counterparty notice were valid, proceeding on that basis; objections as to form often come later. However, by that stage any potential objection might be said to have been waived (unless the objecting party made it clear that it was proceeding on the understanding that it was not waiving its right to object to the validity of the notice before a tribunal).

4.2 The impact of multiple review notices

Another issue arises where it is unclear how many review notices can be served, and/or if responses to those notices are required from the counterparty. Many clauses are not clear as to whether there can be only one review notice served in the relevant review process (in which case, the counterparty must respond to that notice rather than serve its own), or whether either party can opt to serve a review notice in any particular period. In other words, should there be just one review notice (to which the counterparty responds, even if substantively), or can (or even must) a counterparty serve its own notice if it wishes to present its own case in detail?

For example, a clause might begin with: "Each of the Parties is entitled to request a review ..." While the use of "each" suggests that both parties can serve a notice, the reference to "a review" might indicate that there is only to be one of them (although, on balance, the best interpretation in that case is likely to be that both parties can serve a review notice). However, what if the clause makes no provision for a response, whether a simple reply (ie, going no further than responding to the notice served), or what would in effect be a counternotice (ie, not merely responding to the notice, but also raising new, substantive points justifying a different result)? Since both parties appear able to serve their own notice, anything going beyond a simple response might best be contained in a separate, self-standing review notice, rather than in a simple reply document.

That leads to the possibility of competing review notices – and, should matters proceed, competing price review arbitrations. This could become a key procedural issue in any dispute. To some extent, the nature of the dispute resolution provision can assist: since (by definition) the arbitration agreement will be the same for each review, certain arbitral rules provide a relatively straightforward mechanism for consolidation in those circumstances. For example, Article 10 of the International Chamber of Commerce Rules provides such a route:

> *The [International Chamber of Commerce] Court may, at the request of a party, consolidate two or two arbitrations pending under the Rules into a single arbitration where:*
>
> *(a) the parties have agreed to consolidation; or*
>
> *(b) all of the claims in the arbitrations are made under the same arbitration agreement;*
>
> *...*

As such, a likely consequence is that parallel arbitrations started under separate review notices would be consolidated into a single action. That said, it is more likely that the parties would agree to a single set of proceedings, reflecting both claims.

However, without express or incorporated terms (and assuming that the parties do not agree), there is a risk that separate notices will lead to separate arbitrations and, in turn, to separate awards. The importance of addressing the point clearly in the clause is self-evident.

4.3 Procedural impact of time limits

Procedural difficulties can arise in the timing of the notices. Typically, they must be served within a set time frame (or at least by a particular date).

If the notice is served outside the permitted period, it is likely to be invalid. However, although timing is therefore very important, many clauses do not state the time periods clearly. What if the clause provides for the service of a notice "in the 30 days before the third anniversary of the sale and purchase agreement"? Without a clear set of rules, the calculation of dates can vary. To take just two examples:

- Should the start and/or end dates be excluded from those 30 days?
- Can a notice be served on the third anniversary?

In these cases, the best (and obvious) tactic is to take a conservative approach when assessing time periods.

4.4 Fundamental validity of the triggers

To the extent that there are complaints about the notices of a price revision, they tend not to be about the validity of the requests themselves; rather, they tend to concern the triggers contained in them. This may lead to a dispute on whether the tribunal has jurisdiction to proceed with a price review arbitration if the triggers identified in the request are invalid or otherwise groundless.

This is a substantive question rather than a procedural one, and it falls outside the scope of the chapter. However, in practical terms, given the symmetry between the trigger requirements and the process that the arbitrators must follow (which is briefly discussed below), the absence of effective triggers is likely to involve the same process of analysis as a decision not to change the price review mechanism. In general terms, the proper establishment of triggers should be considered a condition precedent before the tribunal embarks on a price review process (subject, as always, to the actual language of the clause).

5. The period of negotiation

Most price review clauses go on to provide for a deadline (usually extended) for negotiation between the parties. As mentioned above, it is important to determine and clarify whether these negotiations are conducted on a without prejudice basis (ie, designed to reach a settlement, and so not disclosable in any subsequent arbitration) or an open basis (so that arguments used in the negotiations can be raised in any future proceedings, and inconsistencies between the parties' stated positions highlighted). Clarity on these issues might avoid a subsequent procedural dispute with the tribunal when it comes to assess all evidence available to it.

Typically, it is only after the end of the negotiation period that formal proceedings may be commenced, often within a set time following the close of negotiations. Within these provisions, there is an important distinction between:

- 'not before' clauses, which prevent proceedings from being started before a certain date, but which provide for no long stop date; and
- 'window' clauses, allowing a party to start proceedings within a fixed time after the end of the negotiation period.

Window clauses are more certain, but pose practical difficulties for claimants to the extent that, should negotiations fail, they must start proceedings within a relatively short period.

In a surprising number of cases, it is not made clear within the clause whether it is a 'not before' or a 'window', which gives rise to inevitable disputes. In particular, inconsistencies can arise between the regime prescribed in the price review clause and the dispute resolution mechanism in the contract. The latter can itself provide for a period of negotiation before proceedings are started, but one which is inconsistent with the regime identified in the price review clause (eg, "failing settlement through negotiations not exceeding 30 days, all such disputes shall be referred to and finally and exclusively settled under the LCIA Rules ..."), whereas the price review provisions tend to suggest a simple not before date. The safest course in these circumstances is to treat the provision as a window clause, with the start date identified in the price review provision and the end date in the general dispute resolution clause.

Other problems can occur if a party, faced with a simple not before provision, chooses not to start arbitral proceedings. How long a delay is required before the right to do so is lost? Furthermore, what if that delay extends beyond the start of the next review period? Can a party still resurrect the earlier debate, running the two review periods together (or even separately)? Clearly, the resolution of such a dispute would depend on the precise terms of the sale and purchase agreement (and any other relevant contractual documents). Also, it is likely to be heavily fact dependent. For example, did negotiations continue, even if intermittently? Was anything done to keep the first price review process alive?

The risk, of course, is that the reappearance of an old price review notice after a lengthy delay – and particularly if it coincides with notices served under a later price review – may be viewed as a tactical manoeuvre rather than a credible claim. In such a case, an arbitral tribunal might be tempted to imply a term requiring a party to commence proceedings within a reasonable period after the not before date.

6. Determination by an arbitral tribunal

6.1 The methodology prescribed for the tribunal

Save for enforcement, the final stage in the price review process is determination by the arbitral tribunal. Within that process, there are several areas which often give rise to procedural and other disputes.

Many of those issues concern the methodology imposed on the tribunal (if any) and, in particular, the relationship between that approach and the earlier trigger events. Thus, although the trigger event is usually a discrete step in the process, certain sale and purchase agreements refer back to it when the tribunal comes to assess the revisions to be made to the price formula. In other words, the trigger does more than merely prompt the review; it also requires the tribunal to reflect the impact of the trigger events in its decision.

As such, common areas of dispute before the tribunal include the extent to which the trigger tests remains relevant. Some clauses refer back to the trigger clause events when mandating the role of the tribunal. As such, they require the tribunal to assess whether the contract price/formula needs amending to reflect the trigger events. It is an easy way of defining the tribunal's mandate. (Other clauses state that the triggers merely prompt the review – with the methodology of any future arbitral tribunal provided for later in the clause. In general terms, the former approach is preferable.)

A related question concerns the identification of the relevant market. In particular, if the trigger market differs from the relevant market, what are the differences and why are they present? A common problem is when clauses use different terminology between the trigger events and the role mandated to the tribunal. For example, this author has seen certain clauses which refer variously (but never consistently) to "the energy market", "the Buyer's energy market", "the relevant market" and "the Buyer's market", all within the same provision.

In addition, the arbitral tribunal will need to determine the point in time at which the relevant changes in value are to be considered. An important element of this is the extent to which the tribunal can have regard to events postdating the review date when considering the revisions to be made (demonstrating the utility of incorporating such language as "not short lived"), mirroring the observations raised earlier in this chapter in the context of the trigger events.

However, in some cases, the precise impact of the trigger events might be unclear. For example, problems might arise when the tribunal is requested to take into account certain factors, typically the trigger ingredients, when reaching its conclusion. One might argue that, as a simple matter of English, 'take into account' requires that data to form part of the analysis and assessment, but would need neither to be conclusive nor determinative. In other words, it must form part of the analysis, but it might not exclude the parties (or the arbitrator in due course) from considering other matters in reaching a decision. In turn, that could allow the introduction of supplementary data, going beyond the express terms of the price review clause. An alternative argument is that by expressly referring to certain factors but not others, the parties intended these factors either to be given exclusive consideration or to be prioritised over other factors.

Ultimately, any dispute will be determined by the terms of the mandate imposed on the tribunal. Nonetheless, subtle ambiguities of this nature do commonly give rise to procedural debates over the extent and type of information that can be put before the arbitrators.

6.2 Relevance of the parties' intentions and questions of privilege

Procedural objections can be made if, as part of the available evidence before the tribunal, a party seeks to introduce evidence of the parties' subjective intentions when they entered into the sale and purchase agreement, particularly over the economics of the project. For example:

- What minutes or notes were kept of the various negotiations and internal discussions?
- What drafts or iterations did the contract undergo from start to signature?
- What internal analyses or reports on the project were carried out, and were any of them ever shared with the counterparty?

Perhaps more commonly, parties raise issues regarding the privileged nature of the discussions – whether affecting the events during the negotiation of the sale and purchase agreement or those concerning the build-up to the dispute and the price review process itself. Since many of these discussions occur in the absence of lawyers (whether in-house or external), problems can arise in determining whether that evidence should be privileged. These questions are complicated by the difficulties of determining the applicable privilege rules in international arbitration.

Much will depend upon the applicable law and the preferred approach of the tribunal. These disputes are often of an international nature. The seller and buyer are likely to come from different legal regimes, which in turn will often be different from the applicable law of the sale and purchase agreement and the legal teams advising them (given the widespread use of English or New York law), giving rise to the most frequent procedural debates in price review arbitrations. From the start of any dispute (which is likely to be long before any formal notice is delivered), all parties must be aware of the importance of keeping internal documents privileged, to the extent possible.

7. Disputes arising from the arbitration clause itself

So far, this chapter has focused on the type of procedural issues common to the multi-staged process found in most price review clauses. However, disputes can also arise from problems with the arbitration clause itself.

7.1 Parallel proceedings revisited

The risk of parallel review notices was discussed in section 4.2. However, a related problem can arise where there are both expert determination and arbitration clauses within the agreement (eg, with the former, focused on index-substitution issues, and all remaining matters directed to arbitration). This can create a different risk of parallel proceedings.

For example, assume that the price review formula contains a reference to a particular index, but that index is no longer relevant, perhaps because the market has changed. In that case, should the formula be amended under the expert determination issues regulating index substitutions, or more generally under the price review arbitration clause?

The tension is clear, but the solution is relatively straightforward: in cases of conflict, the agreement should identify who determines whether it goes to arbitration or to expert determination. Typically, it goes to arbitration. It is surprising how few agreements identify that role clearly – allowing parties to institute separate proceedings under their preferred route, without a clear way of identifying which should have priority.

7.2 Disputing the validity of the trigger notices

A further problem arises in disputes concerning the validity of the trigger notices. To the extent that the price review clause provides for a separate arbitral regime (with its own time lines and procedural aspects), that regime might not apply to a dispute which exclusively concerns the validity of the price review notice and the triggers on which the party relies. Such a dispute may fall instead under the general dispute resolution provisions of the sale and purchase agreement.

In practice, problems arise only if the two regimes are materially different and incompatible. In most cases, the validity of the trigger (and the accompanying notice) is likely to be determined by the same arbitrators, in the same proceedings, as the potential price review itself. Therefore, the need for consistency is paramount, to avoid unnecessary problems from the outset.

8. Concluding remarks

The opening premise of this chapter was that, where dispute resolution clauses are complex and multifaceted, the risk of procedural disputes is greatest. The complex and multifaceted nature of price review disputes brings life to that premise.

With each different stage – the trigger, the notice, the negotiations, the determination – there is a risk of procedural problems. However, in most cases those difficulties (and the potential procedural issues that arise as a result) can be reduced – if not always cured – by careful drafting and foresight from the outset.

The real trick is to be aware of the potential pitfalls (many of which are highlighted in other chapters of this book) from the start. Whether they become procedural difficulties will depend on how the parties conduct themselves and how well they have drafted their agreement. To that extent, the lesson here is no different from any other type of agreement: be prepared.

The trigger phase

Marnix Leijten
Martje de Vries Lentsch
De Brauw Blackstone Westbroek NV

1. Introduction

In this chapter, we examine the trigger phase and discuss the criteria for a price review, identifying issues arising in arbitration where the tribunal must determine whether these criteria have been met. The chapter is based on our experience with mainly European, long-term gas sales agreements related to the sale of pipeline gas, of which many different forms and many different price review clauses exist. Specific contracts can and will differ in many important respects. We aim to provide a general overview of the criteria for a price review we have encountered in these agreements.

Generally, the core of the price review that clause is relatively short. Guidance for both the parties and the arbitral tribunal on its construction is limited because there are only a few publically available awards.[1] Most, but not all, European legal systems consider evidence from the negotiation history when determining the proper construction of the clause. Yet, very often the negotiation history – which is in most cases ambiguous and often dates back to the 1980s and 1990s – shows that the wording of the price review clause is based on commercial compromises, making it difficult to identify the parties' intentions and the underlying principles. Therefore, in practice, establishing the criteria for a price review can be difficult for both parties and tribunals, which may struggle correctly to interpret and apply the price review clause. Since any determination in this respect by a tribunal will have important effects for the parties in future price reviews, and since the financial interests at stake are often significant only in one review, it is crucial to get the interpretation right. It is often difficult to determine the meaning of one specific review clause in a specific contract between specific parties. Making general statements regarding the criteria for a price review is even more so, but that is the aim of this chapter.

It has been established and is commonly accepted that the main rationale of the price review clause is to provide both parties with a tool to restore for the future the economic balance of the contract as it was agreed to in the past. If this economic balance becomes distorted, the price review clause serves to reset it by adjusting the price provisions.[2] As a result, in price review arbitrations the main focus lies on expert

1 There are two well-known International Chamber of Commerce (ICC) awards, in 1999 and 2007, regarding the same long-term gas sales agreements. They were published in 2009 in the ICC *Bulletin*. "Extracts from ICC Arbitral Awards: Price Setting and Price Revision in the Energy Sector", in: *ICC International Court of Arbitration Bulletin*, Vol 20/2, 2009, pp69-76 and 93-109.

2 Final Award in Case 13504, January 2007, "Extracts from ICC Arbitral Awards: Price Setting and Price Revision in the Energy Sector", in: *ICC International Court of Arbitration Bulletin*, Vol 20/2, 2009, p94.

opinions regarding the economic (im)balance of the contract and the adjustments to the price provisions are needed.

Taking the above into account, in this chapter we discuss the main elements of the price review clause and the criteria that typically are derived from it and which must be met in order successfully to request an adjustment of the price provisions. We focus on the relevance of the review period and the various elements of the requirement of a change in the economic circumstances, as well as the buyer's ability economically to market the gas. However, first we discuss a more procedural element of the price review clause: the purpose of the trigger letter and its validity.

2. Validity of the trigger letter

A price review occurs only at the request of one or both of the parties. Under any long-term gas sales agreement the price review clause contains one or more provisions on the formalities of requesting a price review. Generally, the contract provides that this request should be made in writing. In practice, the party requesting a price review does so in a letter to the other party. This letter is referred to as the 'trigger letter'. Although the letter becomes relevant once the parties are in arbitration, its validity is crucial to start a price review and to set the scene for the requested review.

2.1 When to send a trigger letter

The price review clause contains several provisions on the formalities of the request for a price review. Typically, it provides that each of the parties is entitled to request a price review with effect at a certain date. This date is not only the date on which the price review comes into effect (ie, the day that the adjusted price provisions – if any – become effective), but also determines the deadline for sending a request for a price review, which should be made before such trigger date.[3] In general, the price review clause is drafted in such a way that it provides the relevant trigger date for the entire duration of the contract by prescribing a certain set interval of one or multiple years between each price review.

This is illustrated in Example 1.

Example 1

A price review clause may provide that each of the parties can first request a price review on October 1 2006 and then on October 1 every following three years – that is, on October 1 2009, October 1 2012 and so on until the end of the contract. In each case the party that wishes to request a price review will have to send its trigger letter to the other party before the trigger date, for instance, before October 1 2012.

A request for a price review sent after the relevant trigger date is likely to be considered invalid.

3 Final Award in Case 9812, August 1999, "Extracts from ICC Arbitral Awards: Price Setting and Price Revision in the Energy Sector", in: *ICC International Court of Arbitration Bulletin*, Vol 20/2, 2009, p73.

In addition to regular price reviews, some contracts also provide for a limited number of review options within the prescribed intervals, also known as joker or wildcard price reviews. The contract will provide how many of these reviews can be requested by each party during the term of the contract. Normally, they can be requested at any time. The only requirement is that the requesting party must send the trigger letter on or before the date on which it wishes the price review to come into effect.

Thus, in the above example a wildcard price review could be triggered on January 1 2014, which is between the October 1 2012 and October 1 2015 trigger dates. The party triggering a wildcard will have to make a careful assessment and balance its interests to determine when exactly to do so: the later it triggers the wildcard, the clearer the distortion of the economic balance may have become and thus the case for a review will be stronger. However, the disadvantage of waiting is that, usually, the price adjustment will apply only from the date of the trigger.

2.2 Level of specificity

What should be included in a trigger letter? Usually, the contract provisions on this are fairly broad. Typically, apart from a reference to the contract and the date on which the price review comes into effect, the contract provides that a request for a price review should also substantiate the reasons for the request. However, the contract rarely provides the level of detail needed to meet this requirement. Based on the more general requirement of substantiation of the request, it is common practice for a party requesting a price review to specify which significant changes in the economic circumstances it relies on when requesting a price review.[4]

Generally, the description of such changes will be broad to avoid narrowing the scope of the price review too early in the process. As the trigger letter is sent before the effective date and thus some information that is crucial to make a proper analysis is not yet available, parties take into account that further analyses may lead to different conclusions after the trigger letter has been sent.

A party that has included a very specific and detailed description of the changes in its trigger letter but later deviates from this may face a formal defence from its counterparty regarding the scope of the price review. Therefore, typically, the requesting party includes more general market developments justifying an adjustment of the price provisions. Usually, the requesting party does not substantiate its request with relevant data and more in-depth market analyses until the first meetings in the early stages of the negotiations. We do not believe that it would be easy to deem a trigger letter invalid because it is not specific enough. The general purpose of the letter is to inform the other party and, since negotiations are to follow, a high level of detail is not necessary at this stage. However, problems could arise if the triggering party seeks to add review grounds during the course of the negotiations or in arbitration that are not covered by the trigger letter. It should be possible for the parties to conduct and conclude a review relatively quickly after

---

4 Final Award in Case 9812, August 1999, "Extracts from ICC Arbitral Awards: Price Setting and Price Revision in the Energy Sector", in: *ICC International Court of Arbitration Bulletin*, Vol 20/2, 2009, p73.

the trigger letter. Adding review grounds weeks or months after the letter, based on new facts, is inconsistent with that goal.[5]

2.3 Claim to be included?

Should the requesting party's actual claim – the actual adjustment of the price provisions – be included in the trigger letter? Defendant parties have argued this point in arbitrations. Normally, the contract does not explicitly provide for this requirement and so it could be assumed that it is not required. However, it could be argued that substantiating the request would also involve the actual adjustment that the requesting party seeks. Most parties have already spent a considerable amount of time analysing the changes and determining the requested adjustment before requesting a price review. However, as noted above, not all relevant data is available when the trigger letter is sent. This makes it difficult for the requesting party to specify its claim in its trigger letter. The purpose of the trigger letter is to inform the other party that a review is requested and of the general circumstances on which the request is based, so precise details of the changes sought should not be necessary. Clarity on this can and should be given in the negotiations that follow, without much prejudice for the party that receives the trigger letter.

Parties have found a way around the lack of essential data at the date of sending the trigger letter: they can agree to maintain the official trigger date and to enter into commercial negotiations instead of sending a formal trigger letter. If the negotiations fail, the trigger letter can still be sent. Based on the arrangement made, this trigger would then be deemed to be valid as of the official trigger date. This method is applied regularly and allows time not only for commercial negotiations, but also for further analyses of the changes and the required adjustments. Usually, this enables the requesting party to provide a specification or at least an indication of the adjustment of the price provisions that it seeks before the official trigger letter is sent. If a party has prepared an indication of the adjustment that it requires before sending the trigger letter, one could argue that the requesting party should in that case inform the other party of such adjustment (and thus its claim) in the trigger letter. However, price review clauses do not usually explicitly prescribe this, it is not an established practice and we have not seen any arbitral tribunals apply a sanction because the requested adjustment has not been included in the trigger letter (indeed, sometimes a party does not even specify its claimed adjustment in its request for arbitration).

3. Criteria for a price review

As stated above, the main purpose of a price review is to restore the balance of the long-term gas sales agreement if it has become distorted. Although the wording of

---

5 *Ibid*, p73:

> *[I]t must be assumed that the price request may include other not specifically mentioned circumstances, provided they are within the scope of the request for price review and sufficiently connected to the identified circumstance(s) … a party failing to provide convincing arguments cannot be precluded from initiating arbitral proceedings and submitting additional or different 'substantiation' in support of the request, provided that any such further substantiation is within the scope of the price review request.*

the price review clause provides reference to the criteria that have to be met in order for a party to claim a price review leading to an adjustment of the price provisions, these criteria are not as straightforward as they seem.[6] In this section, we discuss the various criteria and the issues that can be identified when determining whether the criteria have been met.

3.1 Changes in the economic circumstances

A typical price review clause first of all requires that the economic circumstances have changed compared with what is reflected in the price provisions of the contract. Thus, the parties should identify:

- the changes that have occurred in the economic circumstances; and
- to what extent these changes are not reflected in the price provisions.[7]

Generally, there is no limit to the type of changes in the economic circumstances that a party can rely on in a price review.[8] They can vary from general economic or market conditions to specific legislation. Commonly, the price review clause contains an explicit requirement that the change must have some impact on the energy market as a whole or on the value of gas specifically, as a change in the economic circumstances which can be reflected in the adjusted price provisions. As most parties requesting an adjustment of the price provisions ultimately rely on a change in the value of gas, this change is discussed separately in section 3.2.

Although there is no limit to the type of changes in the economic circumstances, there are some further requirements that have to be met. A party will have to prove that the change in the economic circumstances:

- has taken place within the review period;
- is significant;
- has occurred in the country or market of the buyer; and
- is outside of the control of the parties.[9]

Although these requirements may seem straightforward, many parties and tribunals struggle to meet them. Each can be considered to refer to a separate element, which is discussed below.

(a) Time element – changes within the review period

In determining whether there has been a change in the economic circumstances, the

6 An example of a typical price review clause can be found in the two awards rendered in 1999 and 2007, "Extracts from ICC Arbitral Awards: Price Setting and Price Revision in the Energy Sector", in: *ICC International Court of Arbitration Bulletin,* Vol 20/2, 2009, pp69-70 and 94-95.

7 A similar approach was taken in the two published awards. Final Award in Case 9812, August 1999 and Final Award in Case 13504, January 2007, "Extracts from ICC Arbitral Awards: Price Setting and Price Revision in the Energy Sector", in: *ICC International Court of Arbitration Bulletin*, Vol 20/2, 2009, pp70-71 and 96.

8 Guy Block, "Arbitration and Changes in Energy Prices: A Review of ICC Awards with respect to Force Majeure, Indexation, Adaptation, Hardship and Take-or-Pay Clauses", in: *ICC International Court of Arbitration Bulletin,* Vol 20/2, 2009, pp59-60.

9 Similar conditions are mentioned in the Final Award in Case 9812, August 1999, "Extracts from ICC Arbitral Awards: Price Setting and Price Revision in the Energy Sector", in: *ICC International Court of Arbitration Bulletin,* Vol 20/2, 2009, pp70-71. These are also referred to by Block, note 8 above, p59.

point at which the change occurred must be established by comparing the position at time A and time B. This is determined by the so-called 'review period'.

As indicated above, the price review clause will provide when a party can request a price review and when such price review comes into effect. Thus, it also sets the period to which the price review relates. This period, also referred to as the 'review period', runs from the date of the previous price review until the date of the current price review.

In Example 1 given in section 2.1: if a party requests a price review with effect as of October 1 2012, the review period runs from October 1 2009 until October 1 2012.

This also applies when a party has triggered a wildcard price review. In that case, the end of the review period is set by the effective date of the wildcard review, whereas the beginning of the review period is determined by the effective date of the previous price review.

In Example 1: when a wildcard price review is triggered on January 1 2010, the review period runs from October 1 2009 to January 1 2010. If triggered on time, the subsequent review period will run from January 1 2010 until October 1 2012.

Thus, the review period plays an important role in a price review, as it defines the period in which the changes in the economic circumstances should have occurred. Traditionally, the general approach in this regard was very strict: the change had to have occurred within the review period.[10] However, there is some flexibility in this area, in particular since the financial crisis began in 2008 and the European spot markets have developed into liquid gas markets.

Today, much of the gas is sold on a forward basis against forward prices for delivery in the future, which can be as much as several gas years later. As a consequence, there have been many discussions on when – if at all – a change in such forward values of gas can be considered to fall within the review period. Is the date of delivery and payment for the gas the relevant date for consideration, the date of entering into the forward sale or any date or period in between, and against which gas price under the parties' contract is this forward sale compared? Even though a change may occur outside of the review period, it can still be relied on if its effects occurred within the relevant review period. Before, a typical example would be new legislation which has been announced to enter into force at a later date. If it comes into effect after the review period, technically this change would fall outside the review period. However, as market participants usually start adjusting their behaviour in anticipation of such new legislation before it enters into force, this adjustment in behaviour may qualify as a change in the economic circumstances within the review period if it affects the value of the gas. However, the risk of a change falling between two periods should at all times be prevented. Similarly, a party cannot rely on the same change twice, unless it can show that the change has not been reflected in the price provisions.

The relevance of the review period demonstrates why a party may opt for a

10 See Final Award in Case 9812, August 1999 and Final Award in Case 13504, January 2007, "Extracts from ICC Arbitral Awards: Price Setting and Price Revision in the Energy Sector", in: *ICC International Court of Arbitration Bulletin*, Vol 20/2, 2009, pp70 and 97.

wildcard price review instead of a regular price review. Typically, this is done when the severity of the impact of the changes in the economic circumstances do not permit the requesting party to wait for the next price review. Alternatively, a party may take a more opportunistic approach by trying to lock in a sudden and perhaps temporary change in the market, thus targeting the ideal moment to request a wildcard price review.

When combining the time element with the required change in economic circumstances, the requesting party should prove that these changes occurred within the review period, and that they are not yet reflected in the price provisions. This is determined by comparing the situation that relates to the change at the start and end of the review period. The observed change should be compared with the change in the contract price (determined by comparing the contract price at the start and end of the review period) to verify the extent to which the change is reflected in the contract price.

(b) *Weight element – significant changes*

Typically, the price review clause also provides that the economic circumstances should change significantly compared with what is reflected in the price provisions. The term 'significant' seems to serve as a minimal threshold, ensuring that the change has sufficient weight to justify an adjustment of the price provisions.[11]

When can a change be judged to be significant? The price review clause does not contain any further quantification of this criterion, and leaves the parties and the tribunal with little guidance in determining whether this requirement has been met. The reference to the price provisions suggest that the significance is related to the change in the value of gas. But what change in value is significant? A reduction of 0.01 eurocent per kilowatt hour may not seem significant, but as under these long-term gas sales agreements extremely large volumes are being sold, this seemingly small change is definitely significant.

What is clear is that the requirement of significance does not intend effectively to turn the price review clause into a hardship clause.[12] However, it forces the tribunal to consider whether the nature and the extent of the change justify a price review and adjustment of the price provisions. This must be assessed on a case-by-case basis.

(c) *Influence element – changes beyond the control of the parties*

In order to prevent misuse of the price review clause, generally it will provide that the changes in the economic circumstances should be beyond the control of the parties (or, at least, the party requesting the review).[13] Thus, the price review clause requires that both parties did not and were not in a position to influence the changes that they invoke in a price review. However, in principle this should not stop the

---

11 See also Final Award in Case 9812, August 1999, "Extracts from ICC Arbitral Awards: Price Setting and Price Revision in the Energy Sector", in: *ICC International Court of Arbitration Bulletin*, Vol 20/2, 2009, p71.

12 See also Peter Roberts, *Gas Sales and Gas Transportation Agreements, Principles and Practice*, Sweet & Maxwell, 3rd edn, 2011, 15-005, p189.

13 See also Final Award in Case 9812, August 1999 and Final Award in Case 13504, January 2007, "Extracts from ICC Arbitral Awards: Price Setting and Price Revision in the Energy Sector", in: *ICC International Court of Arbitration Bulletin*, Vol 20/2, 2009, pp71 and 98.

requesting party from relying on changes that were (allegedly) caused by the other party.

This raises questions regarding state-owned entities and parties subject to regulatory action. When can they be considered to be in control of certain changes? In the case of monopolists or dominant market players that have price-setting power, can they be considered responsible for certain developments in their market? Although these points are known to have been raised and have merit in some cases, today's extensive competition laws and regulations are known to have created a more liberal gas market, where no single player has the ability to control changes. Therefore, typically tribunals will find that the changes are beyond the parties' control. However, the situation may be different if a party shows atypical market behaviour which is related to the change that it invokes in the price review.

(d) Geographical element – changes in the country or the market of the buyer

Typically, the price review clause also includes a geographical element, providing that the change must have occurred in the buyer's country or market. Not all price review clauses define this geographical element, although some do refer to a certain country or region in which the buyer traditionally operates.

The question remains how to interpret this geographical limitation. In general, this interpretation is relatively strict. When the price review clause refers to a specific country, the main focus lies on the changes that have occurred in that country.[14] If there is no clear definition of the geographical area, parties tend to focus on the changes that occurred in the country in which the buyer sells the majority of its gas.[15]

Although this assessment may have been relatively straightforward in the past, it raises a number of questions in today's gas market. Borders are fading as gas companies have expanded their business across country lines. In addition, local gas markets are merging. Finally, over the years spot markets have emerged and expanded across Europe, increasing in liquidity. These developments raise various questions regarding the definition of the buyer's country and market, and create challenges for parties and arbitrators. Depending on the review period and the wording of the price review clause, this may lead to extensive discussion.

These developments also trigger yet another, but related, discussion regarding the market level that should be taken into account in price reviews when determining the value of gas. This is examined in section 3.2.

3.2 Changes in the value of gas

As discussed above, in principle a party may rely on any type of change in the economic circumstances, provided that the requirements discussed above are met. However, most price review clauses contain a specific reference to a change in the

---

14 See also Final Award in Case 13504, January 2007, "Extracts from ICC Arbitral Awards: Price Setting and Price Revision in the Energy Sector", in: *ICC International Court of Arbitration Bulletin*, Vol 20/2, 2009, p97.

15 In the Final Award in Case 13504, the tribunal considered that, although the buyer was reselling the gas only into part of the country of the buyer, "documentation of economic changes in [buyers' state] as a whole would suffice to meet the requirement for a price review". Final Award in Case 13504, January 2007, "Extracts from ICC Arbitral Awards: Price Setting and Price Revision in the Energy Sector", in: *ICC International Court of Arbitration Bulletin*, Vol 20/2, 2009, p97.

value of gas. This is not surprising, as a change in the economic circumstances that has not been reflected in the price provisions will usually relate to such change.

In this section, we consider two questions that are regularly raised when a party requests a price review based on a change in the value of gas. These originate from the wording typically found in price review clauses. From this, it follows that "the value of gas" refers to (i) the value in the market of the buyer, with or without reference to the end-user market and (ii) to the value as it can be obtained, directly or indirectly, by a prudent and efficient gas company. This raises questions related to the applicable market level and to the obtainability of the market value of gas.

(a) *Value of gas in the market of the buyer – market level*

We have already discussed the geographical element that is included in price review clauses, referring to the country or the market of the buyer in which the change must have occurred. We have also pointed out the various questions that have arisen in this regard due to recent market developments. Apart from these more geographical questions, the price review clause also raises questions related to the market level that should be used to determine the value of gas in a price review. These questions, which will be discussed in this section, revolve around the two different market levels found in most gas markets today: the end-user market and the wholesale market.

When most European long-term gas sales agreements were concluded, the gas supply chain was relatively straightforward and consisted of only a few key players. Market players bought gas from producers under long-term agreements and sold the gas onward to a variety of end-users: large industrial clients, gas-fired power plants, medium- and small-sized clients. They also sold gas to households, although this was done through local distribution companies. As there was only a relatively small mark-up included in the gas prices, the distribution companies mostly served as an intermediary.

Today, part of the value of gas is stuck at this intermediate level. As distribution companies have been able partly to buy gas from the increasingly liquid spot markets, but are – at the same time – faced with consumers reluctant to change suppliers and renegotiate better prices, they have successfully negotiated lower purchase prices compared with relatively high sales prices.

As a result, the definition of the term 'market of the buyer' has increased in importance when determining the value of gas. The value of gas can differ depending on the market level that is referred to. Buyers argue that as they mainly sell gas at the wholesale level, this is the relevant market. However, some price review clauses make explicit reference to the value of gas in the end-user market. Sellers argue that this suggests that instead of the intermediate wholesale level, the end-user level is the market of the buyer. Buyers refer to the wording "directly and indirectly" sometimes included in the price review clause to argue that the value of gas at the wholesale level should be taken into account. By contrast, sellers argue that this wording suggests that the value of gas includes the value that is obtained at the wholesale level by distribution companies when they sell gas at a higher price to households, which are considered part of the end-user market. Sellers claim that buyers obtain this value indirectly through their sales to the distribution companies (particularly if the buyer is part of a wider group of companies that includes distribution companies), the value of which should therefore also be included in the calculation of the value of gas in the buyer's market. To our knowledge, no award in which a tribunal considers the validity of either position has been published yet.

(b) Technical market value versus obtainable market value – the obtainability test

When determining the value of gas, price review clauses may refer not only to the value in the (end-user) market of the buyer, but also to the value as it can be obtained (directly or indirectly) by a prudent and efficient gas company. This final part clearly reflects that the price review clause refers to an objective value of gas, although this still leaves room for a buyer to support its value calculations with its own sales prices, as long as the buyer can be considered "prudent and efficient". What causes much more debate is the question of whether the value referred to in this part of the price review clause is the technical market value or the obtainable market value.

When most long-term gas sales agreements were concluded, there was no actual gas-to-gas competition. Instead, gas competed with alternative fuels. In order to ensure the long-term competitiveness of gas, its value and, thus, its price was determined by identifying the best alternative fuel for each type of end-user and pricing the gas competitively in relation to the best alternative.[16] In most cases, the best alternative was oil. Prices in long-term gas supply contracts are therefore mainly linked to oil product prices.[17] The price of gas reflects the value of gas to the end-user in comparison with the costs that end-user incurs when using the most attractive alternative fuel. This is referred to as the 'indifference principle' (also known as the *Anlegbarkeitsprinzip*), which sets the technical market value of gas.[18] At a time without gas-to-gas competition, this was the only and accepted methodology to determine the value of gas in a price review, providing a technical market value.[19]

However, as, generally, price review clauses refer to the value as it can be obtained, this has led to parties and tribunals raising questions regarding the meaning of the term 'value of gas' and the methodology to calculate such value. Some parties have argued that 'the value of gas' refers to the market value or obtainable value of gas, also referring to the wording 'directly and indirectly' which can be included in price review clauses. They argue that this wording confirms the price review clause refers to the value of gas as it can actually be obtained. In that

16 The market value principle was introduced in 1962 by the Dutch minister of economic affairs, JW De Pous, who published a policy paper referred to as "*Nota De Pous*" (Parliamentary Papers II, 1961/1962, 6767, nr 1). See also Anthony J Melling, *Natural Gas Pricing and Its Future, Europe as the Battleground*, Carnegie Endowment, 2010, pp16-17.

17 EU Energy Sector Enquiry, January 10 2007, pp101-104 and International Energy Agency, *Natural Gas Pricing in Competitive Markets*, 1998, p32.

18 In its 1998 publication, the International Energy Agency refers to the netback value of gas, which is determined "on the basis of the weighted average value of the gas in competition with other fuels adjusted to allow for transportation and storage costs from the beach or border and any taxes on gas". Note 17 above, p32. See also Hans K Schneider and Walter Schulz, *Die Gaspreisbildung nach dem Anlegbarkeitsprinzip, Ein Beitrag zu ihrer wirtschaftspolitischen Beurteilung*, R Oldenbourg Verlag, Munich, 1977, which discusses the *Anlegbarkeitsprinzip* and indexation-based pricing.

19 Final Award in Case 9812, August 1999, "Extracts from ICC Arbitral Awards: Price Setting and Price Revision in the Energy Sector", in: *ICC International Court of Arbitration Bulletin*, Vol 20/2, 2009, p75.

regard, in its final award in ICC Case 13504 the tribunal considered that:

> *in the absence of a particular provision in the [Contract] as to the meaning of "the value of Natural Gas", the Arbitral Tribunal considers that this expression should be interpreted as referring to the ordinary market value of gas, and that the market value of gas is to be determined on the basis of prices obtained or obtainable in actual transactions in the various market segments constituting the end-user market of the Buyer.*
>
> *... The value obtained in the market is the payment/revenue/price which the supplier receives from the entirety of all end customers. The principle that any value determination under [the price review clause] has ultimately to be checked against and is finally determined by the prices actually obtained or obtainable in the market was acknowledged by Respondent.*[20]

The discussions on the difference between the technical market value and the obtainable market value have been fuelled by various market developments, such as successful production of US shale gas, the increased number of continental European LNG terminals and the financial crisis. These developments have caused a simultaneous supply surge and a drop in demand, which in Europe has led to oversupply situations since around the second quarter of 2009. Combined with the increased liquidity of spot markets, gas-to-gas competition is considered to have emerged to varying extents in certain key European markets. In addition, these developments have caused a spread between the prices of gas on hubs and the price of gas that is traded based on oil price indexation. These prices tended to be both linked and of similar levels over the mid to longer term, yet this has no longer been the case since the summer of 2009. The influence of this development on the actual obtainable values of gas still depends on the particular market involved in the contract.

Following these developments, parties now argue that the wording of the price review clause allows for a shift from the valuation of gas versus alternative fuels to a valuation of gas versus gas. They argue gas to gas competition allows parties to determine the value of gas based on the value that the buyer can actually obtain in its market, which they argue is currently determined by the prices on the spot market, thus definitively moving away from the more technical market value and instead applying an obtainability test. Advocates of the obtainability test claim that the wording of the price review clause confirms that it refers to the value of gas as it can actually be obtained, which they argue is currently based on gas prices in the spot market.

3.3 Ability economically to market the gas

Usually, the price review clause contains a separate paragraph that provides that in any case the price provisions of the contract will allow the buyer economically to market the gas. This is also referred to as the 'in any case' clause. Generally, the wording of this clause raises two questions on its interpretation:

- Does it provide a separate trigger for a price review?
- Does it provide a margin guarantee?

---

20 Final Award in Case 13504, January 2007, in: "Extracts from ICC Arbitral Awards: Price Setting and Price Revision in the Energy Sector", in *ICC International Court of Arbitration Bulletin*, Vol 20/2, 2009, p99.

(a) *Separate trigger?*

It may be questioned whether the in any case clause constitutes a separate basis to trigger a price review. An argument to that extent may be made based on the phrase 'in any case' at the beginning of the clause. However, it follows from the price review clause that a price review requires the economic circumstances to change significantly and that this is the true core of a price review. The phrase 'in any case' could simply mean that any adjustment of the price provisions reflecting these changes should leave the gas marketable.

In the limited case law that is available, reference has been made to the in any case clause and its interpretation. In an ICC award rendered in 1999, the arbitral tribunal held that:

> *Therefore, the Arbitral Tribunal concludes that a consolidation of both paragraphs has to take place. Such a consolidation entitles the buyer to invoke Article 6.10(a)(2) [the in any case clause] if an application of Article 6.10(a)(1) leads to a result where he cannot economically market the natural gas. Accordingly, the second paragraph therefore works as a protection of the buyer against upward adjustments of the price considering his market situation.*
>
> *... the Arbitral Tribunal has found that an allegation of 'non-marketability' ... cannot be used by the Claimants as an independent basis for its request for price review, but can only be invoked as a defence against the Respondents' request for price increase ...*[21]

In another ICC award, rendered in 2007, the arbitral tribunal did not rule on the question of whether the in any case clause can serve as a separate trigger in a price review.[22] The current case law suggests that if certain changes in the economic circumstances in principle require an upward adjustment of the contract price, the buyer may still resist such a price adjustment if this would make it impossible for it economically to market the gas. So the clause appears to serve as a form of safety net provision for the buyer, and not as a separate trigger for a price review.

It is unclear whether the in any case clause provides greater protection to the buyer. Some buyers argue that if they can identify a change that qualifies as a trigger for a price review, the resulting price adjustment not only has to reflect that change, but is also determined by the in any case clause. The adjusted price should allow the buyer economically to market the gas: if the price adjustment following from the change in economic circumstances does not allow the buyer economically to market the gas, an additional adjustment should be made. Although this interpretation may sound reasonable from a buyer's perspective, to our knowledge there is no publically available award in which a tribunal has ruled on this interpretation.

(b) *Margin guarantee?*

Normally, the in any case clause does not provide an explanation of the term

---

21 Final Award in Case 9812, August 1999, "Extracts from ICC Arbitral Awards: Price Setting and Price Revision in the Energy Sector", in *ICC International Court of Arbitration Bulletin*, Vol 20/2, 2009, pp72-73.

22 Final Award in Case 13504, January 2007, "Extracts from ICC Arbitral Awards: Price Setting and Price Revision in the Energy Sector",, in *ICC International Court of Arbitration Bulletin*, Vol 20/2, 2009, p97. In paragraph 101 of its award, the tribunal does note that: "This clause is regarded by both Parties as a safeguard for the benefit of the Buyer."

'economically market'. Some buyers argue that the in any case clause also provides a margin guarantee. They argue that the fact that they should have the ability economically to market the gas means that the buyer should always be able to make a margin. Clearly, the clause provides that in the end, the gas should be marketable. It is unclear whether this means that a positive margin should be obtained at all times over the duration of the contract. Based on the wording of the contract, arguments can be made both ways.

Buyers could argue that the term 'economically' refers to the buyer's ability to obtain a positive margin. Further, they could argue that whereas the intermediate price risk lies on the buyer, the seller carries the ultimate price risk reflected in the price review clause. This division of risks is addressed in the in any case clause, allowing an adjustment of the contract price so the buyer again has a positive margin at the end of the price review, ensuring that the price risk ultimately lies with the seller.

By contrast, sellers could argue that in the absence of a specific stipulation, the contract cannot be read to provide a positive margin guarantee. In addition, as it is within the buyer's control whether it obtains a margin, providing a margin guarantee would go against the first paragraph of the price review clause.

In any event, arbitral tribunals and parties alike will in each case have to rely on the negotiation history of the contract and previous price reviews to assess whether it can be argued that the in any case clause provides a (positive) margin guarantee.

Some buyers even suggest that the in any case clause provides that they should be able to make the same margin at the start and at the end of the review period, or alternatively, that the margin at the start of the review period provides the benchmark when determining the margin at the end of the review period. Again, arguments can be made for both buyers and sellers. As a general note, we point out that if certain changes in the economic circumstances changed the market conditions, it could be argued that the buyer may no longer be entitled to the same margin. However, whether a buyer would be entitled to a fixed margin largely depends on the facts of the case.

4. Summary

In general, it follows from most price review clauses that a party is entitled to an adjustment of the price provisions if there are changes in the economic circumstances which:

- occurred within the review period;
- are significant compared with what is reflected in the prevailing price provisions;
- are beyond the control of the parties; and
- occurred in the country or the market of the buyer.

These requirements confirm and stress the purpose of a price review: to allow for adjustments of the price provisions so that they properly reflect the changes in the market conditions faced by the parties, thereby ensuring that the contractual balance is maintained. It is questionable whether the in any case clause can be used not only as a shield or protection for the buyer if the seller requests a price increase, but also as a sword or separate trigger and margin guarantee to request a price decrease.

Confidentiality in gas price reviews

Philippe Pinsolle
Quinn Emanuel Urquhart & Sullivan LLP

Gas price reviews are based on a paradox: their purpose is to ensure that the price at which gas is bought matches the price at which it can be sold on a given market, yet the price at which gas can be sold on a given market (or any sub-segment of it) is among the most sensitive information in markets which are not yet entirely dominated by spot prices, as is currently the case in much of continental Europe, especially in the southern part.

Moreover, there is often an imbalance between the parties: the seller knows at which price it sells the gas to all of its buyers, while the buyer knows only at which price it buys the gas from this seller (and possibly other sellers). Conversely, the buyer knows the price at which it can sell the gas to its customers, yet generally the seller, unless it operates on the downstream market, can know about the price on the downstream market only through the information that it receives from its buyers, or possibly the regulator or other publically available sources, where the information published may lack transparency.

As a result, the level of information can vary significantly from one party to another. In addition, most gas supply contracts contain confidentiality provisions which further limit the flow of information. This limited availability of information affects the whole process of gas price reviews, including the pre-arbitration negotiations and the arbitration itself. Confidentiality also plays a role after the arbitration.

1. Confidentiality issues during pre-arbitration negotiations

Although it may not generate as much attention as is the case during the arbitration, the issue of confidentiality during the time leading up to arbitration is of major practical significance. This pre-contractual period may cover either the compulsory negotiation period before any price review arbitration, or the informal discussions which frequently are held between the parties before or during such compulsory negotiations. Practice shows that a major distinction should be made between two situations. When the parties provide for a specific agreement governing confidentiality, either in the initial contract or in a subsequent agreement, generally its terms will be enforced. The real difficulty arises when the parties do not have a specific agreement governing the confidentiality of their discussions, especially when they have differing expectations as to how they can use documents and information exchanged during these discussions in a subsequent arbitration.

1.1 When there is a specific agreement between the parties covering the negotiations

In essence, the issue of confidentiality before the arbitration is the question of whether – or to what extent – the information exchanged between the parties, and the position that they take, can be used in a subsequent arbitration. Practice shows that some parties are aware of this difficulty and attempt to deal with it by entering into various types of agreements. Some examples will be discussed below. The effect of such agreements is that, generally, the documents and information exchanged in the pre-arbitration negotiations cannot be used in a subsequent arbitration – but much will depend on the way in which the specific agreement is drafted.

(a) The issue

Often, the parties enter into informal discussions before formally triggering the price review mechanism. In addition, most price review provisions impose a negotiation period between the parties (generally between three and six months), during which they must attempt to resolve the disputed issues and agree a new price. Most agreements provide that no party may start arbitration proceedings before the end of the mandatory negotiation period.

Typically, during this period the parties will exchange views and economic analysis on the relevant market, and state what they each think the new price should be. The buyer may ask the seller for changes in the price formula, such as a lowering of the P0 and/or the introduction of spot-market indexation to the formula; if the price review is triggered by the seller, it will tell the buyer what type of changes it requires. For this exercise to be meaningful, the parties should be free to exchange views without being bound by them in a subsequent arbitration. The aim of these informal or mandatory negotiation periods is to reach an agreement between the parties and thus avoid arbitration. As a result, frequently the parties make concessions in order to reach a mutually satisfactory commercial agreement, notwithstanding the fact that their strict legal position may be different.

Generally, it is advisable to provide that these discussions will be conducted under a specific confidentiality regime and that the information exchanged will not be used in a subsequent arbitration. This will show that the parties understand the situation, and have taken it into account in their actions during the negotiations. A study of various gas price review agreements, and subsequent correspondence, shows that many parties often provide for a specific confidentiality, regime either in the original agreement or in a subsequent agreement – usually entered into at the beginning of the negotiations. Some examples of these provisions are discussed below.

(b) Examples of provisions

Typically, there are three types of arrangement that the parties may adopt.

The first is an agreement under which the positions expressed by the parties during the negotiation are expressed without prejudice to their rights in an arbitration – that is, in an arbitration they cannot rely on the positions expressed during the negotiation. This is not a confidentiality agreement as the information and documents are not subject to a confidentiality requirement. An example of this type of provision is the following:

The parties hereby recognise that these negotiations are conducted for the purpose of finding a commercial settlement to their price review dispute. As a result, the parties hereby acknowledge that the positions that they express during the course of this negotiation are made without prejudice to their rights in an arbitration.

It is not unusual for such a clause to contain an express prohibition for the parties to rely on the position communicated during the course of the negotiation in a subsequent arbitration: "The parties undertake not to rely on the positions expressed during the course of the negotiation in a subsequent arbitration."

The second type of arrangement is a confidentiality agreement which covers all the information and documents exchanged during the negotiations. The confidentiality agreement can remain in force for an indefinite time. In that case, it can be terminated by either party with notice, which is generally fixed by the contract. Following termination, the information that had been exchanged is no longer confidential. In the alternative, the agreement can provide that the confidentiality period lasts for a specific time. The idea is that by limiting the confidentiality period, the parties will have a good incentive to reach an agreement within that time.

However, the fact that the parties entered into negotiations – as opposed to the content of the negotiations – very often is not confidential.

Generally, this second type of arrangement contains a provision which allows either party to make use in a subsequent arbitration of information that was already in their possession before the confidentiality regime. The aim is to avoid the situation in which a given document or piece of information would become confidential simply because it has been exchanged in the course of the negotiations, if it would otherwise be available. An example of such provision is:

For the avoidance of doubt, documents disclosed or exchanged by a Party in the course of the Negotiations can be used and produced by that Party in any arbitral or other legal or other proceedings.

The third type of arrangement is a variation of the second. It contains virtually the same provisions, but adds a sanction in the event that the agreement is breached. The weakness of any confidentiality agreement is that it is very difficult to enforce if a party decides to breach it. Once the breach has occurred, the information is no longer confidential and in practice the only available remedy is damages. However, in an arbitration this remedy can include excluding the record of the document containing the protected information. Of course, this will not address the fact that the tribunal might have read the document, but at least it will prevent both the party, it in its pleadings, and the tribunal, in its award, from relying on it.

As a result, many agreements provide that, in the event that the confidentiality agreement is breached, the arbitral tribunal must declare the document containing the protected information inadmissible and refuse to include it in the record and/or strike it off the record. This type of provision is best used when it is expressed as a mandate to the arbitral tribunal and, thus, as a limitation of the tribunal's procedural powers.

An example of this type of provision is:

Should a Party produce, or rely on, a document, or a witness statement, relating to discussions or (without limitation) any and all information, documents, statements, views and/or positions taken, disclosed or exchanged by or between any of the Parties in connection with the Negotiations, the Tribunal shall declare such document, or witness statement, inadmissible and strike it from the record.

(c) *Practical effect of such provisions*

The effect of the arrangements described above is that an arbitral tribunal will enforce their terms. Generally, there is no difficulty in enforcing the third type of agreement (ie, a confidentiality agreement which provides for the sanction in case of breach). An arbitral tribunal will have a duty to enforce it, provided that the agreement, to the extent that it is a separate agreement, makes reference to the same arbitration agreement as the one contained in the gas supply contract on which the arbitration will be based.

Similarly, in general the first type of arrangement (ie, an agreement which provides that the positions of the parties are expressed without prejudice) is also enforced without difficulty. An arbitral tribunal will not allow a party to rely on a position expressed during the negotiations. The only practical difficulty with this type of agreement is that the arbitral tribunal will be aware of the parties' positions and may be influenced by them in the course of its deliberations.

The second type of arrangement can lead to difficulties, the main one being what sanction the arbitral tribunal should adopt if the confidentiality is breached. Typically, an arbitral tribunal will decide that the documents or information submitted in breach of the agreement cannot be used in the arbitration, either by excluding it from the record or by declaring it inadmissible in the first place. However, when there is no expressed sanction to this effect, the position that the arbitral tribunal will adopt is not certain. It is recommended that a sanction covering pre-contractual negotiations is systematically included in confidentiality agreements.

Of course, if there is no confidentiality agreement at all, the difficulty is compounded.

1.2 In the absence of specific agreement between the parties covering the negotiations

If the parties have not entered into any agreement covering the status of the pre-arbitration negotiations, the question is whether there is any obstacle to the use of the content of those negotiations in the arbitration. In this regard, the parties can have differing expectations, depending on their legal background and degree of sophistication. An arbitral tribunal has to find possible solutions to this issue.

(a) *The issue*

If the parties have not submitted their price review discussions to a confidentiality regime, the issue is whether the content of these discussions can be used in a subsequent arbitration. This issue is twofold: first, it is necessary to determine whether the documents are admissible and, second, in the event that they are, what weight should be given to them by the arbitral tribunal.

This situation may become even more complicated if parties unilaterally give the documents labels such as "without prejudice", "without prejudice for commercial discussions only", "commercially confidential" or "for the sole purpose of negotiation discussions". The difference with the previous examples is that, in this case, it is often only one party that has signalled an interest in a certain protection, while the other party generally did not react.

(b) Managing the respective expectations of the parties

Often, the parties will have different expectations of the status of pre-arbitration negotiations. For a variety of reasons, sometimes they may not be able – or may not be willing – to clarify the situation by addressing the issue with the other party. In such situations, the arbitral tribunal is confronted with differing and possibly contradictory views of the parties as to the status of those negotiations. An example that the author recently encountered may help to understand this type of situation. In this case, the parties had exchanged documents in the course of pre-arbitration negotiations for the purpose of finding a new price formula. During the negotiations, one party, but not the other, had marked all its documents as confidential and without prejudice. Subsequently, the other party produced those documents in the arbitration and the first party objected. The arbitral tribunal admitted the documents in question in the arbitration. Needless to say, the party that took the precaution of earmarking its documents was disappointed by the arbitral tribunal's decision, especially because the decision did not give the reasons on which it was based.

Situations like these occur more frequently than they should. As a result, it is submitted that an arbitral tribunal should be extremely cautious when confronted with this type of situation. Several options are available to the tribunal.

(c) Possible solutions

An arbitral tribunal faced with the situation in which neither party has requested confidentiality in the pre-arbitration negotiations is in a relatively easy position. In principle, neither party should object to the use of the documents or information exchanged during negotiations in the arbitration. However, should one party object, it seems that the principle should be that the document should be admitted unless, of course, there is a compelling reason why the document or information should be excluded.

It would be possible to raise an objection against the production of such a document (or the use of such information) based on the application by analogy of the rules on settlement privilege. The rationale would be that pre-arbitration negotiations are similar in nature to settlement discussions. They are intended to find an amicable solution to a given dispute. As a result, they should be excluded by nature from the arbitration, if only to protect the parties from any concession that they may have made during those negotiations.

This view may produce rather radical effects in that it excludes from the arbitration record any documents arising from the negotiations. It seems to us that, given that parties in gas price reviews are sophisticated parties, one should not presume that they have intended to protect the information disclosed in the course of negotiations if they have said nothing to this effect.

In other words, it should be determined whether there was a common intention of the parties, expressly or implicitly, to submit the information exchanged during the negotiations to a confidentiality regime. Without this common intention, it should be presumed that the documents can be disclosed unless one party has in good faith attempted to protect its own documents or information. It is a question of fact, and thus it is a case-specific situation. Nonetheless, one cannot exclude the case where one party genuinely believed, or had been led to believe, that the negotiations were confidential. In that case, in our view, the documents should be excluded from the arbitration record.

Assuming that the documents are admissible, another issue is what weight should be given to them. In our view, because these documents represent an attempt by the parties to find an amicable solution, their weight should be limited. It would not be right to read in such documents concessions made by a party and for the tribunal to consider figures or proposed formulas contained in them as a ceiling (or a floor, as the case may be) to a party's claim in the arbitration. This is particularly so since the concessions may be irrelevant and misleading outside the specific context of the negotiations. For instance, the negotiations between the parties may have been broader than the mere price review and included other, unrelated issues, so that a concession on a given point was only made in consideration of an advantage on another matter, which is not to be considered by the tribunal.

For all these reasons, it is submitted that the information and to the position taken by the parties in the course of amicable settlement should be given only a limited weight.

The next issue is the issue of confidentiality during the arbitration process.

2. Confidentiality issues during the arbitration

As the arbitration progresses, the parties will have to discuss the underlying economic data to their respective claims and positions. More specifically, generally the claimant will have to show that there is a significant change in the value of gas on the relevant market in comparison with the date of the previous price review (the wording of the price review provision may vary, but in essence this is the test to be satisfied). In order to do so, both parties will have to rely on variety of economic data, some of which is sensitive, such as pricing provisions in various contracts, which are frequently subject to confidentiality agreements. Even if they are not, one party may not want to disclose them to the other party because they are considered to be highly sensitive. In addition, there is often an imbalance between the parties as the buyer generally knows only at what price it can buy and sell gas on the end-users market while the seller, which will generally have several buyers in a given market, will often have a better picture of the price at which the gas is sold at the entry points of a given market.

As a result, confidentiality may hinder a party's ability fully to present its case or, at least, to present it in a manner capable of convincing an arbitral tribunal.

Against this background, it is useful to describe the tools that are available to the arbitral tribunal in terms of confidentiality, then to discuss the impact of confidentiality on access to information, and, finally, it is important to recall that the standard of proof must be adapted, in our view, to the availability of the information.

2.1 The tools available to the arbitral tribunal

Arbitral proceedings may be confidential because the parties have selected arbitration rules which provide such confidentiality. In addition, certain arbitration laws also provide for confidentiality. This is not specific to gas price review. The parties may have entered into a specific agreement creating a confidentiality regime for their arbitration. Finally, the arbitral tribunal has the power to take appropriate protective measures in order to ensure confidentiality.

(a) Confidentiality of the proceedings in general

Some arbitration rules provide for confidentiality. The most notable are the London Court of International Arbitration Rules, which provide as follows:

> *[U]nless the parties expressly agree in writing to the contrary, the parties undertake as a general principle to keep confidential all awards in their arbitration, together with all materials in the proceedings created for the purpose of the arbitration and all other documents produced by another party in the proceedings not otherwise in the public domain – save and to the extent that disclosure may be required of a party by legal duty, to protect or pursue a legal right or to enforce or challenge an award in bona fide legal proceedings before a state court or other judicial authority (Article 30.1).*

The new International Chamber of Commerce (ICC) Rules merely state that the arbitral tribunal has the power to enact confidentiality measures. Article 22(3) of the 2012 ICC Rules provides that:

> *upon the request of any party, the arbitral tribunal may make orders concerning the confidentiality of the arbitration proceedings or of any other matters in connection with the arbitration and may take measures for protecting trade secrets and confidential information.*

The French legal regime accepts the idea that arbitration should be confidential in domestic proceedings, but remains neutral on confidentiality in international proceedings.[1]

These provisions are not specific at all to gas price reviews and are quite familiar to all international arbitration practitioners. However, they have an impact on gas price review arbitrations, as it is frequent that many cases run in parallel.

When there is a global and significant change on the market, either the sellers or the buyers will want to trigger a price review. These price reviews, depending on the relevant dates of each contract, may occur at approximately the same time. Moreover, many contracts provide for a 'joker' price review which can be exercised at any time and, if the change in the market is significant enough, many parties will invoke it. As a result, many cases raising exactly the same issues may run in parallel or consecutively, but more or less at the same time. As a result, different price reviews may be running in parallel at the same time in the same market under different contracts, which may deal with similar issues and be triggered by similar events.

The issue then becomes whether an award obtained in a given case – or a position taken by a party in a given case – can be used in another case (of course, to the extent

---

1 See Article 1464(4) of the Code of Civil Procedure for domestic arbitration, which has no equivalent in international arbitration. See also P Pinsolle, "The Distinctive Features of the New French Law on Arbitration", in *New Developments in International Commercial Arbitration 99* (C Müller and A Rigozzi, eds, Schulthess, 2011).

that it becomes known to the other party in that other case). In practice, this may happen when several companies belonging to the same group oppose the same buyer (or the same seller, as the case may be), or when various companies are represented by the same counsel, or use the same expert, who may have access to awards rendered in parallel cases.

The provisions described above may or may not allow such use. If they do, for example, by relying on the exception according to which confidentiality does not apply when one party wants to enforce a legal right, a party may nonetheless decide to breach the confidentiality provision. Again, this discussion is not specific to price review arbitrations, but it is worth mentioning here because of its impact in this particular context.

The issue cannot be resolved in the abstract – it requires a case-by-case analysis.

(b) The impact of specific agreements entered into by the parties

A study of the contractual practice of gas supply agreements shows that some, but not all, contain confidentiality provisions applying to dispute resolution. Some of these are quite specific and will be discussed below; others are more general.

The most frequent provision concerns expert determination. Frequently, long-term supply agreements provide that certain limited questions (eg, the quality of gas) must be referred to expert determination instead of or before arbitration. In that case, many of these agreements will require the expert to be bound by a confidentiality obligation. This obligation is complete only when the expert accepts its mandate. Nonetheless, this is the most frequent type of confidentiality provision used in practice.

It is far more unusual to find a similar provision concerning arbitration. A study of 17 different contracts with a price review mechanism has not revealed any such provision. In fact, when it comes to arbitration, the parties may want to tailor the confidentiality obligations to arbitration, but in a more discrete way. As we will see below, there are many different methods to achieve this, but usually they will relate to document production or the possibility for one party to give documents supporting the case of the other party.

(c) Case-specific protective orders and other protective measures

The arbitral tribunal has full power to protect confidentiality of certain information if it believes that the protection is necessary. In our view, this power is part of the general power of the arbitral tribunal to conduct proceedings in a way it sees fit. The most recent ICC Rules confirm the existence of this power, but in our view that power existed before the confirmation.[2] Again, the power is not specific to gas price review disputes – frequently it is used in intellectual property disputes.

The many measures available to the tribunal include the following:

- the possibility for one party to submit redacted documents;
- the possibility for one party to submit redacted documents along with a non-redacted version, which will be shown to the tribunal only in the event of a dispute on the scope of the redaction;

---

2 See Article 22(3) of the 2012 ICC Rules.

- the creation of confidentiality 'rings' or confidentiality 'clubs' consisting of a limited number of designated individuals on each side. Typically, such individuals include the lawyers or some of them, one or more designated experts, and sometimes one or more designated client's representatives;
- the possibility for the tribunal to mandate a third party to review and confirm the accuracy of specific information; and
- any combination of the above, depending of the needs of the parties.

Although sometimes these measures can be cumbersome to implement in practice (eg, if during the hearing some witnesses have to go in and out of the hearing room depending of the subject matter discussed), generally they prove useful when there are confidentiality issues. For gas price reviews, these measures are particularly useful when discussing pricing. As mentioned above, these measures are not specific to gas price reviews. Rather, they are also used in other types of arbitration, especially arbitrations involving IP rights. Nonetheless, they can be used by, or at least be a source of inspiration for, arbitral tribunals when addressing confidentiality issues in the context of a gas price review arbitration.

2.2 Access to information

In price review disputes, one of the most sensitive and difficult issues is access to information. Inevitably, parties will have to demonstrate the value of gas on a given market, and possibly the value of competing fuels. Information relating to the value of gas is commercially sensitive and players are not willing to share such core information on their business. Thus, information relating to price is difficult to access and parties must resort to external sources. Given the scarcity of information, it is even more difficult for the tribunal to determine the reliability of the information put before it. This can have an impact on a claim based on a change in the value of the gas in the relevant market. However, the issue of the burden of proof is separate from that of access to information.

As is often the case, the parties may limit or expand their ability to access the relevant information as between themselves. The arbitral tribunal will have to direct the disclosure process in a way that accommodates the legitimate need of the claimant to access the relevant information, the need of the respondent to keep confidential certain sensitive information and, possibly, the competing interest of third parties.

(a) The distinction between burden of proof and access to information

International arbitration practitioners are familiar with the classic objection that is raised in the context of disclosure requests. Very often, the party trying to resist a disclosure request will respond that the information requested should be produced or obtained by the other party as part of its duty to discharge its burden of proof. In other words, many parties believe that it is not legitimate for their opponent to try to obtain in their own record information which may be useful for the opponent to advance its claim. Those parties will consider that they have no duty to help the other party in this respect.

In reality, the situation is more subtle than this. There is a fundamental difference between the burden of proof and the access to information. An example may help. Assume a party has sold one of its subsidiaries to a third party, and that third party makes a number of claims for breach of representation and warranties. The selling party is aware that the records of its former subsidiary contain relevant information which may help it to resist the claim. In our view, in this particular situation, it is only right that the selling party is able to obtain, through a disclosure process, access to this information. This is not a question of burden of proof – the selling party will still have to support with evidence the fact that it asserts in its defence, but it will be given access to the relevant information, which happens to be in the possession of the other party.

Often, the same is true in the context of gas price reviews. At best, the buyer has a limited knowledge of the market's structure and the prevailing price on the wholesales gas market. This may be increased through consultants that provide a quantitative analysis of a given market. The seller may have additional information on the market because it is selling to more than one party. This may create an imbalance and this imbalance may work to the detriment of the buyer when it is the claimant in the price review process. As a result, and subject to certain conditions, the buyer should be able to obtain, through the disclosure process, access to certain information that the seller holds. Similarly, when there is an imbalance to the detriment of the seller, the seller should be able to access the relevant information held by the buyer.

However, sometimes the parties themselves limit this ability.

(b) The impact of specific agreements entered into by the parties

Gas price review disputes are disputes between sophisticated parties. They are aware of the fact that a tribunal has authority to order the disclosure of documents and information. As a result, they sometimes decide to limit this ability.

Our study of the practice in this regard has identified three types of provisions.

The first is to remove the power of the tribunal to order disclosure of documents, either by expressly excluding this power in the arbitration agreement or by excluding the relevant provisions of the applicable rules of arbitration (eg, Articles 24(3), 27(2) and 16(3) of the UNCITRAL Arbitration Rules 1976, insofar as such provisions relate to the production of the documents).

A second type of provision is a limitation as between the parties, but which does not specifically apply to the tribunal. It may be in the price review provision itself, rather than in the arbitration agreement, and the question then becomes whether it binds the arbitral tribunal too. Typically, this provision will be worded: "No party shall be required to disclose any business secrets nor to provide such information as the other party may need to substantiate its position."

Another provision, which is inspired by this second type of provision, imposes a duty for each party to substantiate its claim without any possibility to have access to information held by the other party:

Each party shall provide all necessary information to substantiate its own claim. No party shall be required to disclose any business secrets or breach any confidentiality undertaking nor to provide such information as the other party may need to substantiate its claim.

In a third type of provision, the parties explicitly exclude information covered by a confidentiality agreement. The provision generally reads as follows:

During the course of any contract sales price review, or any resulting arbitration proceedings, neither buyer nor seller shall have any obligation to disclose any information which it is prohibited from disclosing by confidentiality obligations.

(c) *Shaping the disclosure process*

In view of the above, when considering a request for disclosure an arbitral tribunal should pay particular attention to the specific agreements entered into by the parties. Of course, this is true when the disclosure is excluded altogether. However, very often disclosure will not be completely excluded but merely limited.

The difficulty lies with the interpretation of provisions that partially limit disclosure. In particular, the issue is whether the confidentiality limitation entered into for the purpose of the negotiation will apply also during the arbitration. In our view, the arbitral tribunal should respect the terms of the confidentiality agreements entered into by the parties even though they may not explicitly state that they will apply during the arbitration. We believe that it would be counterintuitive for the parties to have submitted their negotiations to a specific confidentiality regime, but then to adopt a radically different regime for the purpose of the arbitration. If the parties have decided that they should be able to reach an agreement on the basis of a certain set of data, or on a basis of limited information, in principle the same set of data or limited information should be available for the arbitration.

The same applies if the agreement specifically states that the limitation applies during the course of the arbitration.

The existence of this limitation does not mean that the arbitral tribunal is deprived of any powers. In our view, the arbitral tribunal should direct the disclosure process in the most appropriate manner. The aim should be to limit any imbalance between the parties for access to the information, while taking into account any agreement entered into by the parties. In resolving this question, the arbitral tribunal should also take into account the limited availability of information and adjust the standard of proof accordingly.

2.3 Adjusting the standard of proof to the availability of information

There is a direct link between the standard of proof and the availability of information.

(a) *The link between the standard of proof and the availability of information*

International arbitral tribunals have long recognised that the standard of proof and the availability of information should be linked. The issue here is not to discuss the standard of proof in the abstract – that is, to determine whether the appropriate standard is the balance of probabilities or otherwise. Rather, the issue is to adjust this standard in real terms to the information available in a given case.

This is not specific to price review disputes, and practical solutions have been found in other fields. For instance, matters of corruption raise similar issues. For a long time, arbitral tribunals considered that, because corruption is a very serious allegation, the corresponding standard of proof must be very high.[3] The difficulty with this analysis is that, because corruption activities are clandestine by nature, it is often very difficult to satisfy such a standard of proof. As a result, the modern approach has been to adopt the opposite rule and to consider that the standard of proof applicable in corruption issues can be relatively low. The idea behind this reversal is that when sufficient indices show a pattern which can lead to the conclusion that corruption exists, this conclusion is valid unless the other party proves otherwise by providing indication or factual elements which can disprove corruption.[4] In practice, it does not constitute a complete reversal of the burden of proof, but it can amount to a burden of proof which can be satisfied on the basis of *prima facie* evidence.[5] As a result, it is a realistic recognition of the fact that because information is rarely completely available in corruption cases, the standard of proof should be adjusted accordingly.[6]

In our view, the same is true in gas price review disputes, although to a lesser extent. As explained above, the difficulty is that very often information on the value of gas is sensitive and so difficult to obtain. As a result, a party to a gas price review dispute will have to rely on internal evidence or extrapolations based on its own experience. Typically, a buyer will have direct experience of the sales that it has concluded on the end-users market and those that it has not concluded. Quite often, for the sales not concluded, the buyer will have a database reporting the content of conversations between the commercial division and the client on the level of the competing and successful offer. The reliability of such a source is not absolute, but it is an indication. This indication can be completed by quantitative studies that can be provided by some consultancies. Again, the reliability will depend on the size of the sample and on the rigour of the analysis carried out. However, because generally there is no open market that gives a reliable indication of the price, it is submitted

---

3 See Award dated December 19 1991 (Claude Reymond president) in the *Westinghouse* case, reference in 12(2) ASA BULLETIN 244 (1994); Michael Hwang SC and Kevin Lim, *Corruption in Arbitration-Law and Reality*, in 8(1) ASIAN INT'L ARB J (2012, forthcoming [2]); currently available at www.arbitration-icca.org, at 28.

4 Karen Mills, "Corruption and Other Illegality in the Formation and Performance of Contracts and in the Conduct of Arbitration Relating Thereto", in *ICCA Congress Series* No 11 288, 295 (2003). The author affirms that:

> *Because of the near impossibility to "prove" corruption, where there is a reasonable indication of corruption, an appropriate way to make a determination may be to shift the burden of proof to the allegedly corrupt party to establish that the legal and good faith requirements were in fact duly met.*

See also Constantine Partasides, "Proving Corruption in International Arbitration: A Balance Standard for the Real World", in 25(1) *ICSID REV 47*, 60 (2010). Partasides' proposition is that "plausible evidence of corruption, offered by the party alleging illegality, should require an adequate evidentiary showing by the party denying the allegation".

5 A Timothy Martin, *International Arbitration and Corruption: An Evolving Standard*, in 1(2) TDM 6-7 (2004). See also Final Award, ICC Case No 6497 of 1994, XXIVA YB COMM ARB 71 (1999). The arbitral tribunal stated that it:

> *may exceptionally request the other party to bring some counterevidence, if such task is possible and not too burdensome. If the other party does not bring such counter-evidence, the arbitral tribunal may conclude that the facts alleged are proven.*

6 Partasides, note 4 above, at 57: *"in determining an appropriate standard of proof, arbitration tribunals should take account not only of the seriousness or likelihood of the allegation, but also the intrinsic difficulty of proving it."*

that this type of evidence should be accepted by the tribunal and that the standard of proof should be adjusted in view of the scarcity of the information.

(b) *Satisfying the standard of a burden proof in practice*

It follows from the above that the burden of proof of a party triggering a gas price review can be satisfied using one or more of the following sources of information:

- public indices on the given market when they are available and representative;
- written resolutions of the regulator when there are available;
- the party's internal return or experience (realised sales and lost sales);
- any extrinsic evidence showing the price at which the sales are made in the relevant market;
- quantitative studies provided by consultancies; and
- any other evidence that can be collected by experts in the course of preparing their report, which should be relevant for the market.

In turn, some or all of the above evidence can be confirmed by an independent auditor third party, which can test that it corresponds to the company's record. This is particularly useful when a party relies only, or primarily, on its own internal records without any corroborating evidence. If necessary, this data can be completed by direct testimony of the representatives of the commercial division of the party triggering the price review, describing their experience in qualitative terms.

3. Confidentiality issues after the arbitration

In principle, the award decided by the arbitral tribunal is confidential between the parties after the arbitration ends. However, given the similarities between individual gas price review disputes and the contractual provisions in dispute, the access to an arbitral award may often be an advantage for the parties, if only for its interpretative value.

3.1 Limited availability of awards

The confidential nature of gas price review disputes means that is it very difficult to obtain information on the awards. Generally, arbitral awards rendered in commercial disputes are kept confidential by the parties, except when there is a duty to disclose the award (eg, to the stock market), or, at the very least, its result. The price of gas under the relevant contract is sensitive.

However, there are situations in which an award can be made available to the public. The first is when the award is challenged before domestic courts. Although it is possible in some countries to obtain a special regime because of the sensitivity of the information, generally an award challenged before a domestic court will become public, or at least partially public, through the decision of the court itself. The same is true when the award is enforced in a country other than the place of arbitration.

In our experience, awards in gas price review disputes are rarely enforced – generally, they are complied with voluntarily, often following negotiations between the parties, precisely to keep their content secret. Nonetheless, they may sometimes be challenged before the court of the place of arbitration.

Usually, apart from this particular case, awards are kept secret by the parties. This is unfortunate because, provided that it is respected that the price formula is sensitive information which should be kept confidential between the parties, there are other parts of arbitral awards which may be of general interest.

3.2 The interpretative value of certain awards

Gas price review disputes are based on provisions which usually are reproduced from one contract to another. There are significant variations, but there is also language which is found in almost every contract. For instance, clauses such as "In any case, the buyer shall be able to market economically the gas" are often included in price review provisions. Information from arbitral awards that have interpreted this language would be useful for the industry at large. In addition, there are issues which arise in almost all gas price review cases, for example, what use can be made of information which becomes available after the date of the triggering of the price review? Again, access to information from awards on this particular issue would be extremely useful.

(a) The interpretation of the term 'market economically'

Most gas supply contracts contain a clause to the effect that the buyer should be able to market the gas economically on its market. Typically, this protection is granted in addition to the mechanism of the price review and may be used as a corrective device by the arbitral tribunal when determining the new price formula. The new price formula will reflect the value of the gas on the relevant market and enable the buyer to market the gas economically. Sometimes, this provision can be viewed as an independent trigger – it depends on the language of the relevant contract.

'Market the gas economically' is generally understood as enabling the buyer to sell the gas at a profit, at least on the day on which the price is reset, but not as a guaranteed margin for the future. However, there are many uncertainties as to the proper interpretation of these terms. For example, what is the proper margin, what type of costs should be taken into account?

Interestingly, this term is found regardless of the applicable law. The author has seen contracts governed by such laws as the laws of France, England and Wales, Switzerland, Italy, Germany, Denmark and New York that contain it. It is submitted that its proper interpretation is not a function of the applicable law but a function of what the industry thinks it should mean. In carrying out this exercise, it would be useful to look at what the arbitral awards have said about the meaning of 'market economically'/'market the gas economically'. For example, one possibility would be to disclose those parts of the award which do not contain sensitive information. However, to the best of our knowledge, such disclosure is not a common practice today.

(b) The issue of the date and the use of information that follows the relevant date

Another issue that is highly contested in gas price reviews is what use should be made of information on the relevant market which becomes available after the date on which the price review has been triggered. The traditional view is that when the price review is triggered at a given date, the arbitral tribunal should look at the information available on that date to determine whether the price review trigger is valid and, if so, at what level the price should be reset. Subsequent information may be used as a benchmark or for verification purposes.

The difficulty is that, with the time taken for negotiations between the parties and then the arbitration, the award is rendered several months after this date. As a result, the arbitral tribunal has had access to information that is more recent than that which was available on the date of the price review. In our view, arbitrators should at least take this information into consideration during the arbitration. The issue then becomes how the information can be used. One possibility is to use it as a statistical benchmark to make sure that the new formula is not off limits, but that is already in breach of the principles described above. Again, having access to arbitral awards on this particular issue would benefit the industry at large. One can hope that some parts of them will become available one day.

Changes of circumstances as a price modifier

Michael Polkinghorne
White & Case LLP

1. Introduction

This chapter in many respects deals with matters that are foreign to the rest of this book. First, it concentrates on civil, and to an extent Arab, legal systems (whereas many gas contracts are English law beasts); second, it considers the notion of hardship or *imprévision* (whereas we are accustomed to speaking of and dealing with gas price reopener clauses rather than more general calls for contract amendment).

The purpose of this exercise is to explore the relief open to victims of changed circumstances under the law applicable to the parties' agreement. The aim is both to demonstrate that remedies may arise independent of any gas price reopener clauses and to consider how these might apply.

The starting point – whether under civil or common law principles – is that the parties are bound by their agreement.[1] That said, however, courts frequently retain a residual right to intervene in cases where matters change so fundamentally as to change that agreement to something else. While parties are well familiar with the notion of *force majeure*, and much of this book is devoted to contractual price reopeners, other remedies may still lie open, and very often do. This is most notable in civil law countries.

A detailed description of the principle of hardship can be found in the UNIDROIT principles:[2]

SECTION 2: HARDSHIP

ARTICLE 6.2.1

(Contract to be observed)

Where the performance of a contract becomes more onerous for one of the parties, that party is nevertheless bound to perform its obligations subject to the following provisions on hardship.

ARTICLE 6.2.2

(Definition of hardship)

There is hardship where the occurrence of events fundamentally alters the equilibrium of the contract either because the cost of a party's performance has increased or because the value of the performance a party receives has diminished, and

---

1 While this is largely self-evident under common law systems, those unfamiliar with civil law may sometimes overlook the fact that French law, for example, echoes these sentiments.

2 Articles 6.2.1 to 6.2.3 of the UNIDROIT Principles of International Commercial Contracts (2004).

(a) the events occur or become known to the disadvantaged party after the conclusion of the contract;
(b) the events could not reasonably have been taken into account by the disadvantaged party at the time of the conclusion of the contract;
(c) the events are beyond the control of the disadvantaged party; and
(d) the risk of the events was not assumed by the disadvantaged party.

ARTICLE 6.2.3
(Effects of hardship)
(1) In case of hardship the disadvantaged party is entitled to request renegotiations. The request shall be made without undue delay and shall indicate the grounds on which it is based.
(2) The request for renegotiation does not in itself entitle the disadvantaged party to withhold performance.
(3) Upon failure to reach agreement within a reasonable time either party may resort to the court.
(4) If the court finds hardship it may, if reasonable,
(a) terminate the contract at a date and on terms to be fixed, or
(b) adapt the contract with a view to restoring its equilibrium.

By way of comparison, examples of commonly used language in gas price reopeners include the following:

Either party may request a review of the method of determining the Contract Sales Price set forth in clause X if it has a good faith basis for believing that, for reasons outside its control, there has been a material change in the value of imports into Y and/or re-gasified LNG in the Y gas market which is anticipated to have lasting effect.[3]

If … economic circumstances in the buyer's market … have substantially changed as compared to that expected when entering into the contract for reasons beyond the parties' control … and the contract price … does not reflect the value of natural gas in the buyer's market.[4]

---

3 P Hodges, "LNG – a minefield for disputes?" in *Liquefied Natural Gas*, Paul Griffin (ed), 2006, p115.

4 S Farmer, "LNG Sale and Purchase Agreement" in *Liquefied Natural Gas*, Paul Griffin (ed), 2006, p49. See also an example from an Energy Charter Secretariat paper (Energy Charter Treaty Paper, *Putting a Price on Energy*, October 18 2007 at 161 (available from the Energy Charter Treaty website):
(a) If the circumstances beyond the control of the Parties chance [sic] significantly compared to the underlying assumptions in the prevailing price provisions, each Party is entitled to an adjustment of the price provisions reflecting such changes. The price provisions shall in any case allow the gas to be economically marketed based on sound marketing operation.
(b) Either Party shall be entitled to request a review of the price provisions for the first time with effect of dd/mm/yyyy and thereafter every three years.
(c) Each Party shall provide the necessary information to substantiate its claim.
(d) Following a request for a price review the Parties shall meet to examine whether an adjustment of the price provisions is justified. Failing an agreement within 120 days either Party may refer the matter to arbitration in line with the provisions on arbitration of the Contract.
(e) As long as no agreement has been reached or no arbitration award has been rendered all rights and obligations under the agreement – including the price provisions – shall remain applicable unchanged. Unless otherwise agreed or decided by the arbitral award, differences to the newly established price shall be retroactively compensated inclusive of interest on the difference calculated at a rate reflecting the conditions on the international financing market.

Both price review and hardship mechanisms deal with the tension – inherent in any long-term arrangement – between the opposing aims of predictability and flexibility. Parties want to know what they have to do, but recognise that no one can predict the future.

Thus, both reopeners and hardship clauses look at ways of dealing with the unexpected. They provide that in the case of an unforeseen event, beyond the control of the parties, which renders performance unduly onerous (the precise terms and degrees vary), something must be done. That 'something' generally involves the parties seeking to negotiate a solution, failing which a third party (an expert, arbitral tribunal or national court) can often impose a solution by way of contract modification.

Are the underpinnings of the two measures the same? Looking at price reopeners (and this chapter concentrates on the European form), their aim may be discerned as the preservation of the contract's feasibility, which from the outset involves the buyer's ability to market the gas in its end market(s). The clauses involve the recognition that the end game – the ability to market the gas – is one of the *raisons d'être* of the entire arrangement.[5]

Hardship provisions, on the other hand – at least insofar as they are found in national legal systems – are not nearly as specific. They are geared to apply to an undisclosed variety of events, and look more broadly to their overall effect on the parties rather than the commercial viability of the deal struck (although this aim can be the subject of a hardship provision).

Questions of the parties' positions and commercial viability are closely related, particularly when price reopeners speak of adjustments that are "fair and equitable" or refer to contractual "equilibrium"; but the fact remains that they are different animals. The question for this chapter is thus whether – in the face of a well-drafted price reopener – a role remains for hardship principles to operate, and if so, when and how.

And what if there is no price reopener clause at all? What options are open to a party to a long-term contract that is no longer viable?

2. Hardship under national laws

2.1 Common law notions?

It seems fairly settled that English law will not admit of a (non-contractual)[6] power to amend a contract on the basis of changed circumstances.[7] Perhaps the closest one might come to this is the doctrine of frustration, which – while arguably broader than the notion of *force majeure*[8] – results in termination rather than modification of the underlying obligation.[9]

The United States has a doctrine of commercial impracticality, pursuant to which several commentators have posited that the court may not only arrive at a fair

5 Another factor being that the seller receives sufficient revenues to ensure the long-term viability of the deal. While one often speaks of buyers taking volume risk and suppliers price risk, the issues are often more nuanced than this simplified description might suggest.

6 For an example of an English court's treatment of a contractual hardship clause, see *Superior Overseas Development Corporation v British Gas Corporation* [1982], 1 Lloyd's Rep 262. (A French example can be seen in CA Paris, December 28 1976, *EDF v Shell France*, JCP G 1978, II, 18810, obs J Robert.)

7 See, for example, *Total Gas Marketing v Arco British Ltd* [1998] 2 Lloyd's Rep 209 (House of Lords).

distribution of losses, but also modify the parties' agreement going forward.[10] That said, the courts appear to have been parsimonious in the exercise of such powers.[11]

One might also pause to discuss the notion of *force majeure* (which does not exist *per se* under English law – hence the large quantities of ink often spilled in drafting these clauses).

Like the above notions, *force majeure* looks to deal with the unpredictable, but it has its limitations. In the usual case, the occurrence of an event of *force majeure* results in either suspension or termination of the agreement in question (although examples exist whereby the parties undertake to negotiate an accommodation). In addition, the requirement under most *force majeure* provisions is that the supervening event render contractual performance not merely onerous, but impossible. In this regard, there is a fairly consistent stream of authority that problems in end-market conditions are not of a type to render a purchase obligation impossible to perform – the usual test for an event of *force majeure*.

However, as *force majeure* is a contractual phenomenon under the common law, skilful drafting of a *force majeure* clause may lead to a different result. Two examples may illustrate this. One involves the use of the word 'hinder'. It is generally accepted under English law that where a clause refers to performance being hindered, this is a lesser standard than impossibility – as was stated nearly one century ago: "to place a merchant in the position of being unable to deliver unless he dislocates his business and breaks his contracts in order to fulfil one surely hinders delivery."[12] So the use of such language may permit a court to intervene in circumstances falling short of impossibility to perform (although even here a price rise may not suffice).[13]

The other is an example of pure wordsmithing. While end-user market problems would not usually fall into the category of *force majeure*, there are examples of cases where *force majeure* has been established purely due to the fact that the clauses defining the same included language that temporary loss of markets would be covered by the relevant clause.[14] One thus needs to take care in drafting and reviewing clauses of this nature.

---

8 *Davis Contractors v Fareham Urban DC* [1956] UKHL 3, [1956] AC 696, [1956] 2 ALL ER 145 cited at Puelinckx AH, "Frustration, Hardship, *Force Majeure, Imprévision, Wegfall der Geschäftsgrundlage, Unmöglichkeit*, Changed Circumstances", 3 *J Int'l Arb* 1986, No 2, at 47 *et seq*, p50:

> *frustration occurs whenever the law recognises that without default of either party a contractual obligation has become incapable of being performed because the circumstances in which performance is called for would render it a thing radically different from which was undertaken by the contract... it was not this that I promised to do.*

9 *Id.*

10 For a general discussion, see Fred Fucci, "Hardship and Changed Circumstances as Excuse for Non-Performance of Contracts – Practical Considerations in International Infrastructure Investment and Finance", provisional TDM, January 2007.

11 See *Aluminium Co of America v Essex Group Co* 499 F Supp 53 (WD Pa 1980) cited by Fucci (*id*) at p2, not followed in later cases; see White & Peters, "A Footnote of Jack Dawson", *Michigan Law Review* 100, No 7 (202): 1973. See also *Florida Power & Light Co v Westinghouse Electric Corp* (517 F Supp 440 (ED Va 1981)), in which the court noted: "Generally, however, the fact that performance has become economically burdensome or unattractive is not sufficient for performance to be excused... We will not allow a party to a contract to escape a bad bargain because it is burdensome."

12 *Tennants (Lancashire) Ltd v CS Wilson & Co Ltd* [1917] AC 495 at 510. Cited in *Chitty on Contracts,* 31st ed, para 14.146.

13 *Id.*

14 See *Kodiak 1981 Drilling Partnership v Delhi Gas Pipeline Corp,* No 83-CI-10260 (Bexor Co Tex 1984), cited in WJ Legg, "Natural Gas Contract Litigation in Oklahoma", 11 *Okla City UL Rev* 63. 1986 at 78.

2.2 Civil law

In the civil law context, however, the notion of hardship is found in a surprisingly large number of systems and may spring from several bases. The vast majority of examples cited are set out in the annex to this chapter.

(a) Arab law countries

In many Arab countries, the theory of revision for hardship finds its true roots in Islamic law. As a religious system, *Sharia* is concerned above all with questions of individual conscience, good conscience and good faith. Thus, to hold the debtor to performance in circumstances in which it had never envisaged performance would – the argument runs – be unconscionable and inequitable.[15]

According to a general principal of Islamic law, "hardship shall bring alleviation". This general principle of Islamic law emanates from the *Quranic* principle that "Allah intends for your ease and does not intend for your hardship",[16] and from a *hadith*[17] reporting that the Prophet Muhammad said that "you have been sent forth to make things easy, not to impose difficulties".[18]

Hanafi[19] jurists have elaborated a 'doctrine of excuses' (*i'dhar*) under which the aggrieved party is excused from performing its contractual obligations – and the contract may be terminated or modified – if performance becomes prejudicial subsequent to the occurrence of an unforeseen circumstance after conclusion of the contract.[20] *Hanbali*[21] and *Maliki*[22] jurists adopted a 'doctrine of calamity/blight' (*ja'iha*), which is similar to the *Hanafi* doctrine of excuses.[23]

Egypt, followed by other Arab countries, adopted the theory of hardship when incorporating much of the French Civil Code in the 1940s. Article 147(2) of the Egyptian Civil Code provides as follows:

> *The contract makes the law of the parties. It can be revoked or altered only by mutual consent of the parties or for reasons provided for by the law.*
>
> *When, however, as a result of exceptional and unpredictable events of a general character, the performance of the contractual obligation, without becoming impossible, becomes excessively onerous in such way as to threaten the debtor with exorbitant loss, the judge may, according to the circumstances, and after taking into consideration the interests of both parties, reduce to reasonable limits, the obligation that has become excessive. Any agreement to the contrary is void.*[24]

---

15 D Rivkin, "*Lex Mercatoria* and *Force Majeure*", in *Transnational Rules in International Commercial Arbitration* (ICC Publ No 480/4), 1993, p196.

16 *Sûrah al-Baqarah*, 185. The following quotations involve informal translation.

17 A report of the sayings or actions of the prophet or his companions.

18 *Sahîh al-Bukhârî*, Vol 1, Book 4, No 219.

19 The *Hanafi* school is one of the four main Sunni schools of law. It was founded by scholar Abu Hanifa an-Nu'man and is followed by most Sunnis of Iraq, Syria, Lebanon, Bangladesh, Mauritius, Pakistan, India, Afghanistan, Central Asia, Southern Russia, the Caucasus, the Balkans, Turkey and parts of Egypt.

20 A Sanhoury, *Al Waseet fi Sharh al Qanun al Madani*, 2008 edition, Vol 1, pp525-526, para 416; J Whelan, *UAE Civil Code and Ministry of Justice Commentary*, p156, para 2-0273.

21 The *Hanbali* school is one of the four main Sunni schools of law. It was founded by scholar Ahmad ibn Hanbal and is considered very strict and conservative, especially regarding questions of dogma and cult. The *Hanbali* school is followed by most Sunnis of Saudi Arabia.

22 The *Maliki* school is one of the four main Sunni schools of law. It was founded by scholar Malik ibn Anas and is followed by most Sunnis of North Africa, West Africa, the United Arab Emirates and Kuwait.

23 J Whelan, *UAE Civil Code and Ministry of Justice Commentary*, p156, para 2-0273.

In North Africa, this is echoed in Article 107(3) of the Algerian Civil Code and Article 147 of the Libyan Civil Code, among others.

However, it appears that Morocco and Tunisia have not adopted this provision.

In the Middle East, one can look to Bahrain (Article 130 of Legislative Decree 19/2001), Iraq (Article 146(2) of the Civil Code), Jordan (Article 205 of the Civil Code), Kuwait (Article 198 of the Civil Code), Qatar (Article 171(2) of the Civil Code), Syria (Article 148 of the Civil Code), the United Arab Emirates (Article 249 of the Civil Code) and Yemen (Article 211 of Civil Law 14/2002) (see Annex 1, section 5 below). Lebanon has limited the application of this principle to administrative (or public law) contracts (in much the same way as France; see below).

(b) *Europe*

In Europe, the theory has ebbed and flowed over the centuries. Founded on Roman law, the principle of *rebus sic stantibus* (ie, the contract remains binding provided that matters remain as they are) enjoyed some popularity in the 18th century, but fell out of favour in the 19th century. It returned to the fore in the early 20th century, as reflected in *Gaz de Bordeaux*.[25]

In this case a concessionaire for the provision of gas lighting in Bordeaux found that the price of coal had tripled, well outside any contractual range. The French *Conseil d'Etat* (the highest administrative court in France) ultimately ruled that the city of Bordeaux should compensate the concessionaire on the basis of this unforeseen event (*'imprévision'*).[26] As a result, French administrative law admits the notion of hardship, although the same principle does not exist in private law.[27]

Other countries, however, have gone further.

For example, Article 6:258 (complemented by Article 6:260) of the Dutch Civil Code and Section 313 of the German Civil Code deal expressly with the effects of unforeseen circumstances in the commercial sphere, giving the court the power to modify or terminate the contract. Austrian law has a similar approach, albeit on a different basis (as in Germany, based on the so-called *Wegfall der Geschäftisgrundlage* ('disappearance of the basis of the transaction')). Similar provisions are contained in the Portuguese and Greek Civil Codes (Articles 437 and 388, respectively). Along the same lines, Italian case law has interpreted Article 1467 of the Italian Civil Code as giving the courts the power to adapt the contract to the new circumstances.

---

24 Perrot Fanner and Sims Marshall, *Translation of the Egyptian Civil Code*, New World Publisher, p29.

25 *Conseil d'Etat, Compagnie générale d'éclairage de Bordeaux*, Rec 125, concl Chardenet, March 30 1916, quoted in M Long, P Weil *et al*, *Les Grands Arrêts de la Jurisprudence Administrative* (2003) at 188-89. Translation from the award in ISID Case ARB/01/8, *CMS Gas Transmission Company v The Argentine Republic* (May 12 2005); all cited in Fucci (note 12 *supra*), p18.

26 *Id*:

> *Just as the Company cannot argue that it should not be required to bear any increase in the price... it would be totally excessive if it is admitted that such increases are to be considered a normal business risk; on the contrary, it is necessary to find a solution that puts an end to temporary difficulties, taking into account both the general interest... and the special conditions that do not allow the contract to operate normally... ; to this end it is necessary to decide, on the one hand, that the Company is required to provide the concession service and, on the other hand, that during this period it must bear only that part of the adverse consequences that a reasonable interpretation of the contract allows...*

27 Civ, March 6 1876, D 1876 1, 193, Note Giboulot; *Les grands arrêts de la jurisprudence civile*, t 2, F Terre and Y Lequette, Dalloz, 12nd ed, 2008, No 165. Note below, however, that application of the principle of good faith may still have a role to play here.

As is outlined below, Belgium has displayed the same reticence as the French in giving hardship a more limited role (see section 4.3(b) below).

(c) *Nordic countries*

One can also find hardship provisions by way of Article 36 of the Contracts Acts of Sweden, Finland, and Denmark (see Annex 1, section 2 below).

(d) *South America*

In South America, the Civil Codes of Argentina, Peru and Paraguay expressly admit change of circumstances as a ground for relief for the affected party.[28] The exception to this rule appears to be Chile, where (like France) the hardship doctrine has not been embraced by the courts outside the area of administrative contracts.

(e) *Eastern Europe*

Provision can also be found in Eastern European jurisdictions (see Annex 1, section 7 below). For example, Article 709(6) of the Russian Civil Code 1995 provides that a contractor has the right to demand an increase in the price of a contract that contains no price escalation clause where there has been a material increase in the cost of materials or in the cost of services rendered to the contractor by a third party. The necessary change in circumstances is defined in Article 451 of the code as "a change of circumstances ... such that if the parties could reasonably foresee this, the contract would not have been concluded at all by them or it would have been concluded on significantly differing conditions".[29]

Lithuania (Article 6.204 of the Civil Code) provides another example.

(f) *Far East*

In Japan – even though there is no statutory law governing changed contractual circumstances – a judge can adapt the contract if he finds unforeseen, substantially changed circumstances which are not the fault of the parties and which mean that continued performance would violate the principles of good faith and equity.

In his book *The Principle of Changed Circumstances in Civil Law* (1926), Katsumoto Masaaki gave the following definition of the rule:

> *The rule states that when the circumstances releasing a legal act, creating a legal relation, change in an unforeseeable way alter the accomplishment of the act and before expiry of its consequences, due to the influence of facts not attributable to the parties, with the result that the creation of legal consequences in the original sense, or their*

---

28 See Annex 1, section 3 below.

29 A court will amend the contract where:
- the parties assumed that the change in circumstances would not occur at the time of contracting;
- the contractor has not caused the change in circumstances itself;
- performance of the contract given the changed circumstances would cause exceptional damages to the contractor;
- the contractor does not bear the risk of the changed circumstances, according either to custom or the contract; and
- termination of the contract would be contrary to the public interest, or would cause significant damage to the parties which would exceed the cost of performance of the contract as may be amended by the court.

continuation, is to be considered as unreasonable in the light of the rule of equity and good faith, then such legal consequences are to be adapted in equity and good faith.[30]

In China, according to informal sources, the situation appears to be as follows:

- Prior to 1993, Chinese contract law allowed for either termination of the contract or alteration of the contract either for *force majeure* or for an "unavoidable external reason" not caused through the fault of either party. The Chinese courts interpreted this "unavoidable external reason" as a change in circumstances.
- While the new contract laws that came into effect in 1993 and 1999 did not include a provision for alteration of the contract in the event of such a change in circumstances, the Chinese courts continue to apply the earlier rule in extraordinary circumstances.

3. Issues of hardship

While one can speak of general principles of hardship, it should be readily apparent that the manner in which these principles are applied will vary not only between different jurisdictions, but even within those jurisdictions themselves. A discussion of the most common issues of relevance to gas price matters may assist.

3.1 Nature of triggering event

(a) Need the underlying event be general or specific?

Article 147(2) of the Egyptian Civil Code, along with many other national codes in North Africa, provides that the event must be not only exceptional, but also "general" in nature. This means that it should not be specific to the debtor, but should affect a category of persons. Thus, the debtor's individual bankruptcy or a strike of its employees will not ordinarily be considered as a general exceptional event on which the debtor may base an application for hardship.[31]

However, the converse appears to be the case under Hungarian civil law. The Hungarian courts seem to accept that Section 241 of the Civil Code (which reflects the hardship principle) cannot be applied to adapt contracts to deal with fundamental changes in the economic and social climate affecting a wide range or the majority of economic actors. In one judgment, the Supreme Court explained that a change in market demand in itself could not serve as ground to amend a contract, since both parties were affected by the change in that case.[32]

(b) Are price changes foreseeable?

The notion of what is foreseeable will vary from case to case, and the issue of price variations may evoke different views from one jurisdiction to the next. The Federal Supreme Court of Iraq, for example, has ruled that a debtor could not rely on an increase in the general pricing level of raw materials and wages to request the

---

30 Igarashi, K, *Keiyaku to jijohenko*, 3rd ed, Tokyo, Yuhikiaku, 1983, pp147-148 cited at Puelinckx, AH (note 10 *supra*), pp62-63.

31 A Sanhoury (note 22 *supra*), 2008 edition, Vol 1, p532, para 420.

32 See Civil Code 1993.670.

amendment of its contract, since "the increase of prices is a predictable event that cannot be considered as an exceptional general unforeseeable event".[33] (One wonders whether the court might nevertheless have accepted the idea that, even here, an increase of unprecedented proportions might have qualified for correction.)

Fucci[34] cites the following as examples of events which have been ruled to have been foreseeable and hence did not give rise to a claim for hardship:

- dramatic changes in market prices for products;[35]
- unfavourable general economic circumstances in a country;
- currency fluctuations, even severe;
- failure of a central bank to grant authorisation to pay in foreign currency when foreign exchange control regulations were in place at the time of contracting; and
- armed hostilities between countries with a history of antagonism.

While the above is undoubtedly true, the inquiry may nevertheless focus not merely on whether an event itself was foreseeable, but also on whether its gravity was foreseeable. As Fucci himself points out later in his article, the following events appear to have constituted events of hardship (and were hence by definition unforeseeable):

- a tenfold increase in price due to a post-contracting change in government regulation[36] and the imposition of new safety regulations after conclusion of a contract to build a plant requiring installation of additional equipment and 'making [the contractor's] performance substantially more onerous';
- a sudden devaluation of a country's currency (the currency of payment) in the order of 80%;
- the disappearance of a market for a contracted product (as opposed to a contraction in the market for a product).[37]

It seems clear, to the author at least, that each case must turn on its own facts.

---

33 Federal Supreme Court of Iraq, December 7 2009, Decision 1289.

34 *Id* (note 12 *supra*).

35 Fucci (note 12 *supra*) cites a case in support:

In the ICC Award in Matter No. 2216 (1974), the case arose because a Norwegian company failed to perform a petroleum purchase agreement because the price of petroleum had gone down by more than half between the time of contract and scheduled delivery. The Tribunal did not permit an adjustment in the contract price on the basis of a hardship argument. This was not found to constitute a "bouleversement" of economic circumstances, but a simple fluctuation in market prices. In a commentary to this case by Yves Derains, then Secretary General of the ICC Court of Arbitration [Y. Derains, Chronique des sentences arbitrales, Clunet 1975, p. 921], he pointed out that to accept this type of fluctuation as a ground to exonerate the non-performance of a contract 'would put in danger the security of transactions.'

36 Fucci (note 12 *supra*) states:

In that situation a party generating waste entered into a four-year contract with a waste disposal company in a certain country. The price is fixed per ton over the term of the contract. Two years into the performance, the Government of the country prescribes prices for storing waste that are ten times higher than before.

37 Fucci (note 12 *supra*) states:

In that case, a dealer in electronic goods in the former East Germany contracted in September 1989 to buy inventory from a supplier in another former socialist bloc country. The goods were to be delivered in December 1990. In November 1990, the buyer in East Germany informed the seller that the goods were no longer of any use to it on the grounds that after unification with West Germany, there was no longer any market for the electronic products from the socialist country supplier.

(c) Nature of impact of that event

Professor Sanhoury suggests that while there is no objective criterion in Egypt that allows one to know when the performance of an obligation has become "excessively onerous",[38] there does appear to be an element of objectivity when considering whether a given event could constitute hardship (rather than a specific enquiry into the effect of the relevance of an event on a given claimant). According to Sanhoury, it does not appear to matter that the debtor has substantial resources which would allow it to bear the loss with no great pain. If the debtor is threatened with a loss that is several times as large as an ordinary loss resulting from such a contract, the requirement of an excessive burden is met, he states – even if such a burden is not great in relation to the debtor's overall wealth.[39]

However, this seems to be at odds with certain authorities discussed in the European or US context. By way of example, in a case governed by Swiss law, the tribunal expressed the view that if the contract in dispute constituted only a small part of the seller's overall revenues, it would be difficult for hardship to apply (which, in the writer's view, suggests a subjective test).[40] Fucci goes on to state:

> *Therefore, it is possible to extract from this award another principle that a contract affected by a change in economic circumstances must represent a significant portion of a company's revenues for performance to be considered "unbearable". Other arbitral jurisprudence supports the theory that the standard for judging what is bearable is subjective. What is unbearable or "excessively onerous" for a relatively small company for which a particular contract represents a significant part of its revenues may be merely onerous and thus bearable for a large, well-funded company which does not risk serious financial difficulty as a result of continued performance of the contract.*[41]

As the citation from Sanhoury shows, this point appears far from settled. Even under Swiss law, other commentators have posited that the test is in fact objective, and that the fact that a particular seller is ruined is not in itself sufficient to make a successful hardship claim.[42]

(d) Extent of changes required to trigger hardship

One example of where hardship was allowed to operate comes from an Algerian law arbitration in the 1990s. In this case, brought under the United Nations Commission on International Trade Law Rules, the tribunal had to rule under a dollar-denominated contract entered into by an Italian construction company with the government of Kuwait for the construction of a new embassy in Algeria. A majority of the three arbitrators accepted that a depreciation of about 35% in the value of the US dollar with respect to the Italian lira constituted a changed circumstance justifying compensation to the contractor (whose costs were predominantly in

---

38 A Sanhoury, *Al Waseet fi Sharh al Qanun al Madani*, 2008 Edition, Vol 1, pp535-536, para 420.

39 *Id.*

40 International Chamber of Commerce award in Case 2508 (1976), reported in *Journal du Droit International* No 4 (October/November/December 1977), 939.

41 Fucci (note 12 *supra*), p26.

42 H Houtte, *Changed Circumstances and* Pacta Sunt Servanda, p113 4(5) TDM, September 2007 – thus advancing the position that under Swiss law, one must look at whether the event in question would seriously affect anyone in the claimant's position.

Italian lire). However, the award contained a strong dissent by one of the arbitrators, who felt that the depreciation was foreseeable. He also maintained that the majority's reading of the scope of the depreciation did not meet the rigorous demands of the Algerian Civil Code provision.[43]

As has been seen above, different cases have given rise to a range of apparently contradictory outcomes. This could be the result of the unique nature of each case when all matters are considered, or could reflect differing judicial attitudes as to when relief should be granted.

Unsurprisingly, there are variations within Europe itself. The Dutch provisions, in speaking of "reasonableness or fairness", appear fairly liberal in respect of the trigger for modification; whereas other systems tend to reflect more closely the UNIDROIT notion that the change must be fundamental before one can speak of contract change.[44]

Other countries have sought to close this debate. Sudan, for example, even puts a figure on the requisite degree of pain, requiring that "the loss exceeds one third of the obligation" (see Annex 1, section 6).

(e) Relevance of assumption of risk

In European doctrine and jurisprudence, one frequently sees discussion of the importance of a party's assumption of risk (ie, the choice of US dollars as the contract currency indicating assumption of risk of currency movements).[45] Indeed, this is encapsulated in Article 6.2.2 of the UNIDROIT principles (see section 1 above). This may be interesting to consider in the light of the Arabic codified hardship provisions, which purport to override contractual provisions negating hardship (one can see a debate arising as to whether allocation of risk constitutes "agreement to the contrary" under the codes).[46]

(f) Nature of request

Under certain European and South American systems, the mechanism involves a requirement that the disadvantaged party first seek termination of the contract, which can then be avoided only if the other party proposes or agrees to modify the same instead.[47] While one might assume that, in reality, the distinctions between requests for dissolution versus modification could become blurred, one can see cases

43 Description of *In the Matter of Arbitration Proceedings between Icori Estero SpA and Kuwait Foreign Trading Contracting & Investment Co*, published in 9 *Int'l Arbitration Report*, A-1 (1994); found in Fucci (note 12 *supra*), p21.

44 That said, the preparatory works to the Dutch provisions suggest that this remedy should nevertheless be applied sparingly. See *Memorie van Toelichting* pp 228, 772-773; C Van Zeben, J du Ron and M Olthof, *Parlementaire geschiedenis van het nieuwe burgerlijke wetboek, Boek 6, Algemeen gedeelte van het verbintenissenrecht*, Kluwer, Deventer, 1981, 967 at 972; cited by Houtte (note 43 *supra*), p114.

45 In a case arising from the Asian financial crisis, an arbitral tribunal – dealing with the catastrophic depreciation of the Indonesian rupiyah and an economic crisis of profound proportions – held, among other things, that "by pricing in US dollars rather than in Indonesian Rupiyah, the Parties unambiguously allocated the risk of a depreciation of the local currency to PLN":

> *When stipulations like these appear in a long-term agreement like the ESC, with respect to which it is obvious that the surrounding circumstances may change dramatically during the life of the contract, one can only conclude that the allocation of risk is intentional, indeed emphatic.*

See van der Berg, AJ, ed, *Yearbook Commercial Arbitration*, Vol XXV (2000), pp11-432, paras194 and 195.

46 See Article 147(2) of the Egyptian Civil Code at Annex 1, section 5 below.

47 See Article 478 of the Brazilian Civil Code at Annex 1, section 3 below.

where a party seeking a price reduction would nevertheless wish to keep the contract alive and would accordingly be loath even to suggest termination.

(g) *Is consensus needed before contract can be modified?*

Under Japanese law, while some authors assert that a judge can adapt the contract against the will of the parties, the majority opinion appears to be that if, upon a request for adaptation, the other party refuses, the contract will most likely be dissolved.[48] This could well be at odds with the situation in many other countries, in which the court's ability to modify an agreement appears not to be limited by the parties' opinions.[49]

4. Is there an inherent duty to renegotiate?

A broader question arises as to whether – for example, on the basis of the civil law concept of good faith – there exists an inherent duty to renegotiate long-term agreements. While this notion may come as a surprise to contract drafters, it has provoked a good deal of discussion among arbitrators, academics and counsel.

4.1 Judicial hesitation

The first point – as explained by Klaus Peter Berger – is that arbitrators remain loath to imply such a duty where the parties have addressed the issue of unforeseen changes (ie, by virtue of a *force majeure* clause), but have not provided for such an exercise for lesser evils.[50] He cites an *ad hoc* award – from an investor-state case – which sums up this school of thought:

> *It is not for the Arbitral Tribunal to question the motives or judgment of the Parties, but to assess their rights and obligations in light of their legally significant acts or omissions. That is all; that is enough. To go beyond this role would be to betray the legitimate expectations reflected in the Parties' agreement to arbitrate, and indeed to impair the international usefulness of the arbitral mechanism...*
>
> *The arbitrators cannot usurp the role of government officials or business leaders. They have no political authority, and no right to presume to impose their personal view of what might be an appropriate negotiated solution. Whatever the purity of their intent, arbitrators who acted in such a fashion would be derelict in their duties, and would create more mischief than good. The focus of the Arbitral Tribunal's inquiry has been to ascertain the rights and obligations of the parties to the particular contractual arrangements from which its authority is derived.*[51]

Hans van Houtte,[52] cited another arbitrator's views:

---

48 Japanese authority also suggests that the mere presence of a hardship clause does not exclude the operation of general principles. See *Arbitration Court of the Japan Shipping Exchange*, award dated September 20 1975, *Yb Comm Arb*, 1983, 153 at 154.

49 Article 147(2) of the Egyptian Civil Code, cited in full at Annex 1, section 5 below, states:
When, however, as a result of exceptional and unpredictable events of a general character, the performance of the contractual obligation, without becoming impossible, becomes excessively onerous in such way as to threaten the debtor with exorbitant loss, the judge may, according to the circumstances, and after taking into consideration the interests of both parties, reduce to reasonable limits, the obligation that has become excessive. Any agreement to the contrary is void.

50 KP Berger, "Renegotiation and Adaptation of International Investment Contracts: The Role of Contract Drafters and Arbitrators", 36 *V and JTL* 1347.

51 *Id* at 1353, citing UNCITRAL award of May 4 1999, 25 *YB Comm Arb* 13, 61 (2000).

52 H van Houtte, (note 43 *supra*).

> *As a general rule, one should be particularly reluctant to accept it when there is no gap or lacuna in the contract and when the intent of the parties has been clearly expressed... Caution is especially called for, moreover, in international transactions where it is generally much less likely that the parties have been unaware of the risk of a remote contingency or unable to formulate it precisely.*[53]

These observations – dealing with the question of an inherent right to renegotiate – are probably of less impact where the principle is nevertheless espoused in the underlying applicable law.

4.2 Discussion of duty to renegotiate

Another school of thought asserts the existence of such an obligation on the basis of the civil law notion of good faith. Other commentators of a more Latin bent argue that the obligation is the offspring of the *rebus sic stantibus* principle),[54] which should temper the overriding notion of *pacta sunt servanda* (ie, agreements must be kept). Berger cites, among other things, the UN Draft Code of Conduct for Transnational Corporations, which states:

> *In the absence of contractual clauses providing for review or renegotiation, transnational corporations should respond positively to requests for review or renegotiation of contracts concluded with Governments or governmental agencies in circumstances marked by duress, or clear inequality between the parties, or where the conditions upon which such a contract was based have fundamentally changed, causing thereby unforeseen major distortions in the relations between the parties and thus rendering the contract unfair or oppressive to either of the parties. Aiming at ensuring fairness to all parties concerned, review or renegotiation in such situations should be undertaken in accordance with applicable legal principles and generally recognized legal practices.*[55]

While, after a far-reaching analysis, Berger reaches no firm conclusions, he does posit that there are "good reasons to assume the existence of such a transnational legal principle".[56]

A short review of the recent law in two jurisdictions which have not (at least in the private context) embraced the notion of a general right of hardship shows that the debate continues.

---

53 ICC Award 1512 (1971), *Yb Comm Arb*, 1976, 128 at 129.

54 This school of thought asserts that the true agreement of the parties foresaw a *quid pro quo* consistent with the agreement's equilibrium at the time of contracting, and hence any modification is in reality the enforcement of the original agreement.

55 UN-ECOSOC 1979 Transnational Corporations: Codes of Conduct, Formulations by the Chairman, Art 5 reprinted in *Legal Problems of Codes of Conduct for Multinational Enterprises* (Norbert Horn ed, 1980) pp493 and 494. (Even here, however, there is a condition that the contract's applicable law should permit such renegotiation, which is a recurring theme). Other international law sources include Article 62 of the 1969 Vienna Convention on the Law of Treaties:

> *A fundamental change of circumstances which has occurred with regard to those existing at the time of the conclusion of a treaty, and which was not foreseen by the parties, may not be invoked as a ground for terminating or withdrawing from the treaty unless:*
>
> *the existence of those circumstances constituted an essential basis of the consent of the parties to be bound by the treaty; and*
>
> *the effect of the change is radically to transform the extent of the obligations still to be performed under the treaty.*

Houtte also points out, however, that this remains subordinate to the overriding principle of *pacta sunt servanda* (note 43 *supra*, pp112 and, citing other authorities, 121). (One might also note that Article 62 speaks only of termination and withdrawal).

56 Berger (note 51 *supra*).

4.3 Debate in traditionally resistant countries

(a) *France*

In its seminal decision in *Canal de Craponne*, the Court of Cassation – the French supreme court – rejected the notion that a duty to renegotiate in cases of hardship exists outside the realm of French administrative law.[57]

While the *Canal de Craponne* decision was confirmed as recently as 2009,[58] there are cases suggesting a broader obligation. As early as 1992, the Court of Cassation awarded damages against a contract party that refused to modify a contract whose terms drove the counterparty to ruin.[59] In a more recent case the Court of Cassation censured an appeal court which obliged a party to perform a contract without enquiring as to whether changes in the economic circumstances of the same – notably, an increase in the cost of primary materials – affected the contractual equilibrium sought by the parties at the time of its signature.[60]

Furthermore, an International Chamber of Commerce tribunal applying French law invoked, among other things, Article 1134 of the French Civil Code to order negotiation rather than termination of an agreement due to hardship. The tribunal found that the general principle of good faith in contract performance contained in Article 1134 of the code implicitly imposes a duty on parties to negotiate in the face of changed circumstances so that performance of the contract does not cause excessive hardship, especially in long-term contracts.[61]

(b) *Belgium*

A 2009 decision of the Belgian Court of Cassation – which had hitherto denied the existence of such a principle in Belgian law – surprised a number of commentators.[62] The court ruled that changed circumstances which were not reasonably foreseeable at the time of the contract and which make performance more onerous may in certain cases constitute an impediment under Article 79 of the Convention on Contracts for the International Sale of Goods (CISG) excusing non-performance.[63] One might therefore ask whether Belgium will move towards a more general principle of hardship over and beyond the CISG.

---

57 *Supra* note 29. Query, of course, the application of public international law principles to commercial agreements of the type encountered in the energy industry.

58 Cass Civ 3e, March 18 2009, *RTD Civ* 2009.235, obs B Fages.

59 Cass Com, November 3 1992 (Huard), *Bull Civ IV No* 338, JCP G 1993, II, 22164 – sale of petrol to a station service owner at non-competitive prices.

60 Cass Com, June 29 2010, D 2010.2481. See also a decision of the Nancy Court of Appeal in which a supplier was ordered to renegotiate a contract after a post-contractual change in legislation bestowed a windfall profit upon him (in which the purchaser sought to participate: CA Nancy, September 26 2007, No 2073/07). While the status of this decision remains the subject of debate (see P Mazeaud, RC, July 1 2008, No 3.7387), it has been recognised as coming close to a duty of hardship (see O Cachard, "*L'ombre de la révision judiciaire du contrat*", *Revue Lamy Droit Civil* 2008, No 49, p2969).

61 ICC Arbitral Award 9994, Excerpt in *ICC International Court of Arbitration Bulletin*, 2005 Special Supplement, pp79-80.

62 Cass (Belge) June 19 2009, C.07.0289.N, http://jure.juridat.just.fgov.be/pdfapp/download_blog?idpdf=F-20090619-4, Arr Cass 2009 nr. 422, cited at Dewez *et al*, "The Duty to Renegotiate an International Sales Contract Under CISG in Case of Hardship and the Use of the Unidroit Principles", *European Review of Private Law* 1-2011, p101.

63 Article 79 of the United Nations Convention on Contracts for the International Sale of Goods, April 11 1980, 1489 UNTS 3, 19 ILM 671, available at www.cisg.law.pace.edu/cisg/text/treaty.html.

Thus, while there may be scope – in the civil law context, at least – to argue for a more general obligation, such a position appears still to be some distance from mainstream thought.

5. A role for national laws?

So where does this discussion leave us? To the extent that one can speak of general notions of hardship, what role might they play in the context of long-term gas supply agreements? One may consider both cases where a price reopener has been agreed by the parties (will national hardship provisions still operate?) and those where no reopener has been agreed.

5.1 Issues that a hardship claim faces

In considering the utility of this doctrine, one can see the issues that a party claiming hardship under a gas sales agreement may face:

- The hurdle over which the claimant must leap in order to activate the trigger can be high. One finds that in many states, one speaks of "excessively onerous" standards or events that "threaten the debtor with exorbitant loss".[64]
- Some clauses require that the claimant first seek termination before a refusal may trigger a renegotiation. It should be readily apparent that purchasers under many long-term arrangements may think long and hard before risking a situation where a supplier agrees to terminate.
- Some provisions require that the underlying event be of a general nature, thereby arguably omitting cases where the problems are specific to a given claimant (although this notion of generality is also often an implied, sometimes express, requirement under certain price reopeners).[65]
- There is also uncertainty in many cases as to the scope of the underlying enquiry into the claimant's position. Is the investigation subjective or objective? And in this light, is one looking at the situation of the party under the contract in question, or at the overall position of that party (for which losing the contract may not be the end of the world)? Can one go even further and look at the group of which the claimant company forms a part?
- In terms of result, hardship clauses rarely, if ever, provide a roadmap for a tribunal to follow in resolving any impasse (whereas price reopeners sometimes do provide some idea as to where the parties may tread). The risk is that the tribunal may be wary of proceeding without a more substantial contractual arrangement, or conversely could rewrite the agreement in a way that neither party intended.
- In the same vein, hardship provisions can be said generally to seek to establish contract 'equilibrium', which appears to involve an objective analysis, rather than any broader notion of 'fairness' (a more subjective

64 See Italian Civil Code, Article 1467 at Annex 1, section 1 below and Civil Code of Jordan, Article 205, Law 43/1976, Annex 1, section 5 below.

65 However, see Hungarian law, discussed in section 3.1(a).

analysis). For some commentators, this is seen as unnecessarily restrictive.[66] Price reopeners are often tied to the stricter notion of marketability.

- The aims of the two different provisions can also differ markedly. In the simplest terms, hardship is often seen as a means of sharing the pain, which in no way ensures that a buyer will cover its costs or even retain a margin in a hardship situation. This can be compared with many price reopeners, which look to the preservation of the marketability of the gas in question (although even here these questions are the subject of serious debate).

5.2 Is there nevertheless a role?

So does this mean that there is little or no role for hardship principles in the area of long-term gas sales? It may be premature to be so categorical (particularly in light of the events of the past few years):

- Given that the bulk of gas price reopener clauses look (partially or completely) at events in and affecting the buyer's end-user market alone,[67] there may well be cases where the relevant events arise in areas such as the supply chain, which have nothing to do with the end market.
- Certain 'non-price' issues (eg, quantities or quality) can give rise to substantial problems, but may not be covered by a given reopener clause.[68]
- There may be cases (albeit few) where a gas price reopener gives rise to an obligation to negotiate, but the clause does not provide the arbitrators with the power and authority to impose a solution above and beyond a finding on whether that obligation to negotiate was fulfilled.[69] Here again, hardship may be the only avenue open.
- A number of price reopener clauses contain detailed provisions as to the review period to which the parties may refer; hardship provisions are often much more liberal in terms of the period over which the hardship analysis is to be undertaken.

Thus, while for a number of commentators the role for hardship appears limited – particularly in the face of a well-drafted gas price clause – this does not mean that there is no such role. Case law confirms that the two can coexist, and indeed that

---

66 Wolfgang Peter, Jean-Quentin de Kuyper, Bénédict de Candolle, *Arbitration and renegotiation of international investment agreements*, Kluwer Law International (1995), p2.

67 Many (not all) clauses concentrate solely on events in the buyer's market and/or affecting the marketability of the gas in that market.

68 In the writer's experience, this can vary from case to case.

69 See, for example, KP Berger, *supra* note 51 at pp1367-1368, citing *Kuwait v Am Indep Oil Co*, 21 ILM at 1004 ("An obligation to negotiate is not an obligation to agree"); *Wintershall AG v Gov't of Qatar, Ad hoc* tribunal, 28 ILM 795 at 814, 841("It is clear that such a duty [to negotiate] does not include an obligation… to reach agreement… [and] the Government [is not] legally required to enter into such an agreement, however reasonable it may be").

70 See discussion by Guy Block of an award where the indexation clause of a contract, which indexed the price of gas supplied to an electricity producer 100% to the price of coal, caused a significant imbalance when oil prices and electricity prices soared. This brought into play the hardship clause to restore the equilibrium; G Block "Arbitration and Changes in Energy Prices: A Review of ICC Awards with respect to *Force Majeure*, Indexation, Adaptation, Hardship and Take-or-Pay Clauses", *ICC International Court of Arbitration Bulletin*, Vol 20/2 (2009) 51, p56. One can equally see arguments in favour of applying hardship in circumstances where a price clause is found inadequate or inapplicable.

hardship can come into play where a gas price clause exists and is applied.[70] Some legal systems, such as those of North Africa and the Middle East, in fact insist upon a role for hardship regardless of what the parties might say. It may also be the case that contract drafters themselves may want to provide for a hardship clause in order to cover matters which are not the subject of traditional gas price reopener clauses. The possibility of raising a hardship claim thus should not be overlooked.

Annex 1: National provisions on hardship[71]

1. Europe

1.1 Italy

Article 1467 of the Civil Code:

In contracts with continuous or periodical execution or adjourned execution and in case that the obligation of one of the parties has become excessively onerous due to extraordinary and unpredictable events, the party who is obliged to such performance can demand the dissolution of the contract with the effects laid down in Art 1458. The dissolution cannot be demanded if the supervening onerosity is part of the normal risk of the contract. The party against which the dissolution is demanded can prevent this by offering to modify equitably the conditions of the contract.

Article 1468:

In the case contemplated in the preceding Article, if the contract is one in which only one of the parties has assumed obligations, he can demand a reduction in his performance or a modification of the manner of performance, sufficient to restore it to an equitable basis.

1.2 Netherlands

Article 6:258 of the Civil Code:

(1) The Court may, upon request of one of the parties, modify the effects of an agreement or terminate it in part or in its entirety on the basis of unforeseen circumstances of such nature that the other party may not, according to the criteria of reasonableness and fairness, expect the agreement to be maintained in an unmodified form. The modification or termination may be given retroactive effect.

(2) The modification or termination may not be pronounced to the extent that these circumstances are to be borne by the party relying upon them, according to the nature of the agreement or commercial common opinion.

(3) For the purpose of this Article, a person to whom a right or obligation from the agreement has passed, is equated with an original party to that agreement.

1.3 France

Conseil d'Etat, March 30 1916, *Compagnie générale d'éclairage de Bordeaux*:

Just as the Company cannot argue that it should not be required to bear any increase in

71 Free translations. The writer cannot vouch for the accuracy of all translations; in case of particular interest, the reader should have the relevant translation verified.

the price… it would be totally excessive if it is admitted that such increases are to be considered a normal business risk ; on the contrary, it is necessary to find a solution that puts an end to temporary difficulties, taking into account both the general interest… and the special conditions that do not allow the contract to operate normally… ; to this end it is necessary to decide, on the one hand, that the Company is required to provide the concession service and, on the other hand, that during this period it must bear only that part of the adverse consequences that a reasonable interpretation of the contract allows.

1.4 Germany

Section 313 of the Civil Code:

Interference with the basis of the transaction

(1) If circumstances which became the basis of a contract have significantly changed since the contract was entered into and if the parties would not have entered into the contract or would have entered into it with different contents if they had foreseen this change, adaptation of the contract may be demanded to the extent that, taking account of all the circumstances of the specific case, in particular the contractual or statutory distribution of risk, one of the parties cannot reasonably be expected to uphold the contract without alteration.

(2) It is equivalent to a change of circumstances if material conceptions that have become the basis of the contract are found to be incorrect.

(3) If adaptation of the contract is not possible or one party cannot reasonably be expected to accept it, the disadvantaged party may revoke the contract. In the case of continuing obligations, the right to terminate takes the place of the right to revoke.

1.5 Spain[72]

All contracts are binding unless there is a change of circumstances. The question of unexpected circumstances has been approached as an implied *rebus sic stantibus* clause. The Spanish courts have developed a doctrine of *rebus sic stantibus* alongside Article 1091 of the Civil Code.[73] In the event of changed circumstances, this doctrine permits a party that is unduly burdened to be discharged from the contract or to request the adaptation of the contract to the new situation.

The conditions stipulated by the courts for the application of the *rebus sic stantibus* doctrine are strict:

- The contract is a long-term contract or a contract in which at least one of the parties has not yet performed.
- The basis of the contract has been altered. This is accepted if:
  - the contract has become excessively burdensome for one of the parties; or
  - the purpose of the contract has been totally frustrated.
- The change of circumstances is extraordinary in nature and unforeseen.

---

72 This involves private law; see Ugo Draetta, Ralph B Lake, Ved P Nanda, *Breach and Adaptation of International Contracts: An Introduction to Lex Mercatoria*, 1992; Ewoud Hondius & Hans Christoph Grigoleit, eds, *Unexpected Circumstances in European Contract Law*, Cambridge University Press 2011, pp127–128. For public law, see Marta Franch and Joan Torrelles, "Spain," in *Droit comparé des Contrats Publics/Comparative Law on Public Contracts*, edited by Rozen Noguellou & Ulrich Stelkens, 2010.

73 Article 1091 states: "Obligations arising from contracts are legally binding on the contracting parties, and should be fulfilled accordingly."

- Neither party has accepted the risk of the change of circumstances as a contractual obligation.
- The person invoking the change of circumstances is not responsible for this change.

The application of this doctrine can result in either adaptation of the contract, restoring the equilibrium, or termination of the contract. The courts prefer to adapt the contract. Therefore, termination of the contract is granted only when it is not possible to restore the balance between the performances.

1.6 Portugal[74]

Article 437 of the Civil Code:

> *[I]f the circumstances on which the parties based their decision to contract change unexpectedly, the burdened party has a right to terminate the contract, or to alter it according to fair judgment, as long as the requirement of the obligations which it assumed seriously affects the principles of good faith and is covered by the actual risks inherent in the contract.*

1.7 Greece[75]

Section 388 of the Civil Code:

> *Unforeseeable change of circumstances. If having regard to the requirements of good faith and business usages the circumstances on which the parties had based the conclusion of a bilateral agreement have subsequently changed on exceptional grounds that could not have been foreseen and the performance due by the debtor taking also into consideration the counter-performance has as a result of the change become excessively onerous the Court may at the request of the debtor and according to its appreciation reduce the debtor's performance to the appropriate extent or decide the dissolution of the contract in whole or with regard to its non performed part.*
>
> *If the dissolution of the contract has been decided the obligations to perform arising therefrom shall be extinguished and the contracting parties shall be reciprocally obligated to restitute the performances by which each benefited pursuant to the provisions governing enrichment without just cause.*

1.8 Switzerland

Hans van Houtte notes the following:

> *The Swiss Federal Tribunal has admitted that some long-term contracts may be terminated because of an unforeseeable and fundamental change of circumstances on the basis of Article 2 of the Code civil (good faith) (36). Only changes which would unjustly enrich one of the parties give rise to such relief. Rebus sic stantibus, however, has to be applied restrictively.*[76]

---

74 See Hondius and Grigoleit (note 71 *supra*), p135.

75 See Draetta, Lake, and Nanda (note 71 *supra*); Hondius & Hans Grigoleit (note 71 *supra*), pp138-144.

76 H van Houtte (note 43 *supra*), p113. He cites the following authority: Federal Tribunal October 10 1933, ATF (59), 1933, II, 372. See moreover Federal Tribunal January 13 1975, ATF (101), 1975, II, 17, 19; Federal Tribunal September 26 1974, ATF (100), 1974, II, 345; Federal Tribunal December 7 1971, ATF (97), 1971, II, 390; Federal Tribunal September 18 1981, ATF (107), 1981, II, 343.

2. Nordic countries

2.1 Sweden

Article 36 of the Swedish Contract Act:

A contract term or condition may be modified or set aside if such term is unreasonable with regard to the contents of the agreement, the circumstances at the time the agreement was entered into, subsequent circumstances and circumstances in general. Where a term is of such importance to the agreement that it would be unreasonable to demand the continued enforceability of the remainder of the agreement with its terms unchanged, the agreement may be modified in other respects or may be set aside in its entirety.

Upon determination of the applicability of the provisions of the first paragraph, special consideration shall be paid to the need for protection of the party which, as a consumer or otherwise, is in a position of inferiority in the contractual relationship.

See also Article 36 of the Finnish Contracts Act and Article 36 of the Danish Contracts Act.

3. South America

3.1 Brazil

Article 478 of the Civil Code:

For contracts of continuing or deferred performance, if the performance by one of the parties becomes excessively onerous, providing an undue advantage to the other, and as a result of extraordinary and unforeseen events, the disadvantaged party may request the termination of the contract. The effects of a judgment of termination shall be retroactive to the date of the summons.

Article 479 of the Civil Code:

Termination can be avoided if the defendant agrees to modify equitably the terms of the contract.

Article 480 of the Civil Code:

If, in a contract, the obligations of performance apply only to one of the parties, such party may request that its obligations be reduced or modified as to its performance in order to avoid excessive burden.

3.2 Argentina

Article 1198 of the Civil Code:

Contracts are to be made, interpreted and executed in good faith, according to what the parties understood or could have understood, acting with care and foreseeablity.

If, in bilateral contracts with deferred or continued performance, the performance of one of the parties becomes excessively onerous because of extraordinary and unforeseeable events, the prejudiced party may demand the termination of the contract. The same principle shall apply to aleatory contracts when excessive onerousness results from causes extraneous to the very risk of a contract.

In contracts of continued performance termination shall not affect that which has already been performed.

Termination shall not be granted if the prejudiced party has been at fault or in delay.

The other party may prevent termination by offering to improve the effects of the contract in an equitable fashion.

3.3 Peru

Article 1440 of the Civil Code:

Definition. In commutative contracts of continuous, periodic, or deferred performance, if performance becomes excessively onerous due to extraordinary or unforeseeable events, the aggrieved party may request a court to reduce or increase the consideration, such that the excessive burden will cease.

If this were not possible due to the nature of the performance, the circumstances or if the defendant so requests, the court will order the termination of the contract. The termination shall not extend to the obligations already performed.

Article 1441 of the Civil Code:

Scope of the excessive burden of the obligation. The provisions contained in Article 1440 apply:

1. *To commutative contracts of immediate performance, when performance by one of the parties has been deferred due to a cause not attributable to such party.*
2. *To contracts of chance, when the excessive burden arises from causes that are extraneous to the risk inherent to the contract.*

Article 1442 of the Civil Code:

Excessive burden in contracts providing for performance by one party. Where only one of the parties undertook obligations under a contract, such party shall be entitled judicially to request the reduction of the obligation such that the excessive burden will cease.

If the obligation cannot be reduced, the second paragraph of Article 1440 shall apply.

Article 1443:

Inadmissibility of the action for excessive burden. The action for excessive burden of the obligation shall not proceed when its performance is deferred due to fraud or fault of the aggrieved party.

Article 1444:

Nullity of waiver of the action. Waiver of the action for excessive burden of the obligation shall be null and void.

Article 1445:

Expiration of the action. The action for excessive burden of the obligation shall expire upon three months of the occurrence of the extraordinary and unforeseeable events referenced in Article 1440.

Article 1446:

"Term of expiration. The initial term of expiration referenced in Article 1445 shall run as of the moment when the extraordinary and unforeseeable events disappear.

4. North Africa

4.1 Algeria

Article 107(3) of the Civil Code:

When... as a result of exceptional and unforeseeable events of a general character, the performance of the contractual obligation, without becoming impossible, becomes excessively onerous in such a way as to threaten the debtor with exorbitant loss, the judge may, according to the circumstances, and after taking into consideration the interests of both parties, reduce to reasonable limits, the obligation that has become excessive. Any agreement to the contrary is void.

4.2 Libya[77]

Article 147 of the Civil Code:

1. *The contract makes the law of the parties. It can be revoked or altered only by mutual consent of the parties or for reasons provided by for the law.*
2. *When, however, as a result of exceptional and unpredictable events of a general character, the performance of the contractual obligation, without becoming impossible, becomes excessively onerous in such a way as to threaten the debtor with exorbitant loss, the Judge may, according to the circumstances and after taking into consideration the interests of both parties, reduce to reasonable limits the obligation that has become excessive. Any agreement to the contrary is void.*

Article 657 of the Civil Code:

1. *When a contract is concluded on a lump sum basis according to a design agreed with the employer, the contractor has no claim to an increase of price, even if modifications and additions are made to the design, unless such modifications or additions are due to the fault of the employer or have been authorized by the employer and the price thereof agreed with the contractor.*
2. *Such agreement should be made in writing unless the principal contract was concluded verbally.*
3. *The contractor has no claim to an increase of price on the grounds of an increase in the price of raw materials, labour or any other item of expenditure, even if such increase is so great as to render the performance of the contract onerous.*
4. *When, however, as a result of exceptional events of a general character which could not be foreseen at the time the contract was concluded, the economic equilibrium between the respective obligations of employer and of the contractor breaks down, and the basis on which the financial estimates of the contract were computed has subsequently disappeared, the Judge may grant an increase of the price or order the resiliation of the contract.*

---

77 See Thomas J McDonald and Omar A Tarhuni, "Compensation for Payment Delays under Libyan Laws", *The International Construction Law Review*, October 1985.

Morocco and Tunisia appear not to have adopted the principle of hardship, at least in the sense of its codification.

5. Middle East

5.1 Bahrain

Article 130 of Legislative Decree 19/2001, promulgating the Civil Code of Bahrain:

> *When, however, as a result of exceptional and unpredictable events of a general character, the performance of the contractual obligation, without becoming impossible, becomes excessively onerous in such way as to threaten the debtor with exorbitant loss, the judge may, according to the circumstances, and after taking into consideration the interests of both parties, reduce to reasonable limits by lessening its extent or increasing its consideration, the obligation that has become excessive. Any agreement to the contrary is void.*

5.2 Egypt

Article 147(2) of the Civil Code:

> *"The contract makes the law of the parties. It can be revoked or altered only by mutual consent of the parties or for reasons provided for by the law.*
>
> *When, however, as a result of exceptional and unpredictable events of a general character, the performance of the contractual obligation, without becoming impossible, becomes excessively onerous in such way as to threaten the debtor with exorbitant loss, the judge may, according to the circumstances, and after taking into consideration the interests of both parties, reduce to reasonable limits, the obligation that has become excessive. Any agreement to the contrary is void.*[78]

5.3 Iraq

Article 146 of the Civil Code:

> 1. *When the contract is concluded, it becomes legally binding and can only be revoked or modified in accordance with the law or by the consent of both parties.*
> 2. *When, however, as a result of exceptional and unforeseeable events of a general character, the performance of the contractual obligation, without becoming impossible, becomes onerous in such as way as to threaten the debtor with exorbitant loss, the court may after taking into consideration the interests of both parties, reduce to reasonable limits the obligation that has become excessive if justice so requires. Any agreement to the contrary is void.*

5.4 Jordan

Article 205 of the Civil Code:

> *If as a result of exceptional and unforeseeable events of a general character, the performance of the contractual obligation, without becoming impossible, becomes onerous in such as way as to threaten the debtor with exorbitant loss, the court may, according to the circumstances, and after taking into consideration the interests of both*

78 Perrot Fanner and Sims Marshall, *Translation of the Egyptian Civil Code*, New World Publisher, p29.

parties, reduce to reasonable limits the obligation that has become excessive if justice so requires. Any agreement to the contrary is void.

5.5 Kuwait

Article 198 of the Civil Code:

Where after and before completion of performance of the contract, general extraordinary circumstances arose which could not have been foreseen on the execution thereof, and which rendered the performance of the obligation arising therefrom oppressive, if not impossible, to the debtor such as will threaten him with heavy loss, the judge may, after weighing the interests of both parties, reduce the oppressive obligation to a reasonable degree either by narrowing its extent or by awarding a balancing interest; any agreement otherwise shall be null.

5.6 Lebanon

In Lebanon, the situation is similar to that under French law, providing for hardship under administrative, but not commercial law.

5.7 Qatar

Article 171 of the Civil Code:

1. *A contract is the law of the contracting parties and so cannot be revoked or modified except with the agreement of the parties or for such reasons as are prescribed by the law*
2. *Notwithstanding, if any general, exceptional events occur that cannot be foreseen as a result of which fulfillment of the contractual obligation becomes, although not impossible, onerous for the debtor such that he is at risk of incurring a substantial loss, the judge may, according to the circumstances and after weighing up the interests of the parties, return such onerous obligation to a reasonable level. Any agreement to the contrary will be void.*

5.8 Syria

Article 148 of the Civil Code:

The contract is the law of the parties. It can be revoked or altered only by the mutual consent of the parties or for reasons provided by the law.

When, however, as a result of exceptional and unpredictable events of a general character, the performance of the contractual obligation, without becoming impossible, becomes excessively onerous in such a way as to threaten the debtor with exorbitant loss, the judge may, according to the circumstances, and after taking into consideration the interests of both parties, reduce to reasonable limits, the obligation that has become excessive. Any agreement to the contrary is void.[79]

---

79 The Syrian judge would require the debtor to bear all the usual increase, while the unusual increase will be borne equally by the debtor and the creditor (see Cassation 247/80 published in the *Syrian Advocates Bar Journal*, 1981, p445).

5.9 United Arab Emirates

Article 249 of the Civil Code:

> *When… as a result of exceptional and unforeseeable events of a general character, the performance of the contractual obligation, without becoming impossible, becomes excessively onerous in such a way as to threaten the debtor with exorbitant loss, the judge may, according to the circumstances, and after taking into consideration the interests of both parties, reduce to reasonable limits, if justice requires so, the obligation that has become excessive. Any agreement to the contrary is void.*

5.10 Yemen

Article 211 of the Civil Law:

> *The contract is legally binding on the contracting parties and it shall not be voided or modified without both parties' consent or for the reasons stipulated by the law, notwithstanding. If as a result of exceptional and unforeseeable events of a general character such as wars and catastrophes, the performance of the contractual obligation, without becoming impossible, becomes onerous in such as way as to threaten the debtor with exorbitant loss, stopping the debtor from proceeding with the contract, and that does not mean an increase or decrease in the prices, the Judge may, according to the circumstances, whether poverty, wealth or others, and after taking into consideration the interests of both parties, reduce the obligation that has become excessive to reasonable limits.*

6. Sub-Saharan Africa

6.1 Sudan

Article 117 of the Law of Civil Transactions:

1. *If as a result of exceptional and unforeseeable events of a general character, the performance of the contractual obligation, without becoming impossible, becomes onerous in such as way as to threaten the debtor with exorbitant loss, the court may, according to the circumstances, and after taking into consideration the interests of both parties, reduce to reasonable limits the obligation that has become excessive. Any agreement to the contrary is void.*
2. *The obligation is not considered onerous unless the loss exceeds one-third of the obligation.*

7. Eastern Europe

7.1 Russia

Article 709(6) of the Civil Code 1995 provides that a contractor has the right to demand an increase in the price of a contract containing no price escalation clause where there has been a material increase in the cost of materials or in the cost of services rendered to the contractor by a third party.

Article 17 of the Act on Production Sharing Agreements 1995 (as amended July 19 2011) allows for the contract to be amended without requiring a hardship clause should a material change in circumstances take place as defined by the Code.

The 'necessary change in circumstances' is defined in Article 451 of the code as "a change of circumstances ... such that if the parties could reasonably foresee this, the contract would not have been concluded at all by them or it would have been concluded on significantly differing conditions".

Administrative contracts in Russia are also subject to provisions on unforeseeable events.

7.2 Lithuania[80]

Article 6.204 of the Civil Code:

1. *If the performance of a contract becomes more onerous for one of the parties, this party shall be bound to perform the contract in accordance with the procedure established in the other Paragraphs of this Article.*
2. *The performance of a contract shall be considered obstructed under such circumstances which fundamentally alter the balance of the contractual obligations, i.e., either the cost of performance has essentially increased, or the value thereof has essentially diminished if: 1) these circumstances occur or become known to the aggrieved party after the conclusion of the contract; 2) these circumstances could not reasonably have been foreseen by the aggrieved party at any time of the conclusion of the contract; 3) these circumstances are beyond the control of the aggrieved party; 4) the risk of occurrence of these circumstances was not assumed by the aggrieved party.*
3. *If the performance of a contract becomes obstructed, the aggrieved party shall have the right to make a request to the other party for the modification of the contract. Such request shall have to be made immediately after the occurrence of the obstructions and the grounds on which the request is based indicated therein. The request for modification of the contract shall not in itself entitle the aggrieved party with the right to suspend performance of the contract. Where within a reasonable time, the parties fail to reach an agreement on the modification of the contractual obligations, any of them may bring an action in court. The court may: 1) dissolve the contract and establish the date and terms of its dissolution; 2) modify the conditions of the contract with a view to restoring the balance of contractual obligation of the parties.*

7.3 Slovenia[81]

Articles 112 to 115 of the Slovenian Code of Obligations (2002) provide that if there is a significant change of circumstances, the court can dissolve a contract at the request of one of the parties.

However, adjustment of the contract appears not to be possible unless both parties consent; one party cannot be forced to accept an adjustment (see Slovenian Supreme Court, III Ips 17/93).

7.4 Hungary

Section 241 of the Civil Code:

The court may amend a contract when it is injurious to any substantial rightful interest

80 See Hondius and Grigoleit (note 71 *supra*), pp83-84.
81 See Hondius and Grigoleit (note 71 *supra*), p76.

of one of the parties in consequence of a circumstance arising in the long-term relationship of the parties following the conclusion of the contract.

8. The Far East

8.1 China

Prior to 1993 Chinese contract law allowed for either termination of the contract or alteration of the contract for either *force majeure* or an unavoidable external reason not caused through the fault of either party. The Chinese courts interpreted this 'unavoidable external reason' as a 'change in circumstances'.

While the new contract laws that came into effect in 1993 and 1999 did not include a provision for alteration of the contract where there had been such a change in circumstances, the Chinese courts continue to apply the earlier rule in extraordinary circumstances.

8.2 Japan[82]

There is no statutory law governing changed contractual circumstances in Japan. However, a Japanese court can adapt the contract if it finds unforeseen, substantially changed circumstances (without fault of parties) that cause the obligation of continued performance to violate the principles of good faith and equity.

In his book *The Principle of Changed Circumstances in Civil Law* (1926), Katsumoto Masaaki gave the following definition of 'changed circumstances':

> *The rule states that when the circumstances releasing a legal act, creating a legal relation, change in an unforeseeable way alter the accomplishment of the act and before expiry of its consequences, due to the influence of facts not attributable to the parties, with the result that the creation of legal consequences in the original sense, or their continuation, is to be considered as unreasonable in the light of the rule of equity and good faith, then such legal consequences are to be adapted in equity and good faith.*[83]

This definition became traditional in Japan.

The Japanese Supreme Court adopted this doctrine in 1944, but has been very restrictive in its application. However, the lower courts were more lenient in applying the doctrine.[84]

The author would like to thank Samy Markbaoui and Hinda Rabkin for their assistance in the preparation of this chapter, as well as Pedro and Filipa at PLMJ. This chapter represents his personal opinions and as such should in no way be attributed to partners or colleagues at White & Case LLP.

---

82 See Puelinckx (note 10 *supra*), p47 *et seq.*

83 *Id*, pp62-63.

84 *Id*; a typical application of this is as follows:

> *The parties agreed in 1935 that a buyer would have an option to buy a piece of land for a set price, such option to last twenty years. When the buyer asked to exercise its option, in 1955, the actual value of the land was estimated at 620 times the price fixed by the contract, as the result of the enormous inflation and soaring land prices following Japan's defeat in World War II. The change in circumstances meant that upholding the contract would violate principles of good faith and equity.*

The arbitrator's role

George von Mehren
Squire Sanders

1. Introduction

Arbitration is available as a back up for parties that are unable to settle a price review request amicably between themselves. So, price review arbitration is an extension of the normal commercial negotiation requirements provided for in a sale and purchase agreement. Unlike many arbitrations, the arbitration of price reviews in the natural gas industry is not based on allegations that one party has breached a contract or otherwise committed a legal wrong. Instead, arbitrators are asked to determine whether the economics of a contract should be adjusted and, if so, to establish a new price formula. In a sense, they are charged with finding an acceptable commercial agreement so that the parties can continue their relationship, and not with the traditional arbitral role of resolving an earlier dispute.

If they are to fulfil this mandate, arbitrators need to understand the commercial context in which they are required to work. The purpose of price review provisions is to maintain the long-term commercial relationship between the parties. These sale and purchase agreements often contain 'take-or-pay' provisions, which require the buyer each year to pay for a substantial quantity of gas, irrespective of whether it takes shipment of the gas. For the seller, take-or-pay provisions are often essential to obtain financing for the high capital costs of producing and transporting natural gas and liquefied natural gas (LNG). The revenues may be pledged as security for the financing.[1] However, for the buyer, take-or-pay provisions may become a financial burden if it is unable to sell the agreed take-or-pay quantity at an adequate margin.[2] Indeed, a prolonged imbalance in a price formula can destroy a disadvantaged buyer's business. If the price becomes too high, the buyer cannot simply ignore the agreement and purchase from another supplier.[3]

Not all sale and purchase agreements used in the natural gas industry contain

---

1 Ben Holland and Phillip Spencer Ashley, "Natural Gas Price Reviews: Past, Present and Future", *Journal of Energy & Natural Resources Law*, Vol 30, No 1, p29 (2012).

2 For example, in 1985, Distrigas Corporation declared bankruptcy based on its 100% take-or-pay liability to Sonatrach and its inability to pass this liability on to its customers in the United States. Office of Fossil Energy (US), "LNG Trade: Past, Present, Future (?)", *Quarterly Focus*, pV, available at www.fossil.energy.gov/programs/gasregulation/analyses/Focus/3rd95foc.pdf. See also, "Distrigas Files for Reorganization under Chapter 11 of Bankruptcy Code", *Fost Natural Gas Report 1537*, p3 (October 3 1985); "Distrigas Files for Bankruptcy Protection; Algerian lNG Imports Halted," *Platt's Oilgram News*, Vol 63, No 190, p4 (October 2 1985); "Cabot Corp to Take $20 Million Writeoff Due to Unit's Woes," *Wall Street Journal* (October 1 1985); and Agreement for the Sale and Purchase of Liquefied natural Gas of April 13 1976 between Sonatrach and Distrigas Corporation, available at www.fossil.energy.gov/ programs/gasregulation/authorizations/LNG_Contracts/88_37_LNG1.pdf.

price review clauses. For example, in so-called 'spot' contracts (a single delivery or a specified number of deliveries to be made over a relatively short time), usually the parties establish a fixed price, which cannot be changed. However, it is usual for agreements covering a multi-year period to state the price as a formula designed to track the value of natural gas as it changes over time. If the gas is destined for a liquid market that has a reliable market index for natural gas, the formula may be based on such an index. For example, in the United Kingdom, often price formulae are based on the National Balancing Point (NBP). In the United States, the Henry Hub can perform the same function. In these cases, the formula automatically adjusts price to reflect the changing value of natural gas as reflected by changes in the liquid index selected by the parties. Again, usually a price review process is unnecessary.

However, if gas sold under a long-term sale and purchase agreement is destined for a market which does not have a reliable natural gas index, usually the formula is based on the change in price of an oil product or another energy product, or, more frequently, on a 'basket' of several such products. For example, in many European gas markets, price formulae refer to indices for products such as Brent crude, gas oil, high or low sulphur oil, coal and electrical prices. As the price of the products used in a formula goes up or down, the price for each delivery of natural gas changes accordingly. However, the relevant market or economic conditions may eventually cause the value of gas in the end-user market to change in a way that is significantly different from the value of the other product(s) used in the formula. When this occurs, a price review is available to adjust the formula. If the parties cannot agree on a new price formula, either party may invoke the right to have arbitrators decide whether and how the price formula should be changed.[4]

Thus, in price review arbitrations, the arbitrators deal with the commercial realities of long-term contracts when the parties do not have available a clear market index reflecting the changing value of natural gas in the applicable end-user market. For the buyer, price review provisions are a mechanism to align its supply costs to achieve economically viable operations, given that the buyer has a substantial, monetary take-or-pay commitment every year, irrespective of whether it can sell the required volumes at a profit. For the seller, price review provisions are a mechanism to ensure that the buyer does not benefit exclusively from increased values in the

---

3 Sale and purchase agreements usually specify that all rights and obligations remain in full force and effect while a price review is pending. Thus, the seller must sell and the buyer must pay for the natural gas or LNG at the price established by the price formula that is under review. If the price formula is ultimately adjusted, a balancing payment is made to reflect the new price retroactive to the date on which the price review was commenced. See for example, Are Brautaset, Eirik Høiby, Rune O Pedersen, Christian Fredrik Michelet, *Norsk Gassavsetning: Rettslige hovedelementer (Norwegian Natural Gas Sales Main Legal Elements)*, Sjørettsfondet, 1998, p253.

4 It is common for price review clauses to refer to a separate arbitration provision that applies generally to all disputes arising under the agreement. These arbitration clauses are of the kind normally found in commercial agreements. Among other things, they specify the applicable rules of arbitration, the number of arbitrators, the place of arbitration, the applicable law and the language of the arbitration. In the author's experience, parties elect a variety of applicable rules, including those of the UN Commission on International Trade, International Chamber of Commerce, International Centre for Dispute Resolution)or American Arbitration Association) and Stockholm Chamber of Commerce. Usually, the tribunal has three members. The place of arbitration is often a major commercial arbitration venue such as London, Paris, Geneva or New York. The languages typically used in price review arbitrations are English and French.

end-user market that are not appropriately allocated by an existing price formula.

The arbitrator's role is to interpret and apply the price review provisions of the applicable sale and purchase agreement, following the law governing the transaction and the parties' commercial objectives.[5] Throughout this chapter, reference is made to various contract provisions that are central to that aim. The analysis uses contract provisions that are public, and also words and phrases taken from some confidential contracts, familiar to the author, where neither the parties nor the economic terms of the transaction can be identified.[6] While this analysis must, of necessity, speak in generalities about price review provisions, it is essential to remember that not all price review provisions are the same. It is critical for arbitrators to focus on the specific provisions of the parties' contract in the case that they must decide.

2. The arbitrators' jurisdiction

Based on familiar legal principles, the jurisdiction of price review arbitrators depends on what is set out in the contract. Typically, the contract requires the parties to engage in negotiations for a specified time. If the negotiations are not successful, one or both of the parties may initiate arbitration. For example, one sale and purchase agreement provided that, if the parties are unable to agree on a new pricing formula, either party may: "submit the matter to arbitration for decision in accordance with the criteria set out [in the price review provision of the contract]".[7]

Of course, the precise language used to describe the arbitrators' jurisdiction varies from contract to contract. Sometimes, the arbitrators simply are directed to decide "the dispute" rather than "the matter". Sometimes, the contract does not expressly require the arbitrators to make their determinations "in accordance with" the requirements for a price review set out in the contract. Alternatively, the contract simply could say that one or more of the parties may "have the Price Formula reviewed by the Arbitral Tribunal".[8]

Despite the differences in language, it might be clear that the arbitrators do not have jurisdiction to amend or change any part of the contract other than the price formula. Some, but not all, contracts contain express statements such as:

For the avoidance of doubt, any adjustment awarded shall only operate to amend the

---

5 An important factor in price review arbitrations is the applicable law governing the construction and interpretation of the contract. Different legal systems have different approaches. In price review arbitration, an important issue may be the extent to which the parties may introduce evidence about negotiation of the sale and purchase agreement.

6 Sale and purchase agreements are confidential and, therefore, relatively few price review provisions are publically available. To help the discussion of the issues, in addition to references to a few publically available provisions, the author has taken words and phrases from various confidential contracts in a way that does not reveal the parties or any commercial information. The author also refers to the discussion of price review provisions in Norwegian contracts by Brautaset, *et al.*, note 3 above, pp 251-258. For a very useful discussion of price review and related contract provisions, see, G Block, "Arbitration and Changes in Energy Prices: A Review of ICC Awards with respect to Force Majeure, Indexation, Adaptation, Hardship and Take-or-Pay Clauses", *ICC International Court of Arbitration Bulletin*, Vol 20, No 2, p51 *et seq* (2009).

7 The above quoted text is from a sale and purchase agreement considered in the decision of the US district court decision in *Gas Natural Aprovisionamientos SDG SA v Atlantic LNG Company of Trinidad and Tobago*, 2008 US Dist Lexis 69632 (SDNY). The author was lead counsel for Gas Natural in the underlying arbitration.

8 The words and phrases quoted in this paragraph are from confidential sale and purchase agreements.

Contract Sales Price and shall not extend to any other provisions of this Agreement.[9]

If there is no express provision, this limitation may be implicit when the price review provision states that the arbitrators should deal with the price review process and nothing more. Thus, arbitrators are not permitted to change a number of significant contract terms that have an important effect on price but are not part of the price formula – for example, the length of the term, source and quality, volume flexibility, take-or-pay obligations, shipping expense and logistics, and diversion rights to other markets. The price effect of those terms may be very important to the process of developing a new price formula and addressing other issues in the case. Often, arbitrators will need to interpret and consider these terms. However, the tribunal simply may not have jurisdiction to amend them.

The situation may become complicated if one party proposes a change to the pricing formula (in itself within the jurisdiction of the tribunal) which would require an amendment to another provision. For example, if a party asks the tribunal to replace or amend the underlying index on which the price is based, the change might affect other provisions in the sale and purchase agreement which, without amendment, would become unworkable. In these circumstances, the tribunal must decide whether it has jurisdiction to amend the pricing provision in a way that would lead to the need to amend other provisions in the sale and purchase agreement.

Typically, the arbitrators' jurisdiction to decide issues arising from the price review process involves one or more of the following three general questions:

- Have the procedural conditions for a price review and price review arbitration set out in the contract been satisfied?
- Have the substantive conditions for revision of the price formula been satisfied?
- Assuming an affirmative decision on the first two issues, how the price formula be adjusted?

The arbitrators' role in each of these three phases of the process is discussed below.[10]

3. Conditions for a price review

3.1 Procedural conditions

Arbitrators are often asked to decide whether the party seeking a price review has met the procedural conditions established by the sale and purchase agreement. Relevant issues may include:

- the timing of the request for a price review;
- the form of the request;
- the contents of the request; and
- the obligation to negotiate before arbitration.

---

9 *Ibid.*

10 Normally, arbitrators consider the issues in this order. See, for example, Brautaset, *et al*, note 3 above, pp251 and 253.

Commonly, these issues are raised by the party that opposes a change in price and are put forward as a basis for dismissal of the price review claim on preliminary grounds.

(a) ***Timing***

Generally, sale and purchase agreements provide that price reviews may be initiated only at specified intervals during the term of the contract – for example, every three years. A deadline for sending the price review notice may also be set – for example, "before January 1" every three years after the first opportunity for a price review. Additionally, some but not all contracts provide for intermediate price reviews but limit how often they can be requested. The timing requirements are not simply formalistic. Commercially, their purpose is to establish price certainty for a specific period during the term of the sale and purchase agreement. The parties have negotiated a process that permits potential price changes to be addressed at agreed intervals but does not permit constant efforts to adjust price. Both parties take the risk that events between the available opportunities to address price will be unfavourable to them (this risk is lower in contracts that provide for intermediate price reviews). Therefore, the arbitrators may be asked to determine if the price review request was made in a timely fashion and, if not, whether the price review may be regarded as intermediate in contracts that contain such provisions.[11] Subject to applicable law, if the party seeking a price review has not complied with the timing requirement in the sale and purchase agreement, the arbitrators are likely to dismiss the claim.

(b) ***The form of the request***

In general, sale and purchase agreements require that the request is made in writing. Sometimes this requirement is expressly set out in the price review provision.[12] Alternatively, writing may be required by the general notice provisions of the contract.

(c) ***The contents of the request***

Arbitrators may be asked to decide whether the notice contained enough information. Some price review provisions do not address this issue and simply require notice that the requesting party has initiated a price review. Others, for example, specify generally that the requesting party must provide with the notice "information supporting its belief" that the price formula should be revised. Still others require even more detail, specifying that the requesting party must provide "its proposals for a revised [price] formula and an explanation of the basis for such proposal in reasonable detail".[13] Generally, these requirements are not interpreted to require that the party requesting the price review provides a complete and detailed case. Instead, they are understood in the context of their commercial purpose, which is to provide the responding party

---

11 See note 8 above. In addition, see, for example, Brautaset, *et al*, note 3 above.
12 Brautaset, *et al*, note 3 above, p 252.
13 See note 8 above.

with enough information to allow productive negotiations to begin. The parties usually exchange more substantial information about their positions, and data in support of their positions, during the negotiations.[14]

(d) The obligation to negotiate

There may be a dispute about whether the party seeking the price review satisfied its obligation to negotiate. Sometimes, the arbitrators have to decide whether the arbitration had been started before the end of the negotiation period specified in the contract, and, if so, what effect this has on the arbitration proceedings. At other times, arbitrators must deal with claims that the negotiation sessions were not scheduled promptly or that they have reached an impasse, such that a waiver has occurred. In addition, the arbitrators may be asked to consider whether a party made its position sufficiently clear during negotiations and whether sufficiently detailed information about the claim was provided during the process.

There are several ways in which the assertions that a party makes in its request, and subsequently in the negotiations, may impact on the scope of the issues to be arbitrated. One issue is whether a party may rely on grounds that are not related to those set out in the request or in subsequent negotiations.[15] Another is whether either party may take positions in the arbitration that are different from, or even contradictory to, those that it took during the negotiations. For example, both parties may simultaneously seek a price review based on claims that the substantive conditions (discussed immediately below) have taken place. However, once arbitration has started, can one of the parties still defend against the other party's claim on the grounds that there have been no changed conditions? Arbitrators may address these questions in various ways – for example:

- whether communications during the negotiation phase are inherently without prejudice or for settlement purposes only;
- whether, because of the applicable law or party communications on the issue, the parties had legitimate expectations during the negotiations about the admissibility of their discussions if the price review went to arbitration;
- considerations about the efficiency and fairness of the arbitral process; and
- issues concerning the credibility of the party seeking to change its position.

3.2 Substantive conditions

It is usual for price review provisions to set out conditions precedent to the revision of the price formula that must be established before revision of the price formula can be considered. In some sale and purchase agreements, the only substantive condition is the passage of time, as the parties assume that, given the dynamic nature of energy markets, a review is appropriate after a specified period. More often, provisions focus on whether specific changes have occurred since the existing price formula was established that justify a new price formula. For example, a sale and purchase agreement could say:

---

14 See note 8 above.
15 See Final Award in Case 9812, *ICC International Court of Arbitration Bulletin*, Vol 20, No 2, p74 (2009).

If circumstances beyond the control of either of the Parties have induced significant changes in the energy market of the Buyer as compared to such market at the time [the existing price formula was established], then either Party may request, in the manner hereinafter described, a Regular Price Review or a Special Price Review.[16]

In considering changes alleged as the basis for a price review, usually arbitrators must determine whether and when those changes took place. This requires analysis of changes during a comparison period. The arbitrators compare the economic or market conditions when the existing price formula was established with the economic or market conditions on the review date. The typical reason for the comparison is that conditions that were affecting value when the existing price formula was established are not new and, therefore, cannot be a valid reason to adjust the economics of the contract.[17]

In addition, contracts often go on to state that the required changes must have one or more of the following characteristics – that they:

- "justify a revision of the applicable Contract Price";
- were "unanticipated" at the time the price formula was last established;
- are "substantial";
- are "lasting" or "are likely to have a significant and enduring effect on the value of natural gas" in the buyer's end-user market; and/or
- were "beyond the control of the Parties".[18]

Arbitrators may find it difficult to interpret and apply these provisions to the facts of a case because of the very general language used to describe the requirements. What is intended by words such as 'significant', 'substantial' or 'enduring'? The use of general wording is essential to the parties' purpose in using the price review process. When sale and purchase agreements are negotiated, it is impossible to predict what will happen or what kind of changes will occur from time to time in the relevant energy market or markets over the term of the contract – which may be more than 15 or 20 years. Therefore, arbitrators should interpret the meaning of the substantive conditions in the context of their commercial purpose by considering whether the changes advanced in support of a price review affect the economics of the contract in a meaningful way.

For example, consider the common requirement that a change is "lasting". One dictionary tells us that 'lasting' means "continuing to exist for a long time or forever".[19] But this kind of definition is not very helpful if the question to be decided focuses on whether a specific period of months or years is enough to be lasting. Of course, arbitrators must make a realistic judgement, which will be well informed by asking what is commercially reasonable in the context of the interval period between price reviews under the parties' contract. On the one hand, it is unlikely to be commercially reasonable to change the price formula – that will be effective throughout the interval period – to reflect a change that is likely to reduce early in

16 See note 8 above. See, for example, Brautaset, *et al.*, note 3 above, p254.
17 See, for example, Brautaset, *et al*, note 3 above, p256.
18 See note 8 above.
19 Cambridge Dictionaries Online, at www.dictionary.cambridge.org/dictionary/british/lasting.

the interval period. On the other hand, it is not likely to be commercially reasonable to refuse to revise the contract price to reflect a change that is likely to persist for much of the interval period. The facts and the commercial context have a significant bearing on the issue.

Many price review provisions require a relationship between the changes advanced as the basis for a price review and the value of natural gas in the end-user market – providing, for example, that the changes "are likely to have a significant and enduring effect on the value of natural gas".[20] The existence of the relationship is often the subject of expert testimony based on data showing values in the end-user market. The party seeking a price review may choose to use data from a variety of sources, including, for example, publically available information on prices from sources such as Eurostat, market surveys commissioned by the claimant, tariff prices available to residential customers, and/or the buyer's own price experience. Which information is appropriate will depend on the markets at issue and the particular price review.

In dealing with this issue, arbitrators will need to determine the extent to which the sale and purchase agreement requires the party seeking a price review to show the precise degree, amount or quantification of the effect on value. To require absolute precision may set an impossible standard that will prevent the parties' commercial objective of providing a realistic opportunity to change price during the lengthy term of the sale and purchase agreement. Again, the arbitrators' decision usually will be driven by the relevant contract language, commercial reasonableness and the applicable evidentiary standard.

In considering "effect on value", arbitrators may need to consider a more complex matrix than a simple comparison of the delivered prices in the end-user market at the beginning and end of the comparison period. Depending on the parties' contract, the concept of 'value' may involve the relationship between delivered prices and the supply cost that is determined by the contract sales price formula. In the buyer's market, value is reflected by the difference between the buyer's costs and the price that the buyer can obtain for natural gas in its end-user market.[21] In other words, "a change in value" can be measured by the extent of change in the buyer's commercial margin. Taking this approach, changed conditions that increase a buyer's margin may demonstrate that the seller is entitled to a price increase and, at the same time, changed conditions in the buyer's market that decrease the buyer's margin may point to a price decrease.

As noted above, price reviews often take place in situations where either the seller or buyer essentially claims that the price formula has become disconnected from the market price of gas. The claim focuses on how conditions in the buyer's market have

---

20 See note 8 above.

21 To simplify, a buyer's cost may be the sum of the following:
- the cost of the natural gas or LNG at the border of the country that is the buyer's market (established by the existing contract sales price formula plus the cost of transportation to the border, if relevant);
- the reasonable costs of regasification (if LNG);
- the cost of transporting the gas from the border to customers; and
- the reasonable costs of commercialisation.

When the sum of these costs is subtracted from the price obtainable in the buyer's end-user market, the buyer is left with a positive or negative margin.

driven prices for natural gas in relation to the value of the basket of other energy products used in the existing price formula. When that relationship has changed during the comparison period, it may be necessary to adjust the existing contract sales price formula.

4. Adjusting the price formula

If the party seeking a price review has established that the substantive conditions have occurred, the arbitrators will next address the issue of how the contract price formula should be adjusted.

Typically, price review clause provide some guidance to the arbitrators about what the economic result of an adjustment should be. For example, one price review provision states that:

The revision of the price shall consist in adapting it in a reasonable and fair manner to the economic circumstances then prevailing on the imported Natural Gas market and on the market for other imported energy supplies competing with this production in the East Coast and Gulf Coast areas of the United States of America within the framework of long-term contracts. The parties shall take into account the individual characteristics of each of the above products including the quality, the continuity of deliveries, the production and transportations costs, etc[22]

Another provision states:

The Contract Price as revised in accordance with this Article, shall in any event allow the Buyer to market the LNG supplied hereunder in competition with all competing sources or forms of energy ... And such Contract Price shall allow the Buyer to achieve a reasonable rate of return on the LNG delivered hereunder.[23]

Other price review provisions address the issue in less detail, requiring that the revised formula must allow the natural gas to be marketed "economically" or "competitively" in the buyer's market as long as the buyer engages in "sound marketing practices and efficient operations".[24]

Like some of the words used to describe the substantive conditions necessary for a price review, dictionary definitions may not be very helpful to arbitrators in defining the meaning of 'economically' or 'competitively'. Once again, subject to the rules of contract interpretation established by the governing law, the words may be considered in their reasonable commercial context and with regard to the parties' objectives in a long-term sale and purchase agreement. For a business to be competitive, or to function economically, the arbitrators may conclude that the buyer should have an adequate margin as long as the buyer is assumed to engage "in sound marketing practices and efficient operations".[25]

---

22 This is from a sale and purchase agreement between Sonatrach and Distrigas. It is quoted in Holland and Ashley, note 1 above, p33. It is available from the US Department of Energy at www.fossil.energy.gov/. Distrigas Corporation Docket N88-37-LNG, Exhibit E-1: Agreement for the Sale and Purchase of Liquified Natural Gas of April 13 1976.

23 This is from a sale and purchase agreement between Atlantic LNG Company of Trinidad and Tobago and Gas Natural LNG sale and purchase agreement, 1995. It is quoted in Holland and Ashley, note 1 above, p33.

24 See note 8 above.

25 See note 8 above.

Therefore, determining an adequate margin is often central to the arbitrators' role in adjusting a price formula. Typically, the issue is addressed by expert evidence. Arbitrators may approach this in a variety of ways. For example, they may consider whether they should:

- build up a reasonable margin;
- restore a historic margin; or
- develop some other equitable approach.

In any specific case, each approach may have advantages and disadvantages that will be the subject of expert evidence and argument by counsel.

Having considered the margin to be reflected in an adjusted contract price formula, the arbitrators next consider how to change the existing formula to reflect that margin, the changes that have occurred and any other factors set out in the parties' sale and purchase agreement. In addressing this question, arbitrators often begin by considering the words in the sale and purchase agreement to determine whether the parties limited their authority to revise the existing price formula. Some sale and purchase agreements contain limitations on that authority. Others can provide the arbitrators with quite wide authority – for example, authority to determine "a fair and equitable revision of the above-mentioned Contract Price provisions".[26] Moreover, the facts of the case may dictate the extent of the revision required to meet the requirements of the sale and purchase agreement.

Price formulae are often based on two general components:

- a constant (fixed) amount (eg, $2 per MMBtu) – known as P0 – which the parties agreed was an appropriate price as of a specific date; and
- a formula providing after that date for an increase or decrease in P0 based on the price movement of the energy product or basket of energy products that the parties elect to use as their index.

Arbitrators may decide to limit their approach to, for example, applying a correction factor that increases or decreases the value of the price that is produced by the existing formula or simply by reducing P0. In both instances, the parties' reference to competing energy products remains unchanged. A more assertive approach could be to alter the basket of energy products used in the formula or to change the weight given to each product in the basket. An even more aggressive approach could be to change the formula fundamentally by, for example, moving from a basket approach to a net-back approach. A number of other approaches are available.[27]

Whatever approach is adopted, price formulae in the natural gas industry are technically and mathematically complex. Since, usually, arbitrators are not experts in the field, they may be reluctant to impose any changes greater than absolutely necessary when revising a formula. Moreover, arbitrators rarely act without

---

26 This text is from the sale and purchase agreement considered in *Gas Natural Aprovisionamientos,* note 7 above, 2008 US Dist Lexis 69632 (SDNY).

27 See, for example, Brautaset, *et al*, note 3 above, p251.

substantial input from the parties. The parties often provide the arbitrators with proposals for a new price formula during the proceedings, supported by detailed expert evidence about the economic effect of those proposals. If they do not do so, the arbitrators may require it.

In addition to providing for adjustment of the price formula, price review provisions usually require that payments made while the price review was pending are adjusted to reflect the new price formula. This involves reducing the amount of each invoice paid since the effective date of the new price formula and calculating the aggregate amount of the reduction. The arbitrators may establish the amount due as a balancing payment.[28] Alternatively, they may simply state the new price formula and leave the parties to carry out the calculation.

5. Timing and the award

For commercial reasons, a quick completion of the price review process may be extremely important to both sellers and buyers. This is particularly so for buyers, as they face uncertainty about their cost of supply when competing against other companies in an end-user market. It may also be important because there will be even greater uncertainty if more than one price review under the same sale and purchase agreement is pending simultaneously – a situation that will exist if the time for a new, regular price review arrives or an intermediate price review is requested.

Accordingly, some price review provisions establish timing goals for the arbitrators. For example, a sale and purchase agreement might provide that:

> *The Parties intend that the Arbitration Tribunal shall reach determination that the Price Formula shall continue to have effect or determine a Revised Price Formula within 90 (ninety) days after the third arbitrator has been chosen, and the Parties agree to cooperate in order to meet such schedule.*[29]

However, many price review provisions leave the timing of proceedings and delivery of the award to the arbitrators.

The commercial need to resolve the issues quickly may influence the procedural approach taken by arbitrators. Arbitrators in price review cases should be prepared to move the process to conclusion in a reasonable time. This will affect the schedule for written submissions as well as the timing of the hearing. It may also affect procedural issues, such as a request to split the proceedings.

There are no special requirements for the form or content of the award itself beyond those that typically apply to all arbitral awards based on the law of the place of arbitration and the Convention on the Recognition and Enforcement of Foreign Arbitral Awards.

6. Conclusion

It is common for price review clauses to provide for arbitration if the parties are unable to agree on a price review request. Despite the frequency with which sellers and buyers have opted for arbitration, some within the natural gas industry have

---

28 See note 3 above.
29 See note 8 above.

questioned whether the process should be left to arbitrators. Their concern is that arbitrators, who tend to have wide experience resolving commercial disputes, do not have the specialised industry knowledge and background to adjudicate the complex issues involved in the proceeding – particularly those raised by the substantive conditions and the process of adjusting a formula. Some suggest that, instead, the process should be left to expert determination by industry specialists.

In the author's experience, usually price review arbitration is successful. This is particularly so when the process focuses on understanding the commercial realities of the parties' relationship, the economics of the end-user market into which the gas is being sold and all other relevant factors as set out in the sale and purchase agreement. In this context, the parties and their counsel have a critical role in clearly presenting the commercial and other facts which should drive the arbitrators' ultimate decision on whether and how the economics of the contract should be revised. Once they have done so, it is for the arbitrators to make commercially reasonable decisions.

The author would like to thank Stephen Anway and Nathan Santamaria for their assistance in the preparation of this chapter.

The client's perspective

Tristram Kennedy Harper
Sirius Well Manufacturing Services (a Royal Dutch Shell joint venture)

---

1. Introduction

In this chapter, we examine the development of price review clauses, and the issues that arose, through to their current form, which means that there is now a wide variety of tools to address gas price review claims. We discuss the different approaches available to contemporary price reviews, including tactics and potential solutions, and best practice for an organisation and its in-house counsel to adopt to ensure that the outcome is one for which it is prepared.

2. The origins of price review clauses

In the early days of the North Sea gas industry, the only way for upstream suppliers, typically operating in consortia, to underpin their initial investment in developing gas fields was to enter into long-term gas sales agreements (ie, for periods up to 25 or more years). The North Sea gas industry was nascent, and many upstream suppliers were not able or willing to make the investments themselves, so the typical source of capital was bank finance. The banks required reliable long-term income streams to ensure that the projects were able to repay the money being lent: long-term sales of gas dedicated to monopsonistic buyers in geographically separated markets suited this requirement.

Given the new market for gas in Europe, the buyer of the gas wanted to ensure that it could sell the gas to customers. Although it had a monopoly on supply in its geographic area, it had to be able to compete against other potential energy sources such as coal or oil. It wanted to ensure that the price that it paid the upstream supplier for the gas was competitive. At the same time, the upstream supplier wanted to receive a price for its gas that produced the highest revenue possible.

The mechanism to ensure that both parties' aims were met was twofold:

- linking the monthly gas price to prices of other energy sources (which varied monthly) and therefore tracked those prices; and
- including a price review mechanism for unexpected changes in the market, enabling the price to be reset against any new market base forces.

The initial price agreed would have been (at least) implicitly agreeable between the parties, who were freely able to negotiate and understand the economic risks of the agreement, and enabled the gas to be marketed economically by the buyer.

The price review mechanism used in these contracts dealt with changes in obtainable value of gas that were not captured by the dynamic change in the pricing clause. The mechanism evolved from the 1960s agreements in place for the sale of gas from the Dutch Groningen gas field. These were refined into a more or less industry standard during the exploitation of the Norwegian Troll gas field in the 1980s. As the sales were organised through a centralised committee, all producers and the Norwegian government sat in on negotiations, and at the same time buyers organised consortia for negotiating with the Norwegian sellers. This meant that a standardised form of agreement was used, including its price review wording. Even after 2001, in the aftermath of the European Commission's intervention in respect of the consortia's breach of the European Union's competition rules, the wording remained and became used in gas sales from other suppliers, such as from Russia and other sources.

3. Flexibility of language

Therefore, the European gas industry had a 'standard' form of wording for price reviews, the wording of which was deliberately accommodating. It suited both buyer and seller – in different price review periods, the buyer might seek a price reduction or, under different economic circumstances, the seller might seek a price increase; and less prescriptive wording enabled the words to apply in most circumstances. In addition, as it was not possible to foresee all changes of circumstance (otherwise they would be reflected in the original pricing discussion), the wording of the clause needed to be flexible enough to cover a wide range of possibilities.

This is not to say that there was no negotiation of price review clauses in new contracts. Indeed, as parties' experience of operating under price reviews increased, their approach developed and, depending on whether the party approaching the negotiation was a buyer or seller, the model wording offered was different.

But the standard model is still relevant today, whether because its operative provisions continue in existing long-term gas sales agreements or whether the provisions act as a standard for the wording of new contracts.

It could be suggested that the wording of price review clauses has been undervalued in the past, and the focus of negotiations has not been on these clauses. Thus, their importance and potential future impact has been underestimated, and it has not been recognised that mistakes made in drafting these clauses can have an effect over the whole contract life, in some cases for up to 40 years.

It is also possible that the clauses were ignored to an extent. In a number of European markets the question of price reviews, although raised, was seldom a contentious issue. Solutions were reached through commercial negotiations, not through strict observation of the contractual language and contractual mechanisms.

However, in recent years, the amount of money involved has become so significant that parties are more focused on the price review clauses and their wording, and resulting disputes have had much more legal input and direction.

The result is that parties cannot afford to underestimate the importance of wording in clauses, as many disputes may end up in a legal forum for resolution, and the tribunal or expert determination will need clear language in order to make awards consistent with the objective purposes and intentions of the parties involved.

Example 1: An example of the negotiation on meaning in price review language

In the 1990s and into the 2000s, buyers and sellers debated whether gas-to-gas competition was included in the words 'change in economic circumstances'.

Buyers sought to include the following into price review clauses: "If the economic circumstances, including, without limitation gas to gas competition, ... in the market of the Buyer ... should change significantly compared to ..."

Another issue concerned the place in which the change of circumstances occurred. Buyers sought to define this as the 'market of the buyer' in order to cover any territory in which the buyer currently sold gas, whereas sellers sought to restrict this to the country in which the price was originally set – to avoid taking price risk for markets that the buyer chose to sell into later.

Sellers would propose language like this: "If the economic circumstances *in the country of the Buyer*, which are beyond the control of the Parties, should change significantly ..."

The counterbalance to this proposal is that the seller may prefer broader geographic scope if it expects the buyer to sell into the highest price market available; and a buyer may prefer a more limited scope if it does not intend to market/use the gas elsewhere.

4. Evolution

By the mid-2000s, as access to transportation infrastructure became available and market restrictions were being removed, the real impact of deregulation of the European gas market began to be felt. Parties with existing positions in the gas market were able to realise additional value around the longer-term gas supply agreements. The ability to source or supply gas outside the traditional trading partnership had value, and the ability to transfer gas from areas of oversupply to areas of demand had an arbitrage value. In addition, the emerging hub trading facilities offered pricing but, given the low levels of liquidity, they again provided an arbitrage opportunity. Shrewd buyers and sellers began to trade off the back of the existing supply agreements, and these separate arrangements were generally of a short-term nature.

New contract forms developed, and for these shorter-term agreements, typically for less than one but up to three years in length, the commercial drivers were to avoid the typical drawn-out nature of price reviews. Furthermore, given the short-term nature of the agreements, the parties agreed not to include any price review mechanism as they were confident that there were few potential unforeseen events that would undermine the agreed pricing mechanism in the period of supply/sales. Or, if price review mechanisms were included, they tended to be detailed and specific in nature, as the events concerned were thought to be predictable, although the effect on pricing was not.

5. Some lessons learned for the future

For parties who had both sales and supply contracts, the lower risk solution in applying price review clauses was to ensure that the price review wording was the same in both the purchase and the sale contracts. Thus, if a buyer of gas was also selling gas and it received a request from its seller to increase the price, citing economic changes which had increased the value of gas in the buyer's market, the buyer would seek to pass on its cost increase to its own buyers by requesting a price review on its sales contracts, citing the same set of circumstances. It would therefore not be left squeezed in between an increase in costs which it could not pass on to its buyers, but also note that unavoidably the inherent risk remained that the negotiated settlements or adjudicated awards would not necessarily be identical.

Another determining factor in successfully negotiating price reviews was to ensure that the teams involved in the negotiation (and the wording of the clauses initially) were the best available. Further, the individuals involved needed to understand how the selected dispute resolution process would work in practice, so that the process would deliver what was expected later on. Otherwise, there could be a mismatch between the deal that the parties thought they had negotiated and what they actually signed up to.

This important combination – understanding the nuances of wording in the price review clause and the skills in applying them to the facts at hand – ultimately drives an organisation's ability to establish its case logically and evidentially. So, this means that the economic evidence must also to be as robust as possible, and engaging suitable experts at an early stage (at the negotiation stage, before any formalistic legal dispute resolution process) is a key element in increasing the chances of a successful outcome for the party concerned.

Example 2: Some simple 'dos and don'ts' in drafting and negotiating price review clauses

- Do make sure the trigger and measurement language is broad and flexible, and not too specific. Otherwise, the trigger may never be achieved; and the discussion should be focusing on the substantive merits of the claim, not on whether the trigger was valid.
- Do have simple and easy-to-measure/calculate items in price review clauses. It will not be easy to establish the price review claim if they are difficult to measure or prove. For example, it can be difficult to get the parties to attribute changes in value to specific changes in circumstance.
- Do ensure that the clause can address structural change in the market. For example, a review calculated on a change between the contract price and a price benchmark may not capture events which have an effect on value (eg, changes in sales methods or development of alternative price sources).
- Don't make the language and mechanism too complicated, as this will increase the chance of the mechanism failing or ambiguities arising, which may lead to unnecessary disputes.
- Don't forget to consider how the price review clause fits with the pricing clause itself. And ensure that the pricing clause itself does not create a barrier to calling price reviews.
- Don't presume that the same wording will be useful to apply to any contract in any market.

6. Why call for a price review?

The buyer's and seller's positions may be different in the consequent negotiation, but we are presuming that, when either party calls for a price review, they are seeking a review and change of the existing contract price. It is possible that a party may have another motive, such as the termination of the existing agreement or an extension of certain terms (or of the whole agreement), and the options, that they will be considering from the outset may be very different from the standard position in a price review – these other negotiation tools/tactics are considered later.

However, generally, the price review clauses are used by both the seller and the buyer over the duration of the contract, although perhaps with a greater focus and emphasis than they had in the past, for the reasons highlighted above – that is, the money involved has become so significant and parties are relying more on the legal options available under the contract itself.

7. The position of the party calling a price review

Before calling for a price review, a party will look at combined effect of its contractual terms and the context in which the price review clause sits. It may look at other contracts with the same counterparty to see whether there are synergies to bring into the negotiation (eg, same pricing for different contracts) or areas of distinction that it wishes to maintain (a slightly different time period for review may mean that different pricing is appropriate), and it will look at the operational aspects of the existing agreement. Are there other areas that the party wishes to bring into the negotiation at the same time, for example, problems in nomination times, changes in delivery points or accrued levels of make-up gas?

There may be other outstanding claims under the contract, problems with payment (or a desire to introduce provisional billing for its proposed price change), or a range of other non-contractual issues that can also be brought into the negotiation.

These will all be considered from a value perspective – that is, what the value of obtaining the various changes would be, and whether it is worth including any/all of them in the ensuing negotiation.

Example 3: A party (through its affiliates) has two different contracts for gas supply

(1) Sale – from Norwegian supply to a European market at a fixed delivery point to a specific seller (including arrangement of delivery).

(2) Purchase – from the same counterparty, for the same Norwegian supply, into a different country at a virtual point.

Differences in the contracts:

- duration – (1) is until 2029, (2) is until 2018;
- volumes – party sells more under (1) than purchases under (2);
- tax regimes of the affiliates for sale and purchase;
- governing law;
- price review periods;
- market reference – (1) is end-user market in country of buyer, (2) is specific

gas-market sales to specific market groups;
- flex for the two contracts; and
- pricing formulae, but both oil indexed.

Other potential negotiation issues:
- carry forward gas volumes under (1);
- potential new supply deal;
- occasional mismatch in nominations occurring under (2), with unwanted consequences; and
- credit exposure to counterparty increasing.

If the party is a net seller – strategically, does it benefit from linking price reviews under both contracts?
This will be determined by valuing the differing elements and the economic circumstances in the different countries from the two entities' perspectives. Plus, the affiliates may have different motivations – these also must be aligned before the value of other outstanding issues is considered.
Then the party can decide what tactic it should seek to adopt in the price reviews: separately for each or together.

Other contractual provisions under the contract should also be reviewed to make sure that there are no other claims that might be raised (or counter arguments that need proactively to be addressed), or bars to raising a price review claim. These could include 'economic hardship' clauses (or similar under the general governing law), change in pricing indices mechanisms and/or the ability (or obligation) to refer issues to an expert instead of arbitration.

8. A commercial solution?

A party will also consider whether it can achieve its aims through commercial negotiations before any contractually mandated negotiations under the price review clause. This would mean entering into a confidentiality agreement and ensuring that any discussions held were deemed to be 'without prejudice'. Further, it should preserve a party's rights to call for a price review (within a certain reasonable time, on a 'use it or lose it' basis) on the failure of the commercial discussions. This will need to be considered from the perspective of the governing law, as not all jurisdictions recognise 'without prejudice' discussions – and a party will not want to have an open and free discussion with a counterparty if it knows that it may be used against it in any subsequent arbitration (and, therefore, in these jurisdictions, some form of formal confidentiality agreement may be necessary).

If affiliates of the contracting parties are involved in the negotiations, a party may hold the meetings in the counterparty's location, using its local staff from the same city (and with the benefit of discussing the matter in the local language), the confidentiality agreement must cater for information flows to and from affiliates, and the affiliates' relationships with each other must be considered from a tax/corporate governance perspective as well.

9. Internal preparation and management of the price review

Parties should be organised in their approach to price reviews, especially if they have several contracts. By using a common approach (and organisational mandate) and involving an experienced group of people within the organisation, a party will have a common basis for understanding and evaluating its options in each price review, regardless of whether this concerns a sales or a supply contract.

All team members must be trained, not just the key negotiating team. They need to understand that setting the boundaries for information exchanges is important, both from a competition law perspective and from a forward thinking internal approach to document discovery in any future litigation. The organisation's legal function can provide written guidance, training and refresher courses on anti-trust, discovery and the basics of legal privilege, and on the content, tone and distribution of communications generally.

The organisation should consider whether it wishes to engage consultants. This should be decided at an early stage as the pool of consultants with international arbitration experience is limited, and conflicts can be an issue. Consultants could be market experts or providers of external data that support the claim, or those who can support gathering and presenting internal data on sales, costs or other comparative contracts. These experts may also be engaged for use in any future arbitration. If this is the case, the business must understand that an expert in this role is not supporting the claim from the employing organisation, but is an independent person engaged ultimately for the benefit of the arbitral panel or expert determination.

It is important to make sure that contracts for consultants'/experts' services provide appropriate terms and conditions for the work to be carried out, and also consider limitations on their work for the counterparty during their engagement (and any ensuing arbitration). A party engaging a consultant should obtain rights in the work produced (and a licence to use background material), in order to circulate it for the benefit of the organisation generally and, where there are a number of price reviews, share the materials with other teams supporting the different price reviews (and potentially to be able to share it with the counterparties).

Information flows within the organisation should be controlled, especially where there are different affiliates involved in separate supply and purchase agreements, and each price review should be treated as a stand-alone measure – again, to protect the organisation from contamination between different price reviews.

Since most long-term sales agreements have confidentiality provisions, it may be difficult to share information across different price reviews. In addition, organisations should check the terms of the confidentiality clauses, as certain contracts provide for sharing information with customers – this may cause problems in a price review if the counterparty's customer is also separately a customer of the organisation. Will a consistent story be provided by the counterparty to the customer, as the party itself is providing to the same customer?

Example 4: Standardisation is a valuable tool for replicating consistency of approach across the organisation

Consider developing:

- model consultancy/experts' agreements;
- model confidentiality/without prejudice agreements;
- standardised potential arbitrator interview questionnaire (see below);
- guidance notes on confidentiality, anti-trust, legal privilege and discovery;
- a set of principles for the organisation to operate its price reviews consistently;
- a valuation methodology for comparing outcomes in a common 'currency'; and
- a standard set of questions for consultants engaged to carry out market studies.

Ensure that any documentation is also tailored to fit any issues arising from differing governing laws.

10. Considering how the price review will end – arbitration?

From the outset, a party should also consider where a price review will end. If the review is not resolved by negotiation, will the party be willing to undertake arbitration to get its desired outcome? If it is, it must ensure that it has management support, as this will affect the negotiating position that it takes.

Further, does management have a clear picture of the likely costs of arbitration? Budgeting tools are useful here, including for estimating the procedural costs of the arbitration itself (the International Chamber of Commerce provides a useful cost calculator for estimating arbitration fees on its website: see www.iccwbo.org/ products-and-services/arbitration-and-adr/arbitration/cost-and-payment/cost-calculator/). Costs may also include external legal fees, internal legal and management time and resources, and the fees of consultants and experts for the arbitration.

Different arbitral institutions have different cost structures. The International Chamber of Commerce charges by reference to the amount in dispute, but other institutions use hourly rates (eg, the London Court of International Arbitration). As a price review claim could be for a significant amount of money, these fees should be borne in mind, along with the quality and efficiency of the arbitral institution. Hopefully, most costs will be for external counsel, external advisers and experts, not the arbitral institution's fees.

At this early stage, a party should also consider potential party-appointed arbitrators, develop a shortlist, interview them and 'reserve' them for future use.

Example 5: Potential arbitrators – a 'to do' list

- Develop a 'long list' of potential names – for party nominated candidates and as chairperson.
- Develop a standard interview questionnaire.
- Be familiar with the Chartered Institute of Arbitrators Practice and Standards Committee Arbitration Sub-Committee Practice Guideline 16: The Interviewing of Prospective Arbitrators.

- Carry out some initial research on possible candidates:
  - their experience with gas sales agreements and the gas market;
  - do they normally act for the buyer or seller;
  - any language barriers;
  - seniority; reputation;
  - previous types of arbitration involvement;
  - independent or partner in a firm (the firm may object because of the affect on its work for other clients);
  - what their approach is likely to be (legal or commercial outlook), and so on.
- Contact those on the shortlist for an initial conflicts check.
- Interview the candidates – preferably in person, and use at least two interviewers to provide a more balanced opinion.
- Consider how each candidate would interact with other members of a tribunal panel.
- Make the selection (there may be different selection criteria for sales and supply cases) and inform the arbitrators.

11. Defensive tactics

A claiming party should consider what its counterparty will raise in defence. Once a counterparty has been informed of a potential price review, it should consider what defensive positions it might adopt.

In the past, parties had plenty of time to prepare for price reviews, because reviews were held regularly – every three years. The parties would prepare in advance for standard discussions. The recent use in the market of 'wild cards' to trigger a review (ie, the contractual right for a party to call for a certain number of additional price reviews during the term of the contract, outside the regular review periods) has changed this.

In the past, these wild cards, or 'jokers', were viewed as being held in reserve or not even considered for use. Today, parties are more proactive in considering their legal options under their long-term contracts and have identified them as a valuable tool, hence their recent usage. However, the receiving party has little or no time to prepare a response.

Although, generally, the contracts provide for a 120-day negotiation period after receipt of the trigger letter, in practice, this is not enough time to gather market data, take internal soundings, develop a mandated approach and then engage in a series of meaningful discussions with the counterparty. Therefore, a party should consider whether it is appropriate to agree with the other side on a longer time for negotiation.

The internal soundings should include a consideration of the potential approaches to the price review. For a party defending a price review, these could include mechanistic challenges to the validity of the trigger letter, challenges to the calling of the price review on temporal grounds, seeking to steer the process by insisting on certain meeting formats or insisting that the counterparty issue its trigger letter (thereby using one of its price review rights if it is under a wild card) before being willing to enter into any commercial discussion. The claiming party should be aware that its defendant may raise such issues and should consider how to address them proactively.

12. Offensive tactics

A party should also consider any additional issues that it may wish to raise in response to the price review, or provide a list of additional changes to the contract that it wants to address. It should consider whom it might select as its party-appointed arbitrator (and acceptable chairpersons).

If a request for arbitration is issued later, the party may consider making challenges to the other party's nominated arbitrator, on the basis of, for example, conflict of interest or bias. However, although more challenges to the appointment of arbitrators have been made in recent years, and challenges to awards, in general, the governing arbitral bodies are not in favour of such challenges and overall their success has been limited.

Another tactic might be to delay the process, if there is a legitimate basis for doing so. The party seeking the price review may be suffering financially (not necessarily because of this contract, but more generally), and the longer the process takes, the longer it is before that party receives any relief under the contract. Parties with cash flow issues may negotiate less than optimal solutions if they are in financial difficulty (especially as they need to report to shareholders on a periodic basis). This must be carefully assessed by the counterparty.

Delaying tactics by the recipient of a price review claim may be used to try to force the claiming party to reveal information. It could insist that it will not enter into any discussion unless/until the claiming party provides sufficient details of its claim to substantiate its request, arguing that it is not for the respondent to assist the claimant in proving its claim, seeking to establish the claimant's good faith.

At an extreme, the recipient could argue that it will wait until receiving the request for arbitration and will not enter into any substantive dialogue, forcing the claimant either to reveal the details of their claim or to withdraw their request. These tactics may work if the respondent believes the claimant is not willing to take the risk of an arbitral process, and therefore negotiate from a stronger position.

Another tactic for the defendant in commercial or contractual negotiations is to challenge the supporting evidence used by the claimant on the basis that it is unrepresentative, biased or flawed. It may be challenged as not being the claimant's own position (ie, it is not the experience that it has in the market) or, alternatively, challenged for not being independent (ie, it is its own data, which has been manipulated to be favourable to its claim).

All of these tactical choices can be used when seeking to resolve the dispute commercially, but, ultimately, if the dispute goes to arbitration or expert determination (if that is the dispute resolution mechanism), only the specific issue can be referred and determined by the arbitral panel or expert – that is, the review of the contract price. The arbitrators or expert cannot make other amendments to the contract unless the contract so provides, or unless the parties agree to give them that power.

13. Other negotiating tools – potential solutions

A party to a gas supply contract should consider what other items of value might be offered or traded in order to resolve the price review. These will all be based on a question of value for the business, and an estimation of the value to the counterparty. The value can be calculated in various ways, but in order for the business to be able to make comparisons, and to make negotiation moves based on offering various elements, they need to have a common basis.

One important consideration to explore is whether the solution to be offered to the counterparty is temporary or permanent. A temporary solution will mean that the price may need to be revisited within a short timeframe, but it may also mean that it is possible to offer something more than a party may be willing to offer in the case of a permanent solution – while awaiting the real impact of changes in the marketplace to become clear on, for example, the obtainable value of gas. A permanent solution concludes that period, but may be more difficult to resolve. A party may be unwilling to settle for a permanent solution if evidence on what is happening in the end-user market is not yet available, as, for example, comparable import contracts are still subject to outstanding price reviews (and so the position in respect of gas-to-gas competition is unclear).

A example of this was reported by Andrey Konoplyanik in his paper entitled "Pricing gas: evolution not revolution", published in *Energy Economist* in November 2010, in which he stated that the deputy chief executive officer of Gazprom proposed a "stimulating package" for European gas buyers under their long-term contracts, which offered a "temporary change in the pricing linked to oil-products".

14. Duration and termination

A party may then consider whether it will offer to the counterparty a shortening of the contract duration. For example, if a counterparty claims that the current price is unaffordable, one tactic is to offer to terminate the agreement, or to shorten its duration. This will depend on whether the seller has an alternative outlet for the gas, or believes it can market the gas effectively to other customers.

The party being offered early termination or shortened contract duration must assess the benefit of having a continuing long-term security of supply, its need to have the gas (eg, if its own onward sales portfolio is shrinking, or if the forecasts of prices it is able to achieve in onward sales is lower than the contract price even after change in price resulting from the price review), against its ability to source gas from elsewhere in the volumes and in the timescales that it requires.

The acceptability of this solution will depend on the values attached by the parties – it does not need to be the same value (and such value assigned to it will not necessarily be communicated by each party to the other in any event), merely that the solution offered is above the values assigned to it independently by the parties.

While a termination may be negotiated to be effective immediately, it could also be at a convenient time for the parties, for example, the end of a gas year. Similarly, a shortening of the duration is likely to be at a convenient time for both parties either at the end of a future gas year or immediately before a specific further price review. In this instance, a party will seek to remove or limit future price reviews under the shortened contract life.

15. Flexibility and delivery point changes

One possible solution is to vary the flexibility offered under the contract. This will vary according to the specifics negotiated in the original contract (and as varied over its life), but generally there may be intra-day, month and yearly gas take obligation flexibility that will be of value to both parties. Generally, a seller will value the removal of 'flex' in order to increase the guaranteed take of gas and hence its revenues (and therefore may be willing to be more flexible on the price of the gas), and a buyer may be willing to accept a lower flexibility depending on its actual needs profile. It may be willing to accept a lower flex in conjunction with a change in the volumes – so it has a lower overall obligation to the seller.

Another solution is a variation to the delivery point. Typically, many long-term gas contracts were based on dedicated physical transportation and entry/exit capacity, with access prearranged to the country in question. As European markets become more integrated, and as buyers seek to widen the scope of their activities, it is possible that a buyer may wish to have gas delivery at a virtual delivery point such as Gaspool, TTF or NCG, and a seller may be willing to offer this as an alternative. The ongoing cost of transportation and entry/exit capacity must be addressed as part of this analysis, and, depending on which party is contractually required to provide the arrangements, there may be a cost saving to one party.

In many markets, a seller may be willing to offer a change in delivery point as a solution, in order to free up its (over)booked capacity for use for other, more lucrative trades or to balance its physical and virtual deliveries, which may have operational and trading benefits. However, it is possible that deliveries at a virtual trading point lead to a discussion about pricing for the gas – should it be priced similarly to the gas being spot traded at that trading point, or should it remain priced according to the existing contract terms? This will depend on what the buyer plans to do with the gas once delivered.

16. Sweetening the deal – and other possibilities

A party may seek to offer other commercially attractive items to the counterparty to 'sweeten' the deal on the price review, such as additional volumes, geographic or time swaps of gas and new long-term gas sales. This will depend on the willingness and ability of the parties to offer and negotiate the items – and the value that each party places on such new alternatives. They may be of great value to a party, but unacceptable if it leaves the main contract still not performing profitably, or if the counterparty does not want to have further commercial dealings with the party that is resisting the price review (or accepting similar terms again).

There is a range of other options that may be considered (although these options are rarely concluded in practice), including changing payment terms, building in incentive payment structures or options for additional gas. The reason that they are rarely considered is that they are more difficult to value, and in more uncertain times (ie, if the changes in the market are increasing, or increasing more rapidly), the parties will be unwilling to bind themselves into complex arrangements. The simpler buy-sell arrangements will provide less risk and therefore be more acceptable to management.

The price review mechanism itself could also be subject to amendment. A change in price may be acceptable only if the ability to change it in the future is restricted. The parties may determine in advance how the pricing will change in the future, for example, by agreeing a provision to modify the contract price on the occurrence of a specified event, for example, to change the pricing structure from oil-indexation to spot-market pricing when a specified level of 'churn rate' at a gas trading hub is achieved.

One of the most radical solutions might be to reduce the volume of gas being sold under the agreement, creating a new contract with different pricing (and flex) for the carved-out quantities. This may be a mutually acceptable solution if there is some agreed change in the market which does not affect the whole market.

17. The desire for certainty

Underlying the potential solutions is the desire of the business to have certainty. A suboptimal price review solution may still be acceptable to management if it means that at least the pricing of the gas is known, as price reviews can last for years, and until the review is resolved (potentially by costly and risky arbitration), the parties will not know what the actual historic price of the gas is – and a rectifying settlement for past years will need to be effected. This may be of crucial importance to the organisation's accounts if it is reporting on an accrual (and not mark-to-market) basis.

The business itself will evaluate the options of continuing with a price review and the ability to settle it. It will be aware of the management and commercial resources used to manage a price review, as well as the engagement of support staff and external consultants and experts. Overall, the view may be that it is using valuable resource on an issue focused on the past – and it wishes to focus its attention on the future and new sales opportunities. To some extent, this may be dictated by the organisation's priorities.

If the organisation is primarily a buyer of gas and a reseller, its focus may be directly (and at a high level) on the price review because of the critical nature of the pricing on its profitability, whereas if it has a range of businesses, including commodities trading, the focus may focus on a quicker resolution of the dispute.

18. The role for in-house legal support

It is not just an organisation's commercial personnel who are involved in the price review – its legal support is critical for successful negotiation and resolution. The starting point for lawyers is a good understanding of the gas business in general, and detailed knowledge of the specific market in question. This will include the infrastructure, regulation and market dynamics, and particularly the extent of gas-to-gas competition.

The lawyer will also need to know how gas is sold in the market, on what terms, to which types of sector, for what length of time, and so on. The lawyer must be very familiar with the contract in question, including the mechanics for dealing with flexibility. An informed lawyer will be an important part of any negotiation, and can support and develop commercial negotiation strategies which influence the contractual position.

The legal advice will follow the commercial drivers for the negotiation. For example, if the contract is not strategic to the business, the emphasis on a quick commercial settlement may not be the top priority, and indeed the business may wish to use time as negotiating tactic.

It is also the case that the governing law may not be a limiting factor for the legal advice. The interpretation of the wording of the price review clause may be different under different governing laws, but, in general, the key questions in the negotiations are driven by the economics.

The lawyer must also support the business by providing training on an ongoing basis, as discussed in section 9. Raising awareness of the legal framework for conducting price reviews also ensures that the business knows when to raise legal issues and how to behave in accordance with the law, even when there is no legal representation present.

19. Conclusion

An organisation that understands the importance of price reviews generally, and which has a systematic approach to them, will benefit – whether it is defending or prosecuting a price review, and regardless of whether the matter appears to be pre-destined for arbitration or expert determination. The best outcome is one that the organisation has properly evaluated and negotiated, not one that is imposed because it was ill prepared or under informed. The legal role in this is crucial – in training, in making the organisation aware of the issues, and in working collaboratively with the commercial team to deliver robust, creative and defendable solutions.

The opinions expressed in this chapter are those of the author, and do not reflect the opinions, views or policies of Royal Dutch Shell Plc and its affiliates. Suggestions and analyses in the chapter are examples used for illustrative purposes only and are not intended to depict any past, current or future scenarios. Information provided should not be relied on as legal advice, nor should it be relied on as a substitute for obtaining competent, experienced professional legal counsel.

The role of the expert in price review arbitrations

Colm Gibson
Energy and utilities expert
Dr Boaz Moselle
FTI Consulting

1. Introduction

This chapter discusses the role of the economic expert acting as a party-appointed expert witness in price review arbitrations arising from long-term natural gas[1] supply contracts in continental Europe. We distinguish this role from testimony that may be provided by other types of expert (eg, legal expertise, which may be required if specific points of applicable law arise) and from the role of an expert appointed by the tribunal to help it in its deliberations (although much of what we say here will also be relevant to that function).

Nonetheless, a more accurate title might refer to the 'roles' rather than the 'role' of the expert. As we explain below, typically, economic testimony in price review arbitrations covers a wide range of issues, depending on the facts of the case and the price review clause itself. Therefore, the role of the expert may involve discussion and analysis of matters such as:

- market trends, using standard economic tools (eg, analysis of price trends, market concentration, barriers to entry and other factors affecting competition);
- regulatory changes (eg, developments promoting gas-to-gas competition);
- pricing, value and profitability (eg, by comparison of the price of gas under the contract at issue with prices of gas from other sources; by calculating the value of the gas in comparison with competing fuels; or by performing calculations of profitability derived from end-user price data).

In addition, the applicable law affects the role of the expert in a number of ways, including the extent to which the tribunal will be interested in the subjective intent of the parties and potentially in claims of trade practice that might be used to support some elements of contractual interpretation.

Therefore, the expert has many possible roles, which may require the use of a wide range of skills, types of evidence and analytical methodologies. The expert may be asked to act as any of the following:

- competition economist, with specialist skills in the study of industrial organisation and the application of economic theory to the analysis of markets;

1 Whether piped gas or liquefied natural gas (LNG).

- regulatory economist, with expertise in understanding the development of economic regulation and its impact on gas markets;
- accountant, with the expertise to understand company accounts to establish, for example, whether gas is being sold profitably at the current price levels or (where there is a hardship clause in the contract) whether either the buyer or the seller is suffering 'hardship' within the definition;
- statistical expert, to undertake appropriate analysis of data on the market, including potentially large and complex data sets concerning pricing (see later discussion). The expert may need to perform relatively sophisticated analysis (eg, assessing impact of changes on value while controlling for short-term factors such as weather);
- local market expert, to provide detailed local knowledge on pricing, energy use, data sources, regulatory history (which in some cases can be complex and obscure); and
- industry expert, to provide knowledge of industry practice, both current and at the time the contract was agreed.

Indeed, the set of roles is wide enough that it is quite common in our experience for one or both parties to use several experts, since often no individual will have expertise in all the required areas.

Lastly, as in other proceedings, the basic task of the expert or experts is to assist the tribunal in its role by providing clear, non-technical explanations of their analyses.

As the above may suggest, the role of the expert in price review arbitrations can be different from that in other international arbitration proceedings.[2] It is our experience that the role of the expert can be central in price reviews. The expert witness often provides the majority of the testimony, whether measured in terms of the volume of written matter, the time spent in oral testimony or the focus of legal submissions. Factual evidence, if any, may be limited to short accounts of the negotiations that preceded the request for arbitration (since a party may wish to establish that it has followed the contractually required procedures and acted in good faith). To put this in perspective, we often see no more than 10 or 20 pages of factual testimony but several hundred pages of expert testimony, and legal pleadings often largely focus on the content of the expert reports.[3]

Typically, the structure of expert testimony covers three or four areas:

- Economic and financial principles underlying the pricing and related arrangements – commonly, expert testimony is used to set out the relevant economic and financial principles that underlie the pricing arrangements, because it is not possible to discuss changes to those arrangements without a clear understanding of how they currently work. Explanations may cover both the pricing formula used, and important non-price terms such as the 'take-or-pay' mechanism.

2 These comments apply equally to commercial litigation conducted in national courts.
3 Lest this be thought self-serving coming from two experts, we should add that it reflects the views of various international arbitration lawyers with whom we have worked.

- Analysis of 'trigger' – most price review clauses specify certain criteria that must be satisfied in order to justify a price revision (the 'trigger criteria'). Most often, the trigger involves changes in economic or market circumstances that meet certain criteria (eg, "affecting the value of gas in the Buyer's market").
- Analysis of 'adjustment' – if the tribunal finds that the criteria for triggering a review have been met, it must determine whether an adjustment to the existing pricing arrangements is justified and, if so, what adjustment is most appropriate.
- Other areas – these include providing testimony where one of the parties claims that one or more clauses of the contract are anticompetitive, or seeks to invoke a hardship clause. We have seen instances where parties suggest that pricing arrangements in existing long-term contracts are in themselves an abuse of a dominant position, or that the refusal to agree to a price reduction is an abuse.

The second and third points above (trigger and adjustment) reflect the typical structure of price review clauses.[4]

The rest of this chapter follows the structure described above.

2. The expert's role in setting out the economic and financial principles and context

In order to understand how price review clauses generally work (in economic terms), one must first understand at high level the principles behind gas pricing in long-term gas sales agreements. Indeed, pricing arrangements and price review clauses are sometimes said to go hand in hand.

Also, to understand the issues that arise in most price reviews, one must have some knowledge of developments in European natural gas markets. Typically, therefore, the expert will need to include in his or her testimony some or all of the following:

- the mechanism of pricing in long-term gas sales agreements;
- the origins of these pricing mechanisms, including (but not limited to) concepts such as:
  - the 'equivalence principle' (often referred to by the German *Anlegbarkeitsprinzip*) and net-back pricing;
  - benchmarks based on comparison with border prices;
  - the balance of risk in traditional long-term contracts, including the role of take-or-pay clauses under which the buyer takes on the bulk of the volume risk; and
- recent and ongoing market developments (both regulatory and commercial developments may be relevant).

4 We note that in our experience this two-part (trigger and adjustment) structure is one of the few points common to most price review clauses, though not all. In most respects, price review clauses vary widely. Some writers have suggested a 'typical' or canonical price review clause, or claim that price review clauses form a 'single family'. The reality is more complex – as one colleague has said: "The 'family of price review clauses' is like the 'family of dogs' – there are common features across the family, but one clause need not look anything like another."

2.1 Pricing in long-term gas sales agreements

The pricing formulae in long-term gas sales agreements look complex. However, conceptually, the formulae usually represent a relatively simple underlying relationship between the contract price and a 'basket' of prices of alternative fuels (usually some or all of crude oil, refined oil products such as gasoil and fuel oil, and coal).[5] There is often a base price, with an indexation element that tracks this basket of other fuels. This is illustrated graphically in Figure 1.

Figure 1: Illustrative relationship between contract price and basket of other fuels

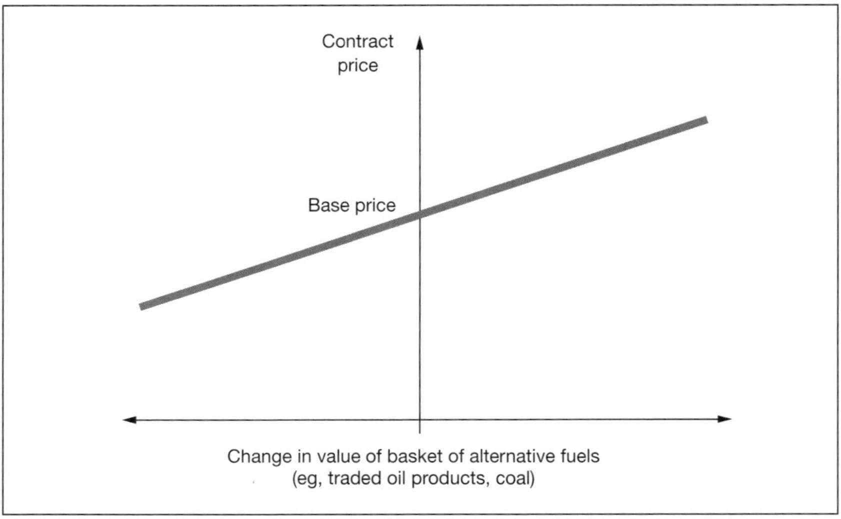

As Figure 1 shows, the price of gas is set at the base price on the day that the pricing arrangements go into operation. It then moves with the basket of alternative fuels: if the price of the basket increases (positive change in value), the price of gas increases, and vice versa.

There have been two general approaches to determining pricing formulae reflected in most long-term contracts. One common approach is based on the difference between an estimate, or proxy, for the end-user price or value of gas in the buyer's market and an assumed gross margin – that is, allowing for reasonable costs and profit:

Contract price = [estimated end-user price/value] – [assumed gross margin]

If the buyer is able to resell the gas in line with the estimated end-user price/value, this formulation will give it the intended margin.

Historically, under this approach the estimated end-user price/value was derived or expressed as the price of a basket of alternative fuels. The composition of that

5 The term 'oil indexation' is often used even if the basket includes other elements such as coal.

basket (ie, the relative weights of the different fuels in it) reflected the composition of the buyer's market. Different sectors of that market were linked to different alternative fuels. In other cases, the price is derived by negotiation, either with or without explicit reference to end-user prices. In such cases the choice of basket and of weights in the basket will also be a matter of negotiation.[6]

Another widely used approach to deriving the pricing formula has been by comparison with other upstream contracts. The underlying commercial logic is that setting a price that is comparable to that in other contracts should allow the buyer to remain competitive, and also reassure the seller that it is not selling at too low a price.

These two approaches may produce price formulae that have the same mathematical form, despite their different bases. However, they are shown in different ways in different price review clauses, which may make reference to one or both as the relevant criterion.

With the development of gas hub trading, a third approach to pricing gas is becoming increasingly relevant: indexation to price levels at EU trading hubs such as the NBP (National Balancing Point) in the United Kingdom or the TFF (Title Transfer Facility) in the Netherlands.

2.2 Take-or-pay clauses

Long-term gas sales agreements often include take-or-pay arrangements. Despite the name, this does not usually mean that if the buyer does not take the minimum volume under the contract it is obliged to pay for gas that it does not receive. Rather, it is better to think of such clauses working more like banking arrangements. Specifically, if less than the minimum volume is taken, the buyer must pay in advance part or all of the contract price for the gas not taken. In return for this, the volume of gas is 'banked', and can later be called upon by the buyer (in return for a payment of the rest of the contract price, if only part-payment was made in advance). Therefore, essentially, the take-or-pay payment gives the buyer the right to take the relevant volume of gas later. However, in our experience, there is typically a time limit requiring banked gas to be taken within a specified number of years. Any gas not removed from the bank at the end of this period would be lost. Moreover, there is obviously a cost to advance payment. Depending on the circumstances, the take-or-pay arrangements may be either advantageous or burdensome to the buyer.

2.3 Recent and ongoing market developments

As experts, we are often asked to analyse recent or ongoing market developments. This is almost always relevant background for consideration of the trigger criteria,[7] but can also be useful to a tribunal when considering a price adjustment, especially if the contract states that any such adjustment must allow the buyer the ability to sell the gas in a downstream market. Typically, expert testimony will cover a number of kinds of ongoing market developments including:

---

6 In reality, it is likely that many elements of a contract formula will reflect the results of negotiation, even if the starting point was an analysis of end-user prices.

7 In relation to whether a specific event has occurred, but also in relation to whether an event was foreseeable, as discussed below.

- European gas market liberalisation – for example, relevant EU and national legislation.
- The effects of liberalisation – for example, the development of hub trading and the corresponding increase in liquidity of hub markets.
- Market events – for example, economic downturns, the decoupling of oil and gas prices, the development of renewable energy, and the possible impact of increasing LNG and shale gas production.

3. Expert testimony concerning 'trigger'

It is common (though not universal) for long-term gas sales agreements to specify various criteria that must be met in order to trigger a price review (usually referred to as 'trigger criteria'). The specific criteria vary between different price review clauses, but typically they refer to changes in certain economic, financial or commercial circumstances. In addition, there are timing criteria: typically, a price review can occur only on a specified date (often every three years from a specified starting date, although in some contracts this requirement is softened by allowing each party one or more 'jokers' – ie, the right to request one or more price reviews outside the normal schedule).

Where the trigger criteria require there to have been "changes in [economic] circumstances" (or similar language), generally, these changes must meet certain additional criteria. These criteria are quite varied, but typically involve various qualifiers on the kind of change that can trigger a price review. For example, they must be "significant", "expected to be long-lasting", "beyond the control of the parties", "not reasonably foreseeable", as well as meet certain geographical criteria, and so on.

The changes are often required to have had an effect on "the value of gas" or a similar concept. Again, the specifics of this criterion vary very significantly. In some cases, the 'value concept' is not defined; in others it is specified relatively clearly (eg, by reference to the prices paid in comparable contracts or by reference to competing energies, if relevant).

In general, these criteria must be assessed by comparing circumstances at two specified dates:

- a start date, which is commonly the date of signing of the contract or of the last price revision; and
- an end date, which is commonly the date on which a formal request for the price review was made by one party to the other (the 'trigger date').

This period is sometimes referred to as the 'trigger period' or the 'comparison period', or simply the 'relevant period'.

Therefore, the expert's role in assessing whether the trigger criteria have been met often involves (conceptually) two elements: describing the alleged changes in economic circumstances and assessing them against the specified criteria. Generally, this requires the expert to develop both qualitative and quantitative evidence. We illustrate with two examples. The first is a relatively straightforward change that is typical for a traditional price review (in contrast to a review that focuses on the impact of liberalisation). The second relates to liberalisation and gas-to-gas competition.

Example 1: A 'traditional' price review

Suppose that the government of the country where the gas is delivered and sold (the buyer's home market) increases/decreases the excise duty (ie, tax) on a certain competing fuel,[8] say fuel oil. Suppose also that this would be a valid trigger for a price review under the price review clause in question, which defined 'value' by reference to competing fuels. First, the expert would need to document the change in excise duty (by reference to official publications), and show by how much it affected the price of fuel oil, in particular in applications where it was a competing fuel for natural gas.

Second, the expert would need to show that the change affected the value of gas, and estimate by how much it did so. In brief, the likely effect would be that an increase in duty would make it possible for the buyer to raise the price that it charged for natural gas to those customers for whom fuel oil was the main alternative to natural gas, since the increase in duty would make that alternative more expensive. Conversely, a decrease in duty would be likely to lead to a lowering of the price charged to those customers. In that case, the expert might need to:[9]

- document that fuel oil was indeed a competing fuel for natural gas, in the market in question, at the relevant point(s) in time;
- estimate the amount or proportion of sales of natural gas from the contract under review that could be considered to be sold in competition with fuel oil, at the relevant point(s) in time;
- show that at the beginning of the period under review, natural gas sold in competition with fuel oil was priced at a level to make it competitive with fuel oil;
- calculate by how much the price should change in those circumstances, taking into account various technical parameters (eg, the relative efficiencies of appliances using natural gas and using fuel oil, in various applications); and
- calculate the average impact on the price that the buyer could obtain for its gas (given that this change affects only part of its market).

Depending on how the 'value of gas' is defined in the relevant contractual provisions, the result of this exercise might be considered to be the impact on the value of gas (it would not be so if, eg, the contract required the value of gas to be assessed on the basis of comparison with the price of gas in other import contracts and not at end-user level).

8 Historically, gas pricing in contracts with end users in continental Europe was often derived by considering the price of alternative fuels that the customer could use for the same purpose (eg, a household might choose to use gasoil for heating if it did not use natural gas). In this context, these were referred to as 'competing fuels'.

9 We do not claim the following list to be either necessary or sufficient. The specific nature of what is appropriate expert evidence will depend on the factual details of the matter in question, and the specific contractual requirements.

Example 2: Review driven by market liberalisation and gas-to-gas competition

Suppose the buyer seeks a price review on the grounds that EU and national legislation that have liberalised the gas market, and this has led to competition from other suppliers that has pushed down the price that it can obtain for its gas (and suppose again that this would be a valid trigger under the price review clause). In this case, the expert might need to:[10]

- describe and document the legislative and regulatory changes that have liberalised the market;
- describe and provide evidence of market responses to these changes. This might involve, for example, evidence concerning the entry of new competitors or changes in pricing that can be linked to gas-to-gas competition. The types of evidence used could include data of the sort commonly used in competition economics (eg, market shares, changes in pricing compared to a competitive benchmark), as well as more business economics types of documentation such as market commentary from trade press, broker notes, and so on. National regulators and academic economists may also prove useful sources; and
- demonstrate that the market response has affected the value of gas in the relevant market. Depending on how the contract defines 'value of gas', this could involve, for example, analysis of import and/or end-user prices, to estimate how they have changed relative to relevant benchmarks such as the price of oil or the price of gas at trading hubs.

In our experience in recent price reviews, debates about liberalisation vary significantly depending on the specific countries and time periods under discussion. The pace of gas market liberalisation across the European Union also varies significantly. In some member states gas markets are highly liberalised, while in others liberalisation remains more a theoretical possibility than a significant factor affecting the market. Therefore, in some cases there may be material debates on the extent to which the liberalisation is sufficient to warrant a price review. In other cases, the effects of liberalisation may be clearer, but experts may disagree on issues of timing and whether the start of competition fell within the contractually relevant time period. In yet other cases, where the price review clause and/or applicable law exclude changes that were reasonably foreseeable at the beginning of the relevant time period, there may be discussion on the extent to which the changes attributed to liberalisation were foreseeable.

The types of evidence that the expert may rely on, and the analyses he performs, can vary considerably. In some cases the expert will rely significantly on personal knowledge, particularly in markets that historically have been less transparent. In other cases, the expert may rely significantly on public documents (eg, legislation, regulations, official publications, as well as trade and business press, analyst

10 As in the previous example, we do not claim the following list to be either necessary or sufficient.

reports from banks). The expert may use a range of different data sources, including:

- data from public sources (eg, EU data, data from national statistical agencies, data from energy regulators);
- data purchased from survey companies,[11] which may be produced specifically for the expert or be generally available; and
- the buyer's internal data on the prices that it achieves as a gas marketer.

In the last case, there are typically disagreements between the parties over the disclosure of data, and the expert must be ready to deal with data at short notice (if disagreements over data provision have led to delays in disclosure, as is often the case) and under potentially burdensome confidentiality requirements. This is particularly so if the data can be accessed and worked on only in a secure data room. The expert may need to have a team able to use business software packages such as SAP, and to process large datasets, both in terms of data handling and in terms of undertaking numerical and statistical analyses.

4. Expert testimony concerning price adjustment

In our experience, the variation between price review clauses is particularly marked with regard to the contractual criteria that apply to a price adjustment. Therefore, it is likely that the expert will be asked to provide an opinion on a range of relevant areas, depending on what is specified in the contract with respect to the adjustment.

The adjustment criteria may be explicitly linked to the trigger criteria (eg, "adjust to reflect the changes"). Alternatively, the clause may specify other criteria for the price adjustment, even if they are not (explicitly) required for trigger. For example, some clauses require any adjustment to take into account a comparison between the contract price and the pricing in other comparable long-term gas supply contracts, even if the trigger does not make any reference to other such contracts.

Some price review clauses also specify that the adjustment should be such that the buyer is "able to market" the gas "economically", subject to certain safeguards for the seller: such requirements may be argued to mean that the price should allow the buyer to sell the gas, cover its costs and earn some kind of a net margin, provided that the buyer acts and has acted efficiently and prudently in its marketing and operations.

Some contracts also exclude certain changes from the scope of the price review clause, so that the buyer is explicitly required to bear the corresponding risk. Examples are pricing clauses that exclude taxes or exclude changes to the taxation regime.

There are also some basically technical issues that arise, depending on what the claimant (whether buyer or seller) is looking to change.

For example, the claimant may wish to reset only the price level in the contract, but not to change the indexation mechanism. This would involve only a change to the P0 parameter in the price formula, as illustrated in Figure 2.

11 In our experience, one or both parties may commission surveys to obtain data on pricing from large customers.

Figure 2: Change in P0

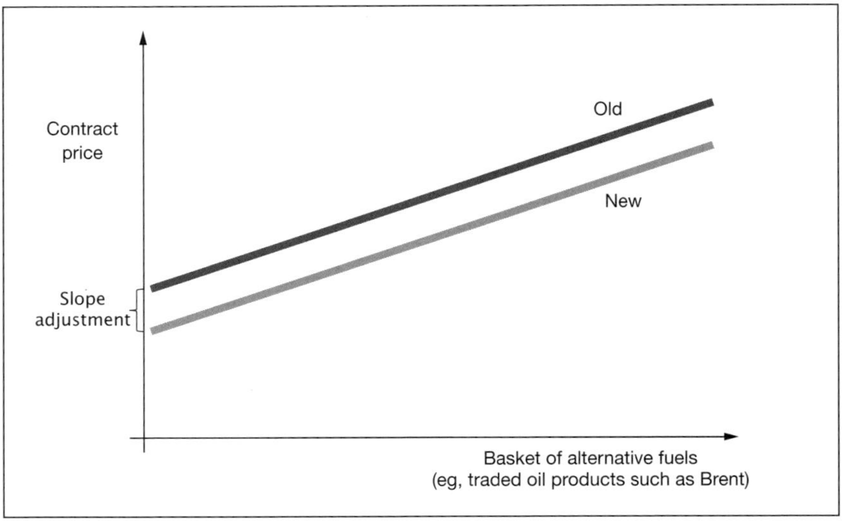

Alternatively or in addition, the claimant may wish to change the 'slope' in the price formula (ie, the percentage of the prevailing oil price that sets the price), so that future changes in the oil price have a lesser or greater impact on the contract price than they would under the pre-award formula. The expert may need to explain carefully the economic significance of a change in slope.

Figure 3: Change in 'slope' in the price formula

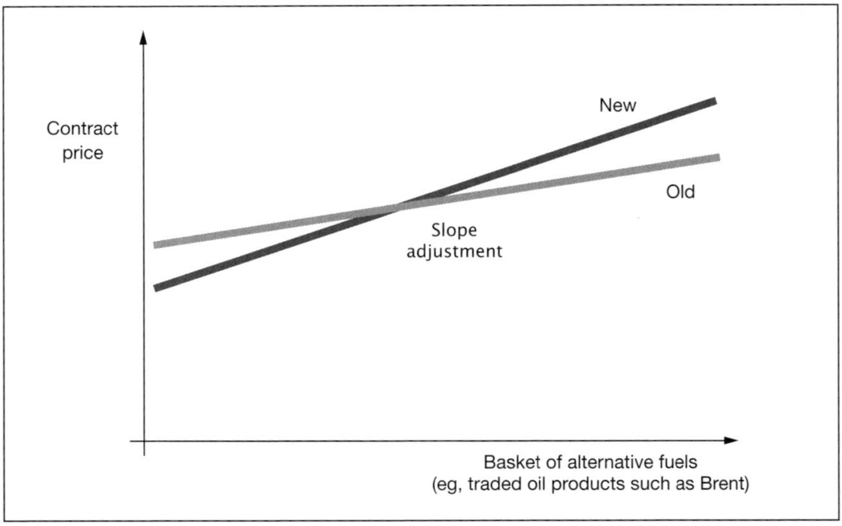

Alternatively, the claimant may wish to change what the price is indexed to (though in some cases the price review clause explicitly forbids this). In particular, in some recent cases the claimant has sought to introduce a new element of indexation to the price of gas being traded on commodity exchanges ('gas trading hubs', giving rise to 'hub indexation').

The introduction of hub indexation is more complex to evaluate and calibrate for the contract than the other adjustments described above. The price of gas on a hub is the price for a basic contract involving the delivery of the same amount of gas each day over a defined time period. In contrast, a typical long-term import contract gives the buyer (and, to a much lesser extent, the seller) a certain amount of flexibility on the amount of gas that it takes over various timeframes, ranging from a day to a year. Depending on the details of the proposal, the price of gas in a hub-indexed contract may therefore need to reflect this difference, which may require complex and potentially challenging calculations.

5. Expert testimony in other areas

In our experience, there are often specific individual features of a contract or of a dispute that require additional expert evidence. These include a range of competition issues, and analysis related to the application of specific contractual clauses, such as hardship clauses.

5.1 Competition issues

It is open to either or both parties to raise additional legal points in the context of arbitrations. We have seen both buyers and sellers introduce competition law-based arguments that require input from economic experts. These arguments may involve a claim that part of the contract itself is anticompetitive, breaching Article 101 of the Treaty of the Functioning of the European Union (TFEU) or the national equivalent legislation,[12] or that some aspect of the contract represents an abuse of a dominant position (eg, on grounds of excessive pricing), contrary to Article 102 of the TFEU or the national equivalent legislation.

In either case, usually the expert is required to provide an opinion on the relevant product and geographical market definitions within which the market shares of the seller and/or buyer should be measured, and to calculate the relevant market shares. Such market shares are potentially important either for the purpose of establishing whether the contract in question is entitled to an exemption under Article 101 of the TFEU, or to help determine whether the buyer or seller was dominant at the relevant point in time, based on standard legal criteria for dominance.

5.2 Hardship clauses

Hardship clauses are clauses that provide some form of relief if one party is suffering from 'hardship' (a concept which may be rather vaguely defined). Some of the long-

12 To clarify, the claims we have seen are not related to allegations of collusive/cartel-like behaviour, but to 'vertical issues' – for example, resale restrictions (so-called 'destination clauses' that limit the ability of the buyer to resell the gas outside its own market area).

term gas sales agreements with which we are familiar include a hardship clause in addition to the price review clause. These clauses are examined elsewhere in this book.

If a party is claiming the benefit of a hardship clause, the expert's role is likely to include an analysis of the relevant financial evidence to reach a view on whether the relevant party is, in fact, suffering hardship, within the definition of the clause. This may involve a rigorous accounting analysis to assess the link between the profit/loss shown in accounts and the underlying economics. For example, it may be due to a provision in the accounts, reflecting an expectation as to future losses, rather than actual operational loss in the period in question. Conversely, an accounting profit may reflect the outcome of financial hedging, rather than the effect of sales to consumers.

6. Some process issues

Lastly, we provide a few comments from an expert's perspective on the process issues that arise in price review arbitrations.

First, we note the obvious: independence is central to the role of the expert. As in other areas, experts should not become advocates for the party that has appointed them.

Second, in our experience the key points of disagreement between experts can be relatively narrow. In some cases, expert reports appear to provide very different views, but the underlying difference arises from the legal view of the contract that they have been instructed to take by counsel. In other cases, we have seen expert reports where there was close agreement on the majority of the facts and analysis. In such instances, it can be useful for the expert to explain to the tribunal the areas of agreement, so as to help focus attention on the remaining areas in dispute. Tribunals often seek to achieve further progress on those areas through techniques such as requesting a joint report from the experts, or the use of witness conferencing.

The adjustment phase

David Mildon QC
Essex Court Chambers

1. Introduction

Elsewhere in this book, we have noted that many price review clauses identify some kind of 'trigger' event which allows the review procedure to be invoked. We have also seen how provision is then made for a process to review the existing price or formula and resolve any resulting disputes. This is what we describe as the 'adjustment phase'.

Typically, the adjustment phase begins with an exchange of views, followed by negotiations and, if agreement is not reached, a mechanism for dispute resolution. The types of dispute resolution are discussed elsewhere in this book. In this chapter, we concentrate on the substance of the dispute where a consensus cannot be achieved. In particular, we look at the criteria for altering the price or formula, the extent to which the existing bargain can be modified and the practicalities of devising new formulae in a contentious environment. We include within the adjustment phase the remedies available if the adjustment remains contentious after the initial contractual steps for dispute resolution have been exhausted.

Before turning to these points, it is important not to overlook the procedure which the parties have agreed to adopt. This matters at two levels. First, at a purely technical level, if the review clause requires negotiations and mediation before arbitration or expert determination can be invoked, these pre-conditions should be followed. Any attempt to go straight to arbitration (or to the expert) is likely to be met with the objection that the exercise is premature and the arbitrator (or expert) lacks jurisdiction.[1]

Secondly, the choice of dispute resolution method may itself provide information on the kind of criteria by reference to which the parties intend the price or formula to be revised. In common law jurisdictions it is sometimes said that the law will not enforce an agreement 'to agree' or 'to negotiate'.[2] The reason given is that such an agreement is too vague and uncertain to be enforced. A court or arbitrator will not have objective criteria by which to determine or to enforce what ought to have been agreed. The same logical objection does not apply where the

1 Compare *Cable & Wireless Plc v IBM UK Ltd* [2002] 2 All ER (Comm) 1041 and *Paul Smith Limited v H & S International* [1991] 2 Lloyds Rep 127. See also Mustill & Boyd: *Commercial Arbitration, 2001 Companion* at pages 139-140.

2 See, for example, *May and Butcher Ltd v The King* [1934] 2 KB 17, particularly per Lord Buckmaster at 20; *Walford v Miles* [1992] AC 128. For a more recent review of the authorities, see *Mamidoil v Okta* [2001] 2 Lloyds Rep 76.

parties agree to refer price review disputes to expert determination. Such an arrangement does not involve an agreement to agree. On the contrary, it is an agreement to abide by, whatever the expert decides.

A number of consequences follow from this. An arbitrator, and particularly a legally qualified arbitrator, is likely to be looking for objective criteria, either expressed or implied from the terms of the agreement and its price review provisions: (see below). Conversely, an expert – and particularly a professional appointed for his skills in valuation – is unlikely to start from the same premise. He will assume that a significant part of his task is to value the gas using his expert knowledge and to come up with a new formula which will continue to put a fair price on the gas in the future. He will not take other criteria into account unless expressly instructed to do so. He is unlikely to be impressed by an analytical lawyer's analysis of the language of the price review clause or its presumed purpose.

Partly for the above reasons, some price review clauses which incorporate expert determination set out in extensive and sometimes prescriptive terms the criteria which the expert is required to apply. There are dangers in this approach. As we shall see later, the circumstances in which an expert determination can be reviewed or challenged are limited, and in some senses rather technical. If the expert departs from a prescriptive term of his mandate, the whole exercise may be void. On the other hand, if superficially he follows the prescribed criteria, but allows his own expert opinion to drive the outcome, there may be little that an aggrieved party can do about it.

The arbitration solution is not without its problems either. As already noted, a legally qualified arbitrator is likely to look at the gas sales agreement only for objective criteria to guide him in his review. There will be a problem if he cannot find any objective criteria. It is unusual, but not unheard of, for lawyer arbitrators to worry over this kind of problem, and exceptionally to find that the whole price review procedure is unenforceable as an agreement to agree.

The common law authorities that deal with this situation are not always easy to reconcile, and there is a tendency to view each case as depending on its own facts and terminology.[3] The result is an unusually high proportion of first instance judgments reversed on appeal and of dissenting judgments in the appellate courts.[4] Despite these concerns, the majority of legally qualified international arbitrators, whether from common law or civil law jurisdictions, will make every effort to find objective pricing criteria somewhere within the terms of the gas sales agreement, even where the agreement is, on its face, entirely silent. Provided such criteria can be found, the price review process will not fail as a mere agreement to agree.

Where dispute resolution is left to arbitral or expert determination in a price review context, some general observations from the case law should be mentioned. As will be seen, these propositions tend to favour the party which is arguing for the enforceability of the price review process.

A distinction must be drawn between substantive contractual obligations and the

---

3 *Mamidoil v Okta* [2001] 2 Lloyds Rep 76 at 89R per Rix LJ.

4 For illustrations see both *Mamidoil* (above) and *Phillips Petroleum Company UK Limited v Enron Europe Limited*, (Court of Appeal, unreported, October 10 1996).

machinery by which they are to be given effect. If a substantive obligation to pay a reasonable price determined by an arbitrator can be inferred, that agreement will be enforced even if part of the machinery breaks down for want of further agreement.[5] In general, an obligation to pay a reasonable price can be inferred, so it is wrong to consider a price review to be no more than an agreement to agree which can be frustrated by the absence of agreement. Equally, it should not be capable of being frustrated by the death or incapacity of an expert determiner.

Particularly in cases where a contract has been substantially performed and much expense incurred in implementing it, the common law is prepared to infer an intention that any uncertainty resulting from a specific agreement to agree should be resolved on as reasonable a basis as possible by an arbitrator.[6] However, the presence of an arbitration clause is not decisive, and it has been said that a "general" arbitration clause in common form is not a sufficient solution to the problem. It has to be possible to infer from the wording of the arbitration clause an intention that any uncertainty arising from the agreement to agree should be referred to arbitration.[7] In a price review context, normally this requirement is satisfied by the inclusion of a dispute resolution mechanism within the price review clause. If that mechanism is arbitration, it will not be a case of using a general arbitration clause. Arbitration is specifically agreed as the solution to a disputed price review.

Even in the absence of an arbitration clause, the common law is willing to stretch the rules on the implication of contractual terms in order to enable the contract to be carried out. The longer the contract has been in force and the greater the parties' reliance on it, the further the courts will be prepared to go down this route.[8]

2. Criteria for revised formula

It is possible to have a price review clause that, once triggered, would require the parties (and in default of agreement, an expert or arbitrator) to re-start the whole pricing exercise from scratch. Such a clause would be unusual. We suggest that one of the reasons why this approach tends not to be favoured is that it would involve an elaborate inquiry, even in cases where the market change which had triggered the review could be addressed using a minor adjustment to the existing formula.

Most of the review clauses in common use try in some way to relate the price revision to the energy market change which has triggered the review. In other words, they seek to value the change rather than valuing the gas. They also recognise that the whole exercise is likely to be either unworkable or capricious unless the expert or arbitrator is given a fairly wide discretion over the content of any revision. Contractual criteria can operate well enough as guidelines, but any attempt to dictate a price revision in a mechanistic way is unlikely to work fairly in all the diverse circumstances in which it may have to apply.

---

5 *Sudbrook Estates v Eggleton* [1983] AC 444; *Didymi* [1988] 2 Lloyds Rep 108.

6 For examples, see *Sykes v Fine Fare* [1976] 1 Lloyds Rep 53; *Didymi* [1988] 2 Lloyds Rep 108 at 115 and 119R.

7 *May and Butcher Ltd v The King* [1934] 2 KB 17. There are serious difficulties in reconciling this House of Lords authority with later Court of Appeal authority in both *Sykes* and *Didymi*.

8 *Mamidoil v Okta* [2001] 2 Lloyds Rep 76 at 89R per Rix LJ.

A further feature in some price review clauses is a stipulation requiring the new price to be set at a level which will enable the buyer to market the gas 'economically' in its own end-user market. These clauses are particularly common where the buyer is a utility which depends on the demand of customers connected to a local infrastructure in order to re-sell the gas. Such 'market economically' clauses usually operate as a cap on the new price. Unless stated otherwise, they tend not to prevent an expert or arbitrator from setting a price below the cap.

In a clause which values the change rather than valuing the gas and which gives the expert or arbitrator some discretion in how he goes about his task, the bargain inherent in the existing price formula can and should carry considerable weight. A few examples illustrate this. For the purposes of the examples, it is assumed that the pricing formula incorporates a prescribed base price which is then subject to indexation by reference to changes in the index values of other energy products.[9]

It is not unusual for an escalation formula to be designed to smooth out changes in the contract price. Various techniques are available for this purpose. A 12-month moving average of an oil price index will provide some smoothing, but in the process it can introduce a time lag effect which means that the contract price is out of phase with movements in the market. There is no unfairness in this, provided the market moves up as well as down (or vice versa) over the life of the formula. The time lag will benefit the buyer for some of the time and the seller at other times. In general, arbitrators (or experts) can be expected to preserve this sort of feature in the existing bargain, so long as it can continue to provide benefits to both sides in the current market context.

Another form of 'smoothing' is to limit the proportion of changes in indicator prices which is passed through into the contract price. This will reduce the effects of peaks and troughs in the energy market. As with moving averages (see above), the benefits and burdens can be expected to be shared so long as the market moves up as well as down (or vice versa), and the market trading range remains centred around the originally agreed (or base) price. However, problems may arise if the market moves permanently into a lower or higher trading range.

If the pass through of oil price indicator to contract gas price is deliberately set artificially low, it may be argued that there can be no need for a price revision just because the market moves into a permanently higher or lower trading range. The resulting prejudice to seller or buyer is said to be a necessary consequence of the bargain. This argument may be met with some scepticism where the evidence suggests that, at the time of contracting, the package of base price and limited escalation[10] was designed to distribute the benefits of the smoothing effect between the parties. An alternative argument is that if a price review is triggered and the market has moved into a permanently higher or lower trading range, the base price should be re-set to suit the new trading range. There may then be a case for preserving some of the smoothing effect of a low pass through factor going forward,

9 See elsewhere in this book for a general description of pricing formulae in long-term gas contracts.

10 That is, an escalation formula incorporating a low pass through factor which only passes through to the contract price for gas a limited proportion of the change in the indicator values of other energy products.

provided that there is some confidence that the benefits and burdens will be shared. In very volatile and unpredictable markets, that may present difficulties.

Another smoothing device is the 'S curve', so called because of its visual appearance when the contract gas price is plotted against oil prices. The formula has a central section between two inflexion points set at the upper and lower limits of the expected trading range of the oil price indicator. Between these points, the contract gas price tracks changes in the oil price. At the upper and lower ends, the effect of extreme movements in the oil price is reduced by a lower pass through factor in the formula.

For price review purposes, this type of arrangement raises specific problems. If a change in the energy market has taken the market trading range permanently outside the inflexion points (whether up or down does not matter), there may be a case for re-setting the inflexion points to suit the new market reality rather than retaining outdated inflexion points for the next 20 years. Whether it would make sense to scrap the S curve altogether raises different issues. The parties clearly wanted some degree of smoothing effect whenever the market moved outside its long-term trading range. An expert or arbitrator could be expected to want to try to preserve that effect even in a different market.

Of course, it is possible for the parties to embark on a deliberate 20-year speculation on the relationship between oil and gas values. If that were the true nature of the bargain, it might be said that there could never be any need to change the price formula because of changes in values, however large these might become. An alternative analysis would be that a deliberate 20-year speculation on the relationship between oil and gas values is inconsistent with the incorporation of a price review clause. The true intention may be more subtle. In a contract incorporating a review clause, the aim may be to track the evolution in the value of gas in the knowledge that the exercise can never be a perfect one, and that both sides are willing to accept an element of imprecision. Ultimately, many price review arbitrations involve questions of degree. Just how far has the price generated by the existing formula deviated from the objective value of the gas? What, if anything, needs to be done to bring the contract price back on track? What, if anything, needs to be done to prevent the price deviating from the objective value of the gas in the future?

In the various examples given above, a recurring feature is the concept of the existing formula operating 'fairly' in the current market context. Most escalation formulae were designed to operate fairly as between buyer and seller in the market context in which they were originally agreed. That fairness will be apparent from the way in which features of the formula (eg, moving averages, pass throughs and S curves) will have brought benefits and burdens to both parties in the original market context. The price review permits the formula to be reviewed so that it continues to operate fairly in the current market context.

There may be exceptional cases where it is clear from the context in which the formula was originally agreed that the formula was intended to be deliberately one-sided. These cases are more problematic. There is an argument for saying that the beneficiary of the one-sidedness has only contracted for that benefit up until the next price review. On the other hand, experts and arbitrators may be prepared to allow some imbalance in the formula to continue into the future, particularly if the imbalance arises regardless of any changes which have occurred in the energy market during the period under review.

3. Foresight and hindsight issues

Under most price review clauses, the expressed objective is to re-set the base price and/or the formula at a defined review date. Thus, under a contract providing for regular, say four-yearly, price reviews, the contract will provide for the new pricing arrangements to be assessed at the review date and to be applicable from that date. Generally, the draftsman will have provided a schedule under which certain procedural steps (including dispute resolution) start before the review date with a view to completion at or around the review date.

If the review proceeds to dispute resolution, the contractual timetable often has to yield to practical considerations, such as arbitrator (or expert) availability, the need to give both sides a fair hearing on what may be complex issues and so on. Most contract wordings recognise that it is neither realistic nor wise to dictate a precise timetable for dispute resolution. There is no point in having contractually binding deadlines which are so tight that none but the most underemployed arbitrator or expert would agree to be bound by them. Equally, there is no point in having deadlines which are so generous that the time spent on dispute resolution expands to fill the time permitted. A contractual schedule should be regarded as an aim which conveys to the tribunal the sense of urgency that the parties have agreed to attach to dispute resolution in a price review context. It should not be regarded as binding.

There are other dangers in being over prescriptive. If an award or determination is conditional on compliance with the contractual schedule, the whole process may be frustrated by events such as arbitrator or expert illness. Questions can then arise as to whether arbitrators or the courts are entitled to fill the gap left by the failure of the agreed process.[11] A well-drawn price review clause should not allow this kind of argument to arise. So long as the schedule is set as an aim rather than a precondition, this kind of argument will be avoided.

It follows that in many cases the decision maker (whether arbitrator or expert) may have to reach a decision at a time other than the review date. If he is making a decision in advance of the review date, should he attempt to anticipate market conditions at the review date? If he is making a decision after the review date, should he ignore hindsight and attempt to reconstruct the market context as it stood on the review date?

In the rapidly changing energy market conditions of recent years, these questions are far from academic. There have been price reviews where the timing of the hearing and award has become critical. If energy prices spike between review date and hearing date, that inevitably gives rise to a perception that a higher contract price may be justified; or, conversely, if prices slump.

While the wording in any particular case must be studied carefully, generally it is

---

11 Cf *Sudbrook Estates v Eggleton* [1983] AC 444.

a reasonable inference from a clause providing for fixed-term reviews (say, every four years) that the price is supposed to be re-set by reference to the market context and circumstances at the review date. The position may be different if the review date is set at the discretion of the party applying for the review, although even then there are often indications in the contractual wording that it is the context on that date which is to count and not what happens subsequently.

If an arbitrator (or expert) is able to convene a hearing before the review date, the logic of the price review clause may require anticipation of market conditions some months forward. This does not usually cause difficulty, and if there is significant uncertainty about how the relevant factors might evolve, the tribunal might defer publication of its decision to allow reference to the actual rather than the anticipated conditions.

If the hearing takes place after the review date, ignoring hindsight creates practical problems, however compelling the contractual logic for doing so. First, the market context at the review date must include the expectations of the market participants as reflected in analysis, futures prices and so on. There is no sensible basis on which such information can be excluded. Secondly, many arbitrators and experts find it difficult to accept, after the event, that what has actually happened is as surprising as it is being made out to be. The person who is arguing for the post-review date information to be excluded from the relevant data set will be met by the argument that all had been foreseen. Thirdly, reliance is sometimes placed on other areas of law where hindsight issues arise.

This latter tendency can be dangerous ground. For example, there is a developed jurisprudence in some common law countries on how post-injury evidence can be used in assessing quantum in personal injuries actions.[12] It is questionable whether such case law is of assistance in a contractual price review context. Much of it is driven by policy considerations which are peculiar to the area of law in question. In a contractual price review, once it is apparent from the contract that the intention is to set the new price by reference to the circumstances prevailing at the review date, subsequent circumstances ought either to be excluded from consideration or, at most, to be admitted solely for the purpose of assessing the reasonableness of the parties' cases on what was anticipated at the review date.

4. Non-price terms

The commercial terms of long-term gas sales agreements include many incidental terms which affect the price the parties are prepared to agree. For price review purposes, in general, terms relating to quality can be ignored. Most gas delivered into regional markets will be required to comply with standards set by third-party distribution systems. For this reason, it is unusual for contractual quality specification to vary very much between one gas sales agreement and another – at any rate, within a regional market. Gas delivered as liquefied natural gas (LNG) will require re-gasification, the cost of which has to be taken into account when comparing LNG values with the value of natural gas delivered in a gaseous state.

12 See McGregor on Damages, 18th edn, paras 35-033 to 35-054.

However, generally re-gasification costs are predictable and form only a small percentage of the overall gas value.

For price review purposes, other non-price terms form a more important consideration, particularly those concerned with the buyer's 'take or pay' obligations, periodic nominations, claw-back of make-up gas, so-called 'swing' and so on. These can vary considerably from one gas sales agreement to another. Flexibility has a cost, which tends to be reflected in the contract price. A buyer that is entitled to make large variations in its nominations from one day to the next and to vary its nominations even at the last minute will expect to pay more than one who enjoys less flexibility.

Non-price terms of this kind can give rise to difficulties in a price review context. Most long-term gas sales agreements are confidential. However, the actual price paid is often required to be reported (eg, for customs or tariff purposes), and the resulting information then enters the public domain in national statistics and other publicly accessible databases. The same is not true of the non-price terms under which the gas has been sold and delivered. Typically, these remain a closely guarded secret. The result is that the information about comparators available on a price review is incomplete. By simply looking at price, it may seem that the contract price has moved out of line with the market as reflected in published statistics. But an explanation for the discrepancy may be that the contract in question incorporates non-price terms which have become more or less valuable than those under other contracts during the review period.

It is not unheard of for parties to seek disclosure of other contracts within their opponents' gas portfolios in order to reveal issues of this kind. Such applications tend to be highly controversial. The other gas sales contracts are themselves confidential. These and other confidentiality issues are considered in more detail elsewhere in this book.

In many cases, the tribunal (whether arbitrator or expert determiner) has to reach a decision on the basis of an incomplete data set. In practice, therefore, expert evidence assumes a particularly important role in assessing issues such as the value of non-price terms. As a general proposition, the relative value of terms going, for example to flexibility, tends not to vary substantially between price reviews and in cases where a material change has occurred it will be related to regulatory or market changes, the effect of which can be expressed through expert evidence.

5. The revision of the formula

Some legally qualified arbitrators find algebra difficult. This should not disqualify them from acting in price reviews, provided that they can understand what is going on inside an existing formula and have the ability to describe in words a solution which others can convert into symbols. But it helps to have a tribunal which is mathematically literate.

If a tribunal decides that a price formula needs to be revised in a particular way, generally it is preferable for the tribunal to describe its preferred solution in a partial final award and leave it to the parties to prepare a revised formula which carries that solution into effect, with liberty to apply for a further award in the event of continued disagreement. It is almost unheard of for this solution to fail in practice, and it avoids the embarrassment of having to challenge an award for an error in the algebra.

The difficulties that arise out of the range of options open to the tribunal are more fundamental. In many cases, the claimant will put forward one or more proposed revisions and the respondent will propose alternatives. In an adversarial procedure, these proposals will inevitably be at opposite ends of the spectrum. It is not unusual for a tribunal to look for some middle way which may involve a 'mix and match' of elements contributed by both sides. Particularly where the review clause gives the tribunal a wide discretion, there is no jurisdictional basis for challenging this philosophy, but it is not without its dangers.

If a price formula is negotiated at arms' length, the end result is a package which may involve, for example, a compromise in which an objectively high base price is traded against concessions on the indexation weights or vice versa. A tribunal cannot replicate this kind of trade-off, and may not have available sufficient information from which to form an objective view of the consequences of a particular mix and match.

Some commentators have suggested that for this reason a price review calls for some kind of 'pendulum'[13] arbitration in which the tribunal is forced to choose between the rival solutions put forward by the parties and has no power to devise a solution of its own making. Such an approach may also discourage the parties from taking extreme positions and so make settlement easier.

Pendulum arbitration is not always the panacea that it is sometimes made out to be. A pendulum arbitration undoubtedly works with a monetary claim, such as where C claims $100 million, R argues for $50 million and the tribunal thinks the correct figure is $60 million. In such a case, the tribunal's mandate under a pendulum arrangement is clear. It has to award $50 million.

A price review is different because of the package nature of a price formula. If the claimant puts forward package C and the respondent puts forward package R, a tribunal which is attracted by some (but not all) elements of both packages will lack objective criteria for working out whether its overall assessment is closer to formula C than R (or vice versa).

A better way forward for a tribunal that is contemplating a mix and match of elements from both sides' proposals is to inform the parties of this before proceeding to an award and give both the opportunity to comment on what the consequences might be. Under this approach, neither side can be taken by surprise, and both sides have the chance to say why a particular mixture might turn out to be one sided.

6. Post-award challenges

An arbitral award or expert determination does not always mark the end of the adjustment phase. Price reviews under long-term gas sales agreements are often very high-value disputes. The losing party will invariably consider its options closely. Whether the adjustment phase concludes or moves into more contentious territory will vary depending on the chosen procedure.

In general, if the outcome of the price review has been determined by arbitration,

13 Or 'baseball' to those from North America.

the scope for challenging the award will be very limited. Even in those (rare) jurisdictions which retain a limited right of appeal on issues of law,[14] that right can be, and generally is, excluded by express agreement in the forms of clause used in many modern international gas sales agreements.[15] In any event, the issues raised on a price review are rarely pure issues of law such as would be capable of challenge on appeal. With a competent tribunal, the scope for challenge on grounds of procedural irregularity should be similarly limited.

Different considerations apply if the outcome of the price review is determined by a third party under an expert determination clause.

Problems with third-party determinations tend to arise:

- because the dispute is not self-contained and what the third party ends up having to determine overlaps with dispute resolution functions allocated to a judge or arbitrator; and
- because of difficulties in defining the scope and content of the third party's mandate.

Third-party determination of the outcome of a price review involves separating out a defined role for the independent third party from the general dispute resolution procedure. This exercise can give rise to conflict between the general jurisdiction provisions (whether court or arbitration) which apply to the gas sales agreement as a whole and the specific jurisdiction which is given to the third-party expert.

At face value, a price review might not appear an obvious candidate for 'turf wars' between the expert and other dispute resolution service providers. Generally, price reviews arise out of a self-contained contractual code. Disputes under such a code should be capable of being isolated from the general dispute resolution provisions of the agreement. However, experience suggests that price review disputes cannot always be kept within a prescribed limit.

As noted earlier, the value of gas is a function not just of its volume and quality, but also of the other non-price terms on which it is supplied. If issues about non-price terms arise, the third-party determiner cannot always avoid having to form a view on the meaning and effect of the take or pay clause, or the nomination clause and so on. If he is drawn into this kind of debate and in the process he makes an error of law, what next?

Perhaps the best recent explanation of the English law approach to this kind of question is found in a dissenting judgment of Hoffmann LJ in *Director General of Telecommunications v Mercury Communications Limited.*[16] The decision of the majority was reversed in the House of Lords.[17] In these circumstances, it is not surprising that reliance is increasingly placed upon Hoffmann LJ's dissent: see, for example, the Court of Appeal decision in *National Grid Company Ltd v M25 Group Ltd.*[18] In the

---

14 For example, England, but the right of appeal can be excluded by agreement: see English Arbitration Act 1996, s 69(1).

15 Standard institutional wordings (eg, International Chamber of Commerce, London Court of International Arbitration) do this automatically.

16 CA, unreported, July 22 1994.

17 [1996] 1 WLR 48.

Mercury case, Hoffmann LJ described the problem as one of identifying "the limits of the (expert's) decision-making authority". He explained matters in this way:

> *By decision-making authority I mean the power to make the wrong decision, in the sense of a decision different from that which a court would have made. Where the decision-maker is asked to decide in accordance with certain principles, he must obviously inform himself of those principles, and this may mean having, in a trivial sense, to decide what they mean. It does not follow that the question of what the principles mean is a matter within his decision-making authority in the sense that the parties have agreed to be bound by his views. Even if the language used by the parties is ambiguous, it must (unless void for uncertainty) have a meaning. The parties have agreed to a decision in accordance with this meaning and no other. Accordingly if the decision-maker has acted upon what in the court's view was the wrong meaning, he has gone outside his decision-making authority. Ambiguity in this sense is different from conceptual imprecision which leaves to the judgment of the decision-maker the question whether given facts fall within the specified criterion.*

As a general rule, the questions arising in a price review involve what Hoffmann LJ described as "conceptual imprecision". They are questions to which there may be several 'correct' answers. Provided that the third-party determiner makes his selection from within the range of 'correct' answers, the aggrieved party will have no basis for challenge just because another 'correct' answer would have been more financially beneficial to it.

A further point to emphasise is that the parties to an expert determination clause can generally be assumed to have chosen such a mechanism as an economical and expeditious means of resolving disputes without having recourse to the formalities and expense of court or arbitration proceedings. In this context, it is unlikely that they will have intended some parts of a dispute to be for the expert and other parts for the court.[19] For this reason, it is sometimes said to be implicit in an expert determination clause that the expert should have power to determine issues of interpretation which arise from the overall decision-making process. For an example of this approach, see the judgment of Sir Donald Nicholls VC in *Norwich Union Life Insurance Society v P & O Property Holdings Ltd*,[20] as upheld and explicitly endorsed by Dillon LJ in the Court of Appeal.[21]

We suggest that if a third-party expert had to engage in a debate about the value of take or pay or nomination obligations in a price review context, he would not be open to challenge if, in doing so, he reached decisions on the meaning or content of those obligations which differed from what a court or arbitrator might have reached.

In summary, where price reviews are referred to expert determination, the adjustment phase normally ends when the expert makes his determination. Although there is scope for challenge either before an arbitrator or, failing that, the court, the scope is more often theoretical than real.

---

18 CA, unreported, December 21 1998, particularly conclusion (6) in the judgment of Mummery LJ.

19 A similar approach is adopted when construing arbitration clauses: *Harbour Assurance Ltd v Kansa Ltd* [1993] QB 701 at 724 per Hoffmann LJ.

20 [1993] EGLR 164.

21 [1993] 1 EGLR 167 at 169L. Recently, some doubt has been cast on these cases by Neuberger MR in *Barclays v Nylon* [2011] EWCA Civ 826. For the present, these doubts remain a minority view.

In the relatively rare case where the expert is found to have departed from his mandate, the strict legal position is that his determination is, for contractual purposes, a nullity. The parties have agreed to be bound only by a determination made in accordance with the mandate. One made outside the mandate does not bind.

Therefore, a question can arise as to what becomes of the adjustment phase in a case where the price review has been referred to expert determination, and (unusually) the expert is found to have departed from his mandate: does resolution of the price review fall back on an arbitrator or the courts? Or can the expert be asked to resume his task in accordance with his mandate as interpreted by some other tribunal?

There is very little legal authority on this issue. A logical answer is that while an initial supposed determination will be a nullity (for want of compliance with mandate), the expert cannot be stopped from putting things right because he has not yet discharged his contractual function.[22] That was the approach adopted in the one English case in point, but the contrary was not argued and so the decision is of limited value as authority.[23] The position may be different if the authority to make the determination is vested in one of the parties (or its representative) rather than an independent third party. In an Australian case, the Supreme Court of Western Australia took the view that where a clause gave one of the parties a power finally to determine the value of certain works in its sole discretion, on its true construction this gave the party only one attempt. If the determination went outside mandate, the party was in breach of the clause and "would not be entitled to perform the valuation again". In such a case, the power to determine value devolved onto the arbitrators under the general arbitration clause in the contract.[24] The reasoning is not applicable to a case where the expert is a third-party neutral chosen for his independence from either side.

In summary, therefore, the adjustment phase can generally be expected to conclude with either an arbitral award or an expert determination (depending on the agreed procedure). The cases in which matters go further are rare, and rarer still are those in which adjustments to the price and/or pricing formula devolve onto a different tribunal not of the parties' choosing.

---

22 In lawyer's language, he is not yet *functus officio*.
23 *Shell UK Limited v Enterprise Oil Plc* [1999] 2 Lloyd's Rep 456.
24 *WMC Resources v Leighton Contractors* (1999) 20 WAR 489 at 509 per Ipp J.

The future for price reviews

Paul Griffin
Frances van Eupen
Allen & Overy

1. A new era for the LNG market

Before 2011 little was known about pricing disputes arising from long-term liquefied natural gas (LNG) contracts – information on only a few such disputes was available in the public domain. For example, the *Atlantic LNG* case became public in 2009 as a result of New York court proceedings (the background to this case is discussed in section 2). Since 2011 the market has seen a substantial increase in media coverage and corporate announcements relating to long-term LNG contract renegotiations and arbitrations. To list some recent examples in Europe:

- in June 2013 RWE announced that Gazprom had to reimburse it for gas purchases since May 2010 under a long-term contract, citing a ruling by the International Court of Arbitration of the International Chamber of Commerce, but declined to comment on the size of the expected payout;[1]
- in November 2012 it was reported that PGNiG and Gazprom had reached agreement on a dispute over the price of natural gas supplied to Poland under a 25-year contract, bringing to an end arbitration proceedings;[2]
- in October 2012 Edison announced that it had won an arbitration against LNG supplier Eni, leading to a reduction in the price of LNG purchased under that contract worth hundreds of millions of Euros;[3]
- in July 2012 E.On announced that it had reached agreement regarding the renegotiation of long-term gas supply contracts with Gazprom, including a retroactive adaptation of pricing conditions, bringing to an end arbitration proceedings;[4]
- in March 2012 it was reported that Eni had reached agreement on the revision of gas supply contracts with Gazprom;[5]
- in June 2011 it was reported that Gas Natural and Sonatrach had reached a settlement agreement following an arbitration award rendered in favour of Sonatrach providing a retrospective gas price increase worth $2 billion;[6] and
- in February 2011 Edison announced that it had successfully completed a

1 www.reuters.com/article/2013/06/27/rwe-gazprom-dispute-idUSL5N0F32ZZ20130627.
2 www.naturalgaseurope.com/russia-and-poland-agrees-on-gas-price-reduction.
3 www.reuters.com/article/2012/10/01/edison-eni-libya-idUSL6E8L1KYD20121001.
4 www.eon.com/en/media/news/press-releases/2012/7/3/eon-reaches-settlement-and-raises-group-outlook-for-2010.html. See also www.icis.com/heren/articles/2012/08/13/9586537/gas/esgm/e.ons-net-profit-triples-after-gazprom-natural-gas-agreement.html.
5 www.reuters.com/article/2012/03/01/eni-gazprom-idUSL5E8E18G420120301.
6 Reuters, "Gas Natural Pays Sonatrach $1.9 bln to End Dispute", June 14 2011.

renegotiation with Eni in relation to the price for gas supplied from Norway under a long-term contract.[7]

Anecdotal evidence indicates that these cases are only a small part of a widespread practice. These renegotiations and arbitrations suggest that the LNG market is entering a new era. Although only limited detail is available in the public domain, the long-term LNG contracts referred to above are probably traditional oil-indexed contracts. These contracts were drafted on the basis of traditional closed markets, with no gas-to-gas competition, and, generally, an oil index would reflect the spot prices for LNG in the relevant intended markets. However, since about 2008 various market forces[8] have undermined this oil-index pricing regime, most notably in Europe. In some markets it is argued that wholesale LNG prices have fallen significantly below oil-indexed contract prices, leading to a mismatch between the oil-linked prices at which importers had contracted to purchase LNG and the lower spot LNG market prices at which LNG could be sold.

As a result, it appears that some LNG importers in Europe have tried to open pricing negotiations with the major suppliers since at least about 2008, if not earlier. Based on records in the public domain, these negotiations have in some cases resulted in a downward price adjustment for the LNG buyers, some of the adjustments have had retroactive effect (although, as the Gas Natural-Sonatrach arbitration award shows, there have been upward revisions of prices too). Historically, LNG suppliers such as Gazprom resisted agreeing to any downward pricing adjustments under long-term LNG contracts, so the recent trend towards renegotiation marks a significant change. Where negotiations have failed, some LNG importers have chosen to refer the matter to arbitration.

Another significant development is that the energy companies involved have become more open in announcing information on these negotiations/arbitrations (see the examples listed above). This marks a break from earlier practice, where renegotiations and arbitrations were kept secret. Given the economic value and financial implications involved, perhaps this trend is not surprising. For example, the renegotiation between E.On and Gazprom referred to above resulted in the payment of about €1 billion over the third and fourth quarters of 2012, and a tripling of E.On's net profits. Similarly, the settlement agreement between Gas Natural and Sonatrach referred to above resulted in the payment of $1.897 billion to Sonatrach.

Against this background, it is a good time to consider whether the price review regime and the typical dispute resolution clause contained in long-term LNG contracts provide the best framework for resolving pricing disputes, and whether alternative approaches might be better in this new environment.

A useful starting point is to consider the *Atlantic LNG* case, which offers a rare glimpse into the approach of an arbitral tribunal to the operation and interpretation of a price review clause in a long-term LNG contract. As explained in section 2, the

---

7 www.edison.it/en/media/press-releases/2011-02-11-edison-completes-renegotiations-with-eni-for-the-supply-of-natural-gas-from-norway.shtml.

8 Stern, J and Rogers, H, "The Transition to Hub-Based Gas Pricing in Continental Europe", The Oxford Institute for Energy Studies, NG 49, March 2011.

case provides a reminder of the potential risks in relying on short form price review clauses and traditional dispute resolution mechanisms to resolve pricing disputes in an evolving LNG market.

2. The *Atlantic LNG* case

The *Atlantic LNG* case concerns a 20-year contact between Atlantic LNG and Spain-based Enagas (later known as Gas Natural) entered into in July 1995. The contract provided for Enagas to buy 1.1 million tons per year from Atlantic LNG, starting in 1999. The LNG purchased was destined mainly for Enagas's receiving terminals in Spain, but with the option for Enagas to sell cargoes to its terminals in Boston. The LNG prices under the contract were calculated using a pricing formula designed to calculate the price of LNG in Spain. The contract provided that regardless of the cargo destination, Enagas would pay only the price stipulated under this pricing formula.

In the early 2000s, following the liberalisation of the Spanish natural gas market, gas prices in the country dropped. At the same time, US gas prices started to rise. Gas Natural decided to enter into a six-year agreement with GDF Suez to sell its full Atlantic LNG offtake into the US market. In 2005 Atlantic LNG triggered the price reopener clause. The parties failed to agree on a new pricing formula and the matter went to arbitration. The arbitral award was handed down in January 2008. Some details of the arbitral award entered the public domain when Atlantic LNG later petitioned the US District Court for the Southern District in New York to vacate the award.[9]

In summary, the arbitral award introduced a two-part pricing scheme into the contract. This provided that if LNG was sold into the United States on a sustained basis, New England prices should be the basis for determining the gas price. However, if the majority of LNG was shipped to Spain, all cargoes for the relevant period would be priced according to a slightly adjusted Spanish pricing formula. The new pricing structure was made effective from April 2005, when Atlantic LNG had first triggered the price reopener clause. The arbitral tribunal's decision is estimated to have resulted in a movement of value from Atlantic LNG to Gas Natural of between $500 million and $1 billion.[10]

Atlantic LNG petitioned the New York court to vacate the award, claiming the arbitration panel had exceeded its authority by imposing the dual pricing structure. In September 2009 the court upheld the tribunal's decision on the grounds that the original contract did not set a limit on how the price revision should be structured, as the reopener clause required only that a "fair and equitable" revision of the price be set.

The *Atlantic LNG* case highlights two issues with respect to LNG price review arbitrations which are addressed further below: first, the amount of money involved in these LNG contract disputes; and, second, the uncertainties involved in

9 *Gas Natural Aprovisionamientos v Atlantic LNG Company of Trinidad and Tobago* (2008) WL 4344525 (SDNY).

10 "Gas Natural v Atlantic LNG: a rare glimpse into price reopener clauses", *Gas Strategies*, 2009. Edited version of an article which first appeared in *LNG Business Review*, July 2009.

arbitrating these disputes, in particular where the clause effectively gives the arbitral tribunal complete freedom in redetermining pricing formulas.

3. Scale

In the *Atlantic LNG* case, the arbitral tribunal's decision was estimated to have cost Atlantic LNG between $500 million and $1 billion – $70 million owed immediately to Gas Natural for payments from April 2005 to December 2007 and the many millions of dollars it is estimated to have lost since then as the gap between US and European prices under the dual pricing structure widened.[11]

Following a dispute involving Gas Natural and Sonatrach[12] which went to arbitration in 2010, the arbitral award rendered in August 2010 provided for retrospective payment by Gas Natural of nearly $2 billion. In June 2011 the parties announced that they had signed a settlement agreement, under which Gas Natural was to pay Sonatrach $1.897 billion and Sonatrach would take a minority equity stake in Gas Natural.

These cases show just how large the commercial interests in price review mechanisms in LNG contracts are. Commonly, LNG contracts are long-term contracts (perhaps around 25 years) and the value of the contract over its life will often amount to several billion US dollars. Before entering into contractual commitments of this size, the parties will have undertaken much research and analysis, and committed a lot of time to negotiating the details of their rights, liabilities and obligations. The parties will have paid particular attention to the price payable for the specified quantities of LNG and the adjustment mechanism under which the contract price will be revised over time. The management of the companies involved will have satisfied their governance duties to obtain the best and most appropriate pricing provisions. However, despite all this, potential uncertainty in arbitrating LNG pricing disputes remains, as highlighted by the *Atlantic LNG* case.

4. Uncertainties in LNG contract arbitration

Traditionally, pricing reviews were expected to involve a relatively amicable re-division of contractual value which the parties assumed they would conduct every few years. However, the *Atlantic LNG* case and other recent cases show that parties to LNG contracts are often unable to reach amicable agreement, with the result that disputes are referred to arbitration. Given the outcome of the *Atlantic LNG* case, some observers have questioned whether arbitration is the most suitable forum for resolving such disputes.

Some commentaries[13] suggest that the outcome of *Atlantic LNG* was unusual, as the arbitral tribunal appeared to reach the new price review mechanisms on the basis of its own opinion without taking into account the submissions made by the parties. In particular, it is understood that neither party had requested a dual-pricing mechanism of the sort adopted by the tribunal. Without details of the arbitration, it

---

11 *Ibid.*
12 Reuters, "Gas Natural Pays Sonatrach $1.9 bln to End Dispute", June 14 2011.
13 See note 10 above.

is difficult to assess how the arbitral tribunal arrived at the award. One possibility often seen in LNG contract arbitrations is that the claimant overreached itself in the claimed amount and the proposed pricing mechanics, and the respondent chose to focus its case on whether the price review trigger was activated at all rather than engaging in the basic dispute (other than by seeking to discredit the claimant's proposal). In this situation, where the price review trigger is found to have been activated, the arbitral tribunal is not adequately assisted in the crucial step of redetermining the pricing mechanism. In any event, there seems to be a general consensus that the outcome of the *Atlantic LNG* arbitration was undesirable, because it resulted in a pricing formula which neither party wanted or expected. Against this background and in considering the future for price reviews, we must examine not only the dispute resolution process, but also the nature of price review clauses themselves.

5. Typical forms of price review clause

Price review clauses allow the existing price formula to be adapted or replaced in certain circumstances. There is no industry-wide standard form. The scope and effect of different provisions vary, although generally they provide for disputes to be referred to arbitration.

Often, price review clauses are not intended to address foreseeable economic change, but to respond to extraordinary and unforeseeable circumstances (although this depends on the wording of the particular clause and its context). Given their nature, they tend to be drafted in general terms and provide little detailed guidance for what are the (necessarily) unforeseen circumstances in which the clause is intended to be triggered. Of necessity, they are different from the usual price adjustment provisions of many LNG contracts which relate to specific foreseeable changes in relation to the parties' chosen price indicators and indices.

Below are two examples of price review provisions are as follows.

Atlantic LNG Company of Trinidad and Tobago and Gas Natural LNG contract (1995)

(a) If at any time either Party considers that economic circumstances in Spain beyond the control of the Parties, while exercising due diligence, have substantially changed as compared to what it reasonably expected when entering into this Contract or, after the first Contract Price revision under this Article 8.5, at the time of the latest Contract Price revision under this Article 8.5, and the Contract Price resulting from application of the formula set forth in Article 8.1 does not reflect the value of Natural Gas in the Buyer's end-user market, then such Party may, by notifying the other Party in writing and giving with such notice information supporting its belief, request that the Parties should forthwith enter into negotiations to determine whether or not such changed circumstances exist and justify a revision of the Contract Price provisions and, if so, to seek agreement on a fair and equitable revision of the above-mentioned Contract Price provisions in accordance with the remaining provisions of this Article 8.5.

(b) In reviewing the Contract Price in accordance with a request pursuant to sub-Article

8.5(a) above the Parties shall take into account levels and trends in price of supplies of LNG and Natural Gas [redacted] such supplies being sold under commercial contracts currently in force on arm's length terms, and having due regard to all characteristics of such supplies (including, but not limited to quality, quantity, interruptability, flexibility of deliveries and term of supply).

(c) The Contract Price as revised in accordance with this Article, shall in any event, allow the Buyer to market the LNG supplied hereunder in competition with all competing sources or forms of energy.... And such Contract Price Shall allow the Buyer to achieve a reasonable rate of return on the LNG delivered hereunder.

Sonatrach and Distrigas Corporation LNG contract (1976)[14]

The parties agree to meet regularly to proceed with the revision of the Contractual Sales Price defined in Article 9 above. They shall so meet for the first time during the first quarter of the year 1980 and thereafter every four (4) years.

The revision of the price shall consist in adapting it in a reasonable and fair manner to the economic circumstances then prevailing on the imported Natural Gas market and on the market for the other imported energy supplies competing with this production in the East Coast and Gulf Coast areas of the United States of America within the framework of long-term contracts. The parties shall take into account the individual characteristics of each of the above products including the quality, the continuity of deliveries, the production and transportation costs, etc ...

These examples show a number of common themes, such as changed circumstances, unforeseeability, events beyond the control of the affected party, good faith and sometimes specific guidance on matters to be taken into account. This may include matters such as guidance on the nature of comparable contracts and the definition of relevant markets. These clauses may also limit the scope of review of the arbitrators in conducting the price review, which may be prudent in light of the *Atlantic LNG* case.

In the context of recent gas market developments, cases such as *Atlantic LNG* raise the question: what is the nature of the price review clause? What function should it perform?

6. Philosophy of the price review clause

There is no market standard for price review clauses and, out of necessity, their terms will vary. However, in general, there are two philosophical approaches: the evolutionary and the revolutionary. A price review clause can contain a mixture of both.

The evolutionary approach places a lot of importance on the parties' original bargain. It recognises that the parties should be returned to the economic balance that they had at the beginning of their relationship, and provides for this to be done by amending the terms of the contract to restore the original economic balance

---

14 Ashley, Phillip Spencer and Holland, Ben, "Gas Price Reviews: past, present and future", *Global Arbitration Review*, August 2011.

under the new, changed circumstances. This approach can be seen as maintaining, over time, the original economic bargain in the changing circumstances.

The revolutionary approach places little weight on the parties' original bargain. The contract is revised to satisfy the new circumstances. The usual intention is that the provisions of the LNG contract will be changed and that the parties will remain in contractual relations, but under different terms from those originally agreed. If the parties cannot agree on the new terms, they will be determined by a third party. This approach refers not to the change, but to the nature and effect of the prevailing market and circumstances, placing less weight on the original market and contractual balance.

For some, a long-term LNG contract is better defined as a sociological rather than a legal arrangement, with mutual trust and willingness for the contracting parties to share risks and (re)balance interests over the long duration of the contract being the definitive characteristics. Such a relational contract is appropriate for the commitments required in the long-term production and disposal of petroleum products, though it is unusual in the common law framework.

Broadly, a relational arrangement identifies the relationship of the parties, but without precision (at the time of contract formation), on the duration, the subject matter or the identification of quantity, price or substance. In this way, it is said to lack 'presentiation', or the making of a present decision about all future elements of the contractual relationship.

A relational arrangement can be viewed as consistent cooperation rather than the optimisation of the separate positions of each party. Such an approach is said to provide the ability to adjust the relationship over time and allow the parties to phrase their commitments in aspirational terms, with a corresponding requirement that courts or arbitrators should be slow to strike down such a long-term contract, which is expressed in general rather than specific terms. The typical price review provisions discussed above reflect this approach and aspiration.

If the parties' prioritise the aspirations of the relationship over their individual interests, the agreement will be able to evolve and develop according to the prevailing circumstances.

However, recent events in the gas market have shown that if their financial and economic interests diverge, the parties are likely to put their own interests first and seek to strengthen their own position. Today, the price of LNG calculated using the oil-indexed pricing formulae in long-term LNG contracts is different from that achieved by commercial activities at LNG trading hubs. This has caused serious problems for the operation of long-term LNG contracts, as has been seen in the *Atlantic LNG* and other LNG contract arbitrations. Market forces have strained the relational and cooperative nature of long-term LNG contract arrangements.

Given the relational nature of a long-term LNG contract (and the significance of the related investments that parties make and their time in negotiating and drawing up the contract), there is a case to be made that the price review clause should provide for a mechanism which encourages the reapportionment of the value of the shared enterprise, in a way which reflects the risk-sharing nature of the long-term LNG contract.

7. Renegotiation, arbitration or other approaches

7.1 Renegotiation

The *Atlantic LNG*, *Sonatrach* and *Edison* arbitrations raise another question. What is the most appropriate way to deal with price reviews – renegotiation, arbitration or another approach?

Given the relational nature of the long-term LNG contract, in general, settlement between the parties is preferable to adversarial proceedings in carrying out price reviews. Revisiting the price provisions when unforeseen circumstances occur is not so much a matter of dispute as a matter that has been left for agreement at a later date by reference to a contractual system or a third party. It is a matter more for agreement than for dispute, so renegotiation between the parties should be the preferred approach and the first option. Indeed, the preference for meeting and renegotiation between the parties is reflected in the price review clauses that are generally seen in LNG contracts.

Usually, price review clauses provide for a two-tiered approach to price reviews, such that if the condition for price review has arisen and a party has submitted a notice for price review, the parties will meet to examine whether an adjustment of the price provisions is justified and, if so, what adjustments need to be made. The clause's approach is that the best solution is to try to modify the contract and resolve any differences through renegotiation. Normally, it is provided that the renegotiation must take place within a stipulated time.

In recent years, there have been a significant number of LNG contract renegotiations, suggesting that many potential disputes have been settled through renegotiation. For instance, in 2012 it was reported that Gazprom, the major LNG supplier to Europe, had agreed to reduce LNG prices under its oil-indexed long-term contracts with a number of European counterparties, including Germany's E.On, France's GDF Suez, Germany's Wingas, Slovakia's SPP and Turkey's Botas.[15] This resulted in a reported payment of about $24 billion for readjustments of contracts for the period 2010 and 2011.

Usually, the price review clause will provide for one of three next steps if the parties fail to reach agreement within the time for renegotiation stipulated under the LNG contract:

- The LNG contract will terminate (even if otherwise it has many years remaining);
- The LNG contract will continue unamended; or
- There will be reference to an external party.

The external party might be a mediator, who will try to steer the seller and the buyer towards reaching their own agreement. Mediators are not able to force agreement or to make a binding decision. If mediation is not successful (or often without that step at all), typically, long-term LNG contracts provide for binding resolution of the matter by reference to arbitration.

---

15 "Gazprom Gas Price Adjustment Payments to European Customers Total $2.4 bil in Q1", Platts, September 6 2012 (www.platts.com/RSSFeedDetailedNews/RSSFeed/NaturalGas/8700304).

7.2 Arbitration

The *Atlantic LNG* case raises the question of whether arbitration is the best forum for price reviews. Under the arbitration process, the LNG contract will be read in the context of an adversarial relationship and a procedure of dispute resolution. This is likely to polarise the parties into self-interested positions, which is the opposite of the consensual nature of both their original bargain and their agreement for any periodic re-setting of the price provisions.

Controversial cases such as *Atlantic LNG* may encourage parties to resolve their disputes over price adjustment at the first-tier renegotiation stage rather than have an arbitral tribunal impose a possibly undesirable contractual adjustment. However, despite the potential shortcomings of arbitration, long-term LNG contracts must provide a binding dispute resolution mechanism for the event that the parties fail to reach an agreement on price review by consensual means, and arbitration is still the best dispute resolution option in the LNG market. It offers the advantages of:

- neutrality in international LNG deals, which often involve state participants;
- cross-border enforceability through the New York Convention;
- flexibility; and
- confidentiality.

7.3 Other approaches – borrowing from the redetermination mechanism in unitisation agreements

Are there alternatives to renegotiation and arbitration? For gas price reviews, there is a case to be made for appointing a third party to help with the long-term implementation of the contract, in the same way as other well-recognised mechanisms to 'fill in the gaps'. An example is the redetermination process in hydrocarbon reserves development long-term unitisation agreements. It is not suggested that the redetermination mechanism would provide a complete answer to the current perceived drawbacks of referring price review disputes to arbitration, but it could be considered as a potential alternative model.

Commonly, unitisation agreements arise in situations where, for instance, different entities are planning to exploit and develop a hydrocarbon reservoir straddling two or more areas owned by different parties. In essence, unitisation means treating hydrocarbon reserves which straddle interest boundaries as a single unit for the purpose of joint development and operation, and for apportioning costs and profits based on where the reserves lie in relation to the boundaries. As these are long-term projects and require substantial investment, they are unified to avoid competitive drilling (which may lead to sub-optimal exploitation). A major obstacle to unitisation is that, since the respective owners' geological and technical information at the time of unitisation may be limited, a fair allocation of costs and profits at the time of agreement is difficult. To overcome this, unitisation agreements often include a redetermination element, under which the parties agree periodically to revisit or redetermine the allocation of reserves when more data become available, and with the assistance of experts. Unitisation agreements usually provide for managed expert determination if the parties cannot agree on the redetermination.

While the redetermination mechanism in unitisation contracts does have problems,[16] with adaptation it might offer an alternative to the typical renegotiation and arbitration provisions contained in long-term LNG contracts. In particular, the redetermination process offers a workable mechanism under which substantial values are periodically moved between parties over the course of a long-term contract. The contract readjustments are set by managed expert determination. Often, the experts are involved from the start of the contractual relationship and continue throughout its term. The involvement of an expert with whom the parties are familiar may assist in smoothing the process for readjustment negotiation. Moreover, the decision arrived at by the redetermination process is not a 'spot decision' handed down by an arbitral tribunal, but a periodic readjustment which arguably better reflects the relational, cooperative nature of long-term contracts.

The following extract from a unitisation agreement entered into in 2003 between Australia and Timor-Leste in relation to the unitisation of the Sunrise Troubador Fields provides an example:[17]

ARTICLE 8

Reapportionment of Unit Petroleum

(1) *Technical redetermination of the Apportionment Ratio from the Unit Reservoirs may take place in accordance with the following:*

   (a) *Either Australia or Timor-Leste may request the Unit Operator to undertake a redetermination of the Apportionment Ratio.*

   (b) *Australia and Timor-Leste shall have regard to the desirability of minimising the number of reviews of the Apportionment Ratio.*

   (c) *Any redetermination of the Apportionment Ratio shall not occur within five (5) years of any prior redetermination, except that a redetermination may occur within twelve (12) months of the commencement of production from the Unit Reservoirs.*

   (d) *The Unit Operator shall use only commercially available software in a redetermination of the Apportionment Ratio. Only data that is available to both Governments as at the date the redetermination is requested shall be utilised by the Unit Operator and all data and analyses pursuant to the Unit Operator's proposal for the redetermined Apportionment Ratio shall be provided to both Governments with the proposal. The Unit Operator shall use all reasonable endeavours to complete the redetermination within 120 days.*

   (e) *Any change to the Apportionment Ratio arising from a redetermination requested under subparagraph (a) has effect when it is agreed by the Regulatory Authorities or, if referred to an expert for determination, when the expert makes a final decision.*

   (f) *Any change to the Apportionment Ratio shall be retrospective and past receipts and expenditures shall be adjusted.*

---

16 See, for instance, Nwete, Bede, "Mitigating Redetermination Problems in Unitised Hydrocarbon Fields", *International Energy Law & Taxation Review*, 2005, which discusses problems with the redetermination and dispute resolution process in unitisation agreements, and ways to mitigate them.

17 Agreement between the Government of Australia and the Government of the Democratic Republic of Timor-Leste relating to the Unitisation of the Sunrise Troubador Fields dated March 6 2003.

(2) *Notwithstanding paragraph 1, either Australia or Timor-Leste may request a review of the Apportionment Ratio. Following such a review, the Apportionment Ratio may be altered by agreement between Australia and Timor-Leste.*

ARTICLE 26

Settlement of Disputes

(1) *Any disputes about the interpretation or application of this Agreement shall be, as far as possible, settled by consultation or negotiation.*

(2) *Subject to paragraph (3), if a dispute cannot be resolved in the manner specified in paragraph (1) or by any other agreed procedure, the dispute shall be submitted, at the request of either Government, to an Arbitral Tribunal set out in Annex IV.*

(3) *If a dispute arises concerning a proposal for a redetermined Apportionment Ratio pursuant to Article 8(1) or concerning the measurement, pursuant to Article 24, of quantities of gas and liquids, an expert shall be appointed by Australia and Timor-Leste to determine the matter in question. The two Governments shall, within 60 days of notification by either of them of such a dispute, try to reach agreement on the appointment of such an expert. If, within this period, no agreement has been reached, the procedures specified in Annex V shall be followed. The expert appointed shall act in accordance with the terms of Annex V. The expert's decision shall be final and binding on both Governments and on the Sunrise Joint Venturers, save in the event of fraud or manifest error.*

ANNEX V

Expert Determination Procedure

1. *If no agreement is reached on the appointment of an expert within the period specified in Article 26, each Government shall forthwith exchange with the other a list of not more than three independent experts, putting them in order of preference. In each list, the first shall have three points, the second two points and the third one point. The expert having the greatest number of points from the two lists shall be appointed.*
2. *If two or more of the experts named on the lists exchanged by the Governments share the greatest number of points, the Governments shall, within 30 days of exchange, by agreement or, failing that, by lot, select which of the experts shall be appointed to decide the matter in question.*
3. *If the expert to be appointed is unable or unwilling to act, or fails, in the opinion of both Governments, to act within a reasonable period of time to decide the matter in question, then the expert with the greatest number of points among the experts remaining shall be the expert to decide the matter in question. If two or more such experts share the greatest number of points, both Governments shall, by unanimous agreement or by lot, select which expert shall be appointed as the expert to decide the matter in question.*
4. *If a Government fails to respond to any request or notice within the time specified under this Annex, the Government shall be deemed to have waived its rights in respect of the subject of the request or notice but nevertheless shall be bound by the actions of the other Government in selecting an expert and by the decision of the expert.*

5 The task of the expert is to reach an independent determination of whatever matters are in question. Where the matter in dispute is in relation to technical redetermination of the Apportionment Ratio pursuant to Article 8, the expert's decision must be made in accordance with any technical procedures and calculation formula pertaining to redetermination as set out in the relevant Joint Venturers' Agreement.

6. The expert may engage independent contractors to undertake work which is necessary to enable the expert to reach a decision, provided that any contractor nominated by the expert for that purpose is approved by the Governments and gives an undertaking that neither it nor any of its personnel has a conflict of interest which would prevent it from undertaking the work.

7. The fees and costs of the expert shall be paid initially by the Government which first:

(a) initiated the redetermination of the Apportionment Ratio; or

(b) disagreed with the measurement, pursuant to Article 24, of quantities of gas and liquids;

and shall be recoverable from the Unit Operator. The latter shall be required to use best efforts to reimburse the initial payer within 12 months of the payment of those fees and costs.

8. Except as set out in this Agreement, the expert shall establish its own procedures. The expert shall only meet with a Government jointly with the other Government. All communications between the Governments and the expert outside those meetings shall be conducted in writing and a person making any such communication shall at the same time send a copy of it to the other Government.

9. The expert shall use only commercially available software in a redetermination of the Apportionment Ratio. Only data that was available to both Governments as at the date that the redetermination was requested shall be utilised by the expert and all data and analyses relevant to the expert's preliminary and final decisions for the redetermined Apportionment Ratio shall be provided to both Governments with those decisions.

10. Forthwith upon the appointment of the expert, the Unit Operator shall supply the expert with its data and analyses. Within 30 days of that appointment, each Government will make an initial submission and provide a copy to the other Government. Within 20 days of receiving a copy of that submission, the Government concerned may make a supplementary submission (again providing a copy to the other Government).

11. The expert shall issue a preliminary decision within a period of 90 days, or such other period as the Governments may decide, commencing from the date the expert was appointed. The preliminary decision shall be accompanied by such supporting documentation as is necessary for the Governments to make a reasoned assessment of that decision. Each Government has the right, within 90 days of receipt of the expert's preliminary decision, to seek clarification of that decision and the supporting documentation, to request the expert to review its preliminary decision and to make submissions to the expert for its consideration. If such a request is made, the other Government shall, within a period of 15 days after receipt of a copy of those submissions, have the right to make further submissions. The expert shall issue its final decision on the matter in question no later than 140 days from the date of issue of the preliminary decision. The expert's final decision shall be in writing and the expert shall give detailed reasons for that decision.

12. *The Sunrise Joint Venturers shall cooperate fully in supplying information required by the expert and otherwise in facilitating the expert to reach its decision.*
13. *The Governments shall require the expert and any independent contractor engaged by the expert to give an undertaking to safeguard the confidentiality of any information supplied to the expert.*

In practice, a process has developed where the independent expert (once agreed upon) is involved not only in the 'dispute phase' of the redetermination, but also in the 'agreement phase', where the parties seek (often in the context of contractual commitments of good faith and reasonable endeavours) to adjust the contractual terms towards the changed circumstances. A carefully chosen expert, with the necessary skills, will help the contractual relationship, for example, in maintaining the approach of seeking the best outcome for both parties (as in the original negotiation process) rather than pursuing an outcome based on the individual party's perceived rights or entitlements. The presence of a third party throughout the process (and with the powers to make binding determinations as the parties will disagree from time to time) can reinforce the parties' common interests and discourage the approach of 'winning today's argument' that can arise in some processes of dispute resolution outside of long-term, relational contracts. Among other things, the expert will be aware of the parties' approaches and arguments during the agreement phase and so can address any inconsistent approaches and arguments during the dispute phase.

A different process, which is often discussed (although in our experience rarely adopted) in relation to price reopeners, is a 'pendulum' or 'baseball' procedure. In essence, this is an agreed, limited procedure in which each party must make a specific submission for the resolution of the dispute in its favour, and the appointed expert is required only to choose between the submissions. Often, the submission selected will be the one which is closest to the expert's own opinion. It is sometimes said that, rather than seeking to find the right answer to a dispute, the expert in this procedure is seeking to find the less wrong of the two proposals. The 'all or nothing' nature of such a process sometimes brings the parties' positions closer together (for reasons such as the fear of losing all by claiming too much), and in cases of a relatively simple or single question and the availability of extensive and detailed relevant data eg, a baseball player's performance from which the process takes one of its names) this may be the case. However, it is rarely considered to be appropriate in the context of the multi-faceted considerations of fact, law and markets which are usually required in relation to a price reopener provision; and, particularly, where there is likely to be little relevant information or data, and, to the extent it exists, it is likely to be available to one party more than the other.

While none of these examples is particularly appropriate for price reopener provisions, nevertheless, they may form a basis for the development of alternatives to the more traditional approach, which has recently been seen to carry the real risk that, after a comparatively short time, an unknown group of third parties might rewrite the agreed pricing provisions for, potentially, the majority of the life of the LNG contract so painstakingly put together by the parties, often over long periods of negotiation.

8. Some suggestions on improving the price review regime to cater for the new realities

8.1 Suggestions regarding price review clauses

Given the discussions above and in light of the recent *Atlantic LNG* decision, it is suggested that the usual form of price review clause could be improved in a number of general ways.

First, it seems that the traditional two-tiered approach to price review – renegotiation, failing which, arbitration – does not do enough to assist or encourage the parties to come to a mutual and voluntary agreement before resorting to adversarial arbitration proceedings. Given the relational nature of the long-term LNG contract, more emphasis could be placed on effecting the price review through mutual agreement. For this, it is suggested that an extra tier could be inserted between the renegotiation stage and the arbitration stage, thus encouraging the parties, with the help of a properly qualified third party, to come to a voluntary agreement. Such three-tiered dispute resolution provisions – renegotiation, mediation and then arbitration – are commonly seen in other commercial contexts. Of course, there is nothing to stop parties agreeing to refer a pricing dispute to mediation at any stage, but incorporating this requirement in the dispute resolution provisions may provide additional encouragement to the parties to reach agreement without having to resort to adversarial proceedings.

Second, in light of the surprising rewriting of the pricing formula in *Atlantic LNG* decision, there is much to be said for restricting the ambit of a price review arbitration. Potential restrictions could include limitations on the factors the tribunal should or should not take into account in considering the price review and which aspects of the contract or the price formulae could be subject to change. These could be provided contractually in the price review clause.

Third, the parties could contractually provide to divide the arbitration process to deal first with the often heavily contested initial issue of whether the price review mechanism has been triggered, and if the tribunal concludes that it has, secondly, deal with how the price formula should be readjusted. Splitting the arbitration in this way could also be agreed or proposed to the tribunal at the procedural stage after arbitration has been initiated. This approach would help the parties to focus the preparation of their case on one issue at a time, and arguably avoid a situation where the tribunal is not fully assisted by the parties on price adjustment submissions because the claimant overreaches itself in the claimed amount and the respondent focuses on fighting the trigger issue but not the price adjustment issue (which is what the authors suspect happened in the *Atlantic LNG* arbitration). Also, this approach would save time and costs if the tribunal decided that the circumstances did not trigger the price review provisions.

8.2 Nature of third party

Irrespective of which dispute resolution mechanism is adopted – arbitration, expert determination or another procedure – the involvement of an expert in the field who understands the technical aspects of LNG pricing is more likely to produce an appropriate outcome. Clearly, an expert will be required if the contract provides for dispute resolution through expert determination.

However, it is often difficult to find a suitably qualified expert who is willing and able to act. In highly specialised areas such as the LNG market, the pool of experts is small, and those best qualified may be employed (perhaps by the competitors of the parties in dispute) and therefore unavailable.

Other important qualities for any mediator or arbitrator are the ability to control contentious proceedings, to deal with a large volume of witness and paper evidence and to interpret the relevant provisions in the contract. These skills are more often found in lawyers and professional arbitrators than in LNG pricing experts.

Unfortunately, very few experts in LNG pricing possess legal training. The solution may be for any mediation or arbitration to be conducted by a combination of industry experts and lawyers. Alternatively, the expert contribution in arbitration proceedings can, of course, come in the form of expert witness evidence.

8.3 An industry issue; an industry solution?

Some would argue that the issue of LNG pricing disputes is an LNG industry and market issue that requires an appropriate response. Despite the move in some markets to liquid gas or LNG prices, many of today's LNG sale and purchase agreements still have price reopener clauses and, given the long-term nature of these contracts, many of these clauses will continue to apply from some time past and for some time to come. The increase in LNG pricing disputes in recent years stems from market forces which are undermining LNG prices based on oil-indexation under long-term LNG contracts as a result of the widening gap compared with LNG prices in the more liquid markets for gas, which are now present in certain parts of the world. One potential approach to this problem is for the industry to produce a reliable and industry-recognised pricing or dispute resolution system to improve what are seen by many people as the difficulties of the traditional model. Given the significant sums at stake in long-term LNG contracts and the growing number of renegotiations and disputes arising in the evolving market, it may now be time for the industry to revisit traditional price review and dispute resolution clauses and consider how best to optimise the process. A number of suggestions to this end are made above. Ultimately, price review clauses are unusual provisions, often with complex terms and circumstances of application. In these unique circumstances, it seems right to question why the prescribed processes for resolving periodic disputes should continue to be those of a more standard model.

The authors would like to thank Cliff Chow, Allen & Overy, Hong Kong, for his kind assistance in the preparation of this chapter.

Appendices

A. PRICE REVIEW DECISIONS

1. *Esso Exploration & Production UK Limited v Electricity Supply Board* (2004)
2. *Atlantic LNG Company of Trinidad & Tobago v Gas Natural Aprovisionamientos SDG,* S.A Decision of the US Federal Court (2008)

B. EXAMPLES OF PRICE REVIEW CLAUSES IN GAS SUPPLY CONTRACTS

1. Sonatrach and Distrigas Corporation LNG SPA (1976)
2. ICC Cases 9812 (August 1999) and 13504 (January 2007)
3. SPA between Atlantic LNG company of Trinidad and Tobago and Gas Natural LNG (1995)
4. *Esso Exploration & Production UK Limited v City Supply Board* [2004] EWHC 723 (Comm)
5. Sample price review clause from the Energy Charter Secretariat (2007)
6. Clauses suggested as typical price review clauses

A. PRICE REVIEW DECISIONS

1. *ESSO EXPLORATION & PRODUCTION UK LIMITED V ELECTRICITY SUPPLY BOARD* (2004)[1]

1. The applicant, Esso Exploration and Production UK Ltd ("Esso"), is a member of the well-known Exxon group. The respondent, Electricity Supply Board ("ESB"), is the Irish state-owned electricity generating company which operates a combined cycle gas turbine power station at Poolbeg near Dublin.
2. On 27th November 1997 Esso and ESB entered into a contract for the sale and purchase of certain quantities of natural gas each year for a period of 15 years from the date when deliveries began. In the event that was 1st October 1999. The contract provides for adjustments to be made from time to time in the price payable for gas supplied under it and a dispute has arisen between the parties as to the meaning of certain of those provisions. Esso has sought to refer that dispute to arbitration, but ESB has challenged the arbitrators' jurisdiction on the grounds that certain prerequisites to a valid reference to arbitration have not been satisfied. The matter comes before me by way of an application by Esso for

1 [2004] EWHC 723 (Comm).

a declaration that the tribunal has jurisdiction to determine the dispute. It is made under section 32(1) of the Arbitration Act 1996 with the consent of ESB.

3. The contract in question is lengthy and complex, but for the purposes of the present application it is only necessary to refer in any detail to some of the provisions of clause 12 which deals with the price and the manner in which it is to be adjusted during the period of the contract.
4. The price itself is made up of two elements, an Energy Charge and a Delivery Point Capacity Charge. Only the terms dealing with the adjustment of the Energy Charge are relevant for present purposes. Clause 12.2 provides that the Energy Charge is to be reviewed and adjusted every 6 months by reference to four markers: (i) the price of gasoil (30%), (ii) the price of low sulphur fuel oil (30%), (iii) the price of natural gas (30%) and (iv) the rate of inflation in Ireland as reflected in the industrial wholesale price index (10%). In each case the relevant marker is the average over the 12 month period ending 3 months prior to the review date. The prices to be taken for the three commodities are in effect the spot prices for delivery North West Europe.
5. The Energy Charge contains two elements: an amount expressed in pence per kilowatt hour ("Po") and an amount in respect of transportation. Clause 12.6 records that the parties had fixed the initial value of Po by agreement at a level that reasonably reflected the market price at the date of the agreement obtainable for the sale of reasonably similar quantities of gas over a reasonably similar period on reasonably similar terms and conditions between parties of reasonably similar commercial and financial standing for use in a reasonably similar type of power station in the UK or Ireland.
6. In addition to the automatic review and adjustment provided for by clause 12.2, clause 12.6(1) allows the parties to give Price Review Notices requiring a separate review of the Energy Charge at carefully regulated intervals throughout the life of the contract. By clause 12.6(6) a Price Review Notice cannot be given by the seller unless

   "...it is reasonably satisfied in good faith that the Energy Charge ... is at the time of giving such Price Review Notice eighty five per cent (85%) or less than the Comparator."
7. The Comparator referred to in clause 12.6(1) is defined in the opening section of clause 12.6 as follows:

   "The market price ... at the date of the relevant Price Review Notice for natural gas being supplied on the basis described above...",

   that is, on the basis of the sale of reasonably similar quantities over a reasonably similar period on reasonably similar terms and conditions between parties of reasonably similar commercial and financial standing for use in a reasonably similar type of power station in the UK or Ireland.
8. By paragraph (8) a party giving a Price Review Notice is obliged to specify in the notice itself the value of the Energy Charge which it is requesting; it is also obliged to provide the other party with a reasonably detailed explanation of how it has reached that figure and to provide it with all reasonably available published and other non-confidential information to support its position. The parties are then to negotiate with a view to agreeing an adjustment to the Energy Charge,

but in default of agreement within 90 days the Price Review Notice must be withdrawn or the matter referred to arbitration to determine the Comparator and the consequent adjustment to the price.

9. On 1st November 2002 Esso wrote to ESB giving notice under clause 12.6(1) that it required a review of the Energy Charge. In that letter it stated that it was reasonably satisfied in good faith that the Energy Charge was 85% or less than the Comparator and gave its explanation for reaching that view. From that explanation it was apparent that it had determined the value of the Comparator by taking the price quoted in the Heren Report for delivery of a fixed quantity of natural gas to be delivered daily at the Bacton terminal for a period of a year (which it considered to be a generally recognised base market indicator) and adjusting it to reflect the particular terms of the contract with ESB.
10. ESB rejected Esso's Price Review Notice on the grounds that it did not comply with the contract. Its detailed reasons for rejecting it were not explained as clearly as they might have been at the time, but it has now become clear that its objection is based on the fact that the Comparator adopted by Esso is based on the market price for deliveries over 12 months rather than on prices actually being paid in the market for gas being supplied under long-term sale contracts. In these circumstances the parties were unable to reach agreement on an adjustment to the Energy Charge and arbitrators were appointed. However, ESB maintained that, since Esso had used the wrong Comparator, the Price Review Notice was invalid and therefore no dispute had arisen of a kind contemplated by the contract. Accordingly, there was no dispute capable of being referred to arbitration and the tribunal lacked jurisdiction. In those circumstances Esso made this application to the court.
11. The dispute between the parties falls within a very narrow compass. It ultimately turns on the construction of the second sentence of the opening section of clause 12.6 which defines the Comparator, although both parties pray in aid the nature of the contract and what they suggest are the underlying commercial considerations. Esso says that the purpose of clause 12.6 is to ensure that the Energy Charge does not become too far out of line with the current market price for natural gas. Accordingly, if it is not possible to obtain evidence of the price being paid in the market for long-term supplies of gas for power generation under contracts between first class sellers and buyers, an appropriate "market rate" should be calculated by taking the prices being paid for short term supplies and making suitable adjustments. ESB, on the other hand, says that the Comparator is defined as the market price for natural gas actually being supplied under contracts between similar parties on similar terms for similar purposes. If, as seems to be the case, there is currently no market for long-term supplies, the Comparator does not exist and no adjustment to the Energy Charge can be made under clause 12.6.
12. Although Esso is seeking a declaration that the arbitrators appointed in this case have jurisdiction to determine the amount of the Comparator under paragraph (11), the real dispute between the parties relates to the construction of clause 12.6 and the true nature of the Comparator. The line between the nature of the

Comparator and its amount may be a fine one, but in my view the jurisdiction of arbitrators appointed pursuant to paragraph (10) is limited to determining its amount. Accordingly, I do not think that they have jurisdiction to determine the question now in issue in any event.

13. Both parties have proceeded on the assumption that the service of a valid Price Review Notice is necessary if the arbitrators are to have jurisdiction to determine the amount of the Comparator under paragraph (11) and it is for that reason that argument has been directed to the validity of Esso's notice. In my view that is correct. The arbitrators' jurisdiction, as I have pointed out, is limited to determining a dispute that falls within the terms of the contract and has been properly referred to them. The mechanism leading to the creation of a dispute of that kind begins with the service of a Price Review Notice. If a notice is given that does not in substance correspond with the requirements of the contract, it is invalid and ineffective and the other party is free to ignore it. It follows that none of the machinery for determining the Comparator can be invoked against him, no dispute can arise that is capable of being referred to arbitration and any arbitrators appointed to determine the amount of the Comparator will necessarily lack jurisdiction.

14. The terms governing the service of a Price Review Notice are set out in paragraphs (1)-(8) of clause 12.6. One question that arises is whether compliance with paragraph (6) is a pre-condition to the validity of the notice. Mr. Rabinowitz Q.C. on behalf of Esso was inclined to accept that it is, though he submitted that the requirement that the seller be reasonably satisfied in good faith that the Energy Charge has fallen to, or below, 85% of the Comparator is essentially subjective in nature. Accordingly, if the information available to the seller has given rise to a reasonable level of satisfaction on his part that the Energy Charge had fallen to that level, the notice is valid even if in reaching that view the seller has applied the wrong test.

15. Mr. Howard Q.C. for ESB did not accept that construction of paragraph (6). He submitted that the expression "reasonably satisfied" means "satisfied on reasonable grounds". I think that is right. If the parties had wished to impose a purely subjective test it would have been sufficient to require the party giving the notice simply to be satisfied in good faith that the relevant circumstances existed. To go further and specify the necessary degree of satisfaction would be surprising and largely pointless; it would also give rise to an unnecessary element of uncertainty and consequent difficulty of application. An element of objectivity, however, in the form of the existence of reasonable grounds for satisfaction has the merit of providing a degree of protection to the other party by ensuring that there is a proper basis for putting the machinery of clause 12.6 into motion.

16. The right to give Price Review Notices is tightly controlled by paragraphs (2) (5). Both parties have the right to give such notices, but only four in all can be given throughout the life of the contract and those at carefully defined intervals. Accordingly, unless it is later withdrawn, a notice given by one party, whether it results in an adjustment to the Energy Charge or not, necessarily affects the rights of the other, both as to the number of notices that it can give and as to

their timing. That makes it much more likely, in my view, that the parties intended that the procedure should only be invoked when circumstances really justified it and one obvious way of achieving that end is to require the party giving a notice to have reasonable grounds for doing so. That conclusion is reinforced by the terms of paragraph (8) which requires the party giving the notice to explain how it has determined the adjustment to the Energy Charge it is seeking and to support its case with all reasonably available published and other non-confidential information. I conclude, therefore, that the expression "reasonably satisfied" in paragraph (6) means "satisfied on reasonable grounds".

17. The next question is whether, as Mr. Howard submitted, a Price Review Notice given contrary to the terms of paragraph (6) is invalid and ineffective. Clause 12.6 does not directly address that question, but the terms of paragraph (6) suggest that the existence of circumstances that are capable of justifying the conclusion that the existing Energy Charge has diverged to the necessary extent from the Comparator is intended to be a pre-condition to the right to invoke the procedure. It is highly desirable, of course, that the validity of a notice of that kind should be apparent on its face, but in the present case the requirements of paragraph (8) ought to ensure that it is. I find it difficult to accept that the parties intended that a Price Review Notice given in contravention of paragraph (6) was to count as one of the four notices allowed by paragraph (5). Equally, I find it difficult to accept that they intended that the procedure in paragraphs (9)-(12), including, where necessary, arbitration proceedings, could effectively be set in motion unless there were circumstances to justify it. Indeed, the opening paragraph of clause 12.6 states that the Energy Charge shall be subject to review "in either of the circumstances as defined in paragraphs (6) and (7) of this clause". I agree with Mr. Howard, therefore, that a Price Review Notice given by a party who does not have reasonable grounds for being satisfied that the Energy Charge has diverged to the required extent from the Comparator is invalid and ineffective.

18. I turn next, therefore, to the meaning of the Comparator. Mr. Howard submitted that the expression used in clause 12.6, namely, "the market price . . . . . for natural gas being supplied on the basis described above" (i.e. between parties of similar standing under a long-term contract on similar terms and for similar purposes) was intended to refer to the price for gas actually obtainable in the market under a similar long-term contract at the date of the Price Review Notice as ascertained by reference to other contracts of a similar kind. This might be called an 'actual' market price. Mr. Rabinowitz submitted, on the other hand, that the expression was intended to refer to the price at which gas would be supplied under a similar contract negotiated in the market between a willing buyer and a willing seller at the date of the Price Review Notice, if any business of that kind were to be done. This might be called a 'notional' market price.

19. As with any question of construction, the starting point must be the words chosen by the parties themselves to express their intentions, but with due regard to the commercial and contractual context in which they are found. The contract bears all the signs of having been carefully drafted with considerable attention to

detail, so I think it is right, as Mr. Howard submitted, to approach it on the assumption that the words used in clause 12.6 were chosen with some care. I accept that the expression "market price" is not a term of art, but it is fair to say that over the course of time it has acquired a reasonably well-recognised meaning as the price at which goods or services of the relevant kind can be bought or sold among a body of willing buyers and willing sellers: see *The Arpad* [1934] P. 189 at page 202 per Scrutton L.J., approved in *Attorney-General of the Republic of Ghana v Texaco Overseas Tankships Ltd* (The '*Texaco Melbourne*') [1994] 1 Lloyd's Rep. 473. Moreover, it is here found in a contract for the sale of goods and in a clause the first sentence of which refers to the "market price" in terms of the price actually obtainable in the market for goods of the kind in question.

20. On the face of it, therefore, there are powerful indications that the parties used the expression "market price" in this case to mean the actual market price as opposed to a notional market price. It was common ground, however, that by November 2002 neither producers nor consumers were interested in entering into long-term contracts for the sale and purchase of gas and that there was therefore no active market for the sale of gas on terms comparable to those of the present contract. However, I do not think that that of itself matters, even if it has rendered the machinery temporarily unworkable. What matters for present purposes is whether at the time they entered into the contract the parties contemplated that there would be such a market. The terms of the contract suggest that they did, and indeed Mr. Rabinowitz did not submit otherwise. His case was that the parties could not have intended the price review to be carried out by reference to a Comparator derived from the actual market for long-term supplies because that would have been unworkable. They must, therefore, have intended it to be carried out by reference to other material so as to produce a notional rather than an actual market price.

21. Mr. Rabinowitz's argument was based mainly on what he submitted was the practical impossibility of obtaining any reliable information about prices being obtained under other comparable contracts. He drew attention to the fact that the present contract contains a clause which requires the parties to treat its terms and conditions, as well as all information disclosed to each other pursuant to it or in the course of their negotiations, as confidential throughout the period of the contract and for 5 years thereafter. He submitted that a clause of that kind was usually included in such contracts, a view that was supported by the evidence filed on behalf of both Esso and ESB.

22. In the light of that evidence I think one must accept that the parties proceeded on the footing that most, if not all, long-term contracts would be likely to contain confidentiality provisions of some kind. No doubt they could be waived on request, if the parties to the contract in question were so inclined, but there is no reason to think that the parties to the present contract made any assumption one way or the other about that. It must also be remembered that the market for the long-term supply of gas to power stations was necessarily very small. There were only a few companies willing and able to promise long-term non-interruptible supplies and only a few power generators seeking to buy gas on

such terms. Mr. Rabinowitz submitted that the parties must have been aware of these matters and must have appreciated that they could not expect to obtain, or, if necessary, place before the arbitrators, sufficient reliable information of prices actually being paid in the market under comparable contracts to enable price reviews to be carried out on that basis.

23. I think it is helpful to begin by considering the fundamental purpose of the price review provisions insofar as that can be discerned from the contract. The price at which gas or any other commodity is sold under a long-term contract will reflect many different factors. These will usually include, among other things, the current price for prompt delivery, any price being quoted for delivery at a future date, the parties' perception of the likely movement of prices in the longer term and the particular terms of the contract. In the present case the parties took account of future movements in the price of fuel used for power generation by providing for regular adjustments of the price by reference to the average over the preceding 12 months of the prices of three different fuels for immediate delivery. It is true that the indexation formula was not linked to the price of gas alone and to that extent could not be expected directly to reflect changes in the price of gas, but that was the parties' choice. It seems to me, therefore, that insofar as the parties intended to adjust the price by reference to changes in short term fuel prices, clause 12.2 was the means they chose. What clause 12.2 by its very nature could not achieve, however, was an adjustment to reflect the other factors that have a bearing on the price payable under a long-term contract, such as the value to be attributed to non-interruptibility of supply, to take but one example.

24. The effect of a price review under clause 12.6 is to alter the value of the Energy Charge which forms the basis for the subsequent periodic adjustments under clause 12.2. Accordingly, I think its purpose must have been to reflect changes in the value being attributed to the other factors that influence the price payable under a long-term contract, not simply to reflect changes in the spot or short term future price for gas. The extent to which factors of that kind affect the price paid under any given contract must depend to a considerable degree on the particular terms of the contract. It is essential, therefore, that any comparison be based on contracts between similar parties on similar terms, as clause 12.6 requires. However, there remains the problem of how one is to determine the impact of such factors in monetary terms.

25. At this point one comes back to the language of the second sentence of clause 12.6 itself. I think that some significance is to be attached to the fact that it refers not to "the market price obtainable" for natural gas supplied on similar terms and under similar circumstances, as the first sentence does, but to "the market price for natural gas being supplied" on that basis. Mr. Rabinowitz submitted that those words were used simply to identify the purpose of the Comparator, i.e. to show that it is intended to be the price for gas supplied under a long-term rather than a short-term contract, but in my view the change in language reflects the intention of the parties to direct the reader to the price at which gas is currently being supplied under contracts broadly similar in all respects to the present

contract rather than to a notional market price based on the current price for short-term delivery. That in my view is the natural meaning of the words used, but I can see at least two practical reasons why the parties should have looked to similar long-term supply contracts to provide the Comparator. First, because setting a long-term price taking into account all the relevant factors involves a substantial element of commercial judgment; it also depends on the parties' negotiating strengths. Prices set by negotiation in the market place are likely to reflect on average all the factors that have a bearing on the outcome more reliably than the assessment of any arbitrators. Secondly, because, if there really is no market in the long-term sale of gas to power stations, there is no need to re-base the price in order to keep it in line with current market prices under contracts of that kind. If the parties had intended that a new base price should be calculated in any event using whatever information was available, I think that clause 12.6 would have been worded in a way which made that clear. In my view the language used throughout the clause is more consistent with determining the actual price at which gas is being supplied than with calculating a notional market price. For completeness I would only add that I do not think that the second sentence of clause 12.6 limits the parties to contracts made within any particular period prior to the giving of a Price Review Notice. Clause 12.6 defines the Comparator as the market price for natural gas being supplied on the basis described above which will include reasonably similar price review terms. Where gas is currently being supplied under long-term contracts made through the ordinary operation of the market in previous years, the price at which it is currently being supplied may be as relevant as the price payable under a contract negotiated within the last few months.

26.The only question that remains, therefore, is whether the parties cannot have intended to refer to actual market prices because they did not think that it would be possible to obtain sufficient reliable information about the terms on which gas was being supplied. I am not persuaded that that was their view or that as a result they intended to adopt instead a notional market price as the Comparator. Although there is evidence, which I accept, that most long-term sale contracts include confidentiality clauses, there is no concrete evidence that the parties acted on the common assumption that reasonably reliable information about prices currently being charged under long-term contracts would not become available either to them or to arbitrators appointed by them to determine the Comparator. It is interesting to note that paragraph (12) of clause 12.6 allows the arbitrators to rely on all information available to them, not just that provided by the parties. That would entitle them to make use of any knowledge they may have acquired, for example, in the course of their own work. Moreover, if the parties had thought that reasonably reliable information about prices currently being paid under long-term contracts was not likely to be available, I think it most unlikely that they would have left the matter as it stands instead of recognising the difficulty and stating more clearly how the notional market price was to be determined.

27.For these reasons I am satisfied that the Comparator mentioned in clause 12.6 is the actual market price of natural gas currently being supplied under comparable contracts rather than a notional market price derived from the prices for spot or short-term deliveries. It is apparent that in giving its Price Review Notice Esso was proceeding under the mistaken impression that the Comparator was a notional market price and that it was not satisfied, nor, as far as one can tell from the notice, did it have reasonable grounds for being satisfied, that the Energy Charge had diverged to the required extent from the true Comparator. In those circumstances the notice was invalid and no dispute arose that was capable of being referred to arbitration. It follows that the arbitrators lack jurisdiction to make any determination under clause 12.6 and that this application must be dismissed.

2. *ATLANTIC LNG COMPANY OF TRINIDAD & TOBAGO V GAS NATURAL APROVISIONAMIENTOS SDG,* S.A DECISION OF THE US FEDERAL COURT (2008)[2]

DENISE COTE, District Judge

Petitioner Gas Natural Aprovisionamientos, SDG, S.A. (GNA) has filed this petition for confirmation of an arbitration award, and for attorney's fees and costs Respondent Atlantic LNG Company of Trinidad and Tobago (Atlantic) has opposed the petition and filed a motion to vacate the arbitration award. Atlantic principally disagrees with the arbitrators' solution to a dispute over a pricing formula. Unhappy with the arbitration panel's resolution of this hotly contested issue, Atlantic contends that the panel "exceeded its authority." For the following reasons, the arbitration award is confirmed and the motion to vacate is denied. Petitioner's request for attorney's fees is also denied.

BACKGROUND

Atlantic, a company organized under the laws of the Republic of Trinidad and Tobago, is a producer of liquefied natural gas (LNG). In July 1995, it entered into a sales contract with a Spanish company that was GNA's predecessor in interest. The long-term supply contract provides for Atlantic to sell LNG to GNA that Atlantic produces at a facility in the Caribbean (Train 1 LNG), with deliveries beginning in 1999 and continuing for a term of 20 years. The contract further specifies that GNA may transport the LNG to its receiving facilities in Spain or to a facility in New England (New England Receiving Facilities).

Although GNA has an unlimited right under the contract to transport its deliveries of Train 1 LNG to the New England Receiving Facilities, at the time the contract was drafted, the parties expected that the Train 1 LNG would be consumed in Spain. The pricing formula specified in the contract is thus tied to the European energy market. The formula consists of a base price and a multiplier indexed quarterly to the European prices for certain substitute petroleum products.

The contract also includes a "price reopener" provision, whereby either party may request a revision of the pricing formula if it establishes that certain

2 2008 WL 4344525 (SDNY September 16 2008).

preconditions have been met. Specifically, Article 8.5(a) of the contract provides:

> If at any time either Party considers that economic circumstances in Spain beyond the control of the Parties, while exercising due diligence, have substantially changed as compared to what it reasonably expected when entering into this Contract *or, after the first Contract Price revision under this Article 8.5, at the time of the latest Contract Price revision under this Article 8.5,* and the Contract Price resulting from application of the formula set forth in Article 8.1 does not reflect the value of Natural Gas in the Buyer's end-user market, *then such Party may, by notifying the other Party in writing and giving with such notice information supporting its belief, request that the Parties should forthwith enter into negotiations to determine whether or not such changed circumstances exist and justify a revision of the Contract Price provisions and,* if so, to seek agreement on a fair and equitable revision of the above-mentioned Contract Price provisions *in accordance with the remaining provisions of this Article 8.5.*

(emphasis added). If the parties are unable to agree upon a new pricing formula within six months, Article 8.5(f) permits either party to "submit the matter to arbitration for decision in accordance with the criteria set out" in the contract for price reopener proceedings. An arbitration clause in the contract provides generally for arbitration to be conducted in New York City and in accordance with the UNCITRAL Arbitration Rules.

After the parties entered into the contract in 1995, Spain's natural gas market was substantially liberalized. As Spanish gas prices decreased, the New England market became more attractive and GNA entered into a long-term agreement to resell all of its Train 1 LNG deliveries at the New England Receiving Facilities.[3] Indeed, GNA has not delivered any Train 1 LNG to Spain since at least October of 2002. Citing these circumstances, Atlantic notified GNA on 21 April 2005 that it was seeking a revision to the contract price. Because the parties were unable to agree on a new formula, Atlantic demanded arbitration on 21 October 2005, requesting an upward revision to the contract price to reflect the value of natural gas in the New England market.

A three-person arbitration panel (the Tribunal) was formed, and it held an initial conference with the parties on 26 July 2006. After denying a motion by GNA to dismiss Atlantic's price reopener claim, and in accordance with a schedule jointly submitted by the parties, the Tribunal conducted hearings over the course of 12 days in April, May, and June 2007. The parties submitted post-hearing briefs in August and October 2007, and they presented their post-hearing arguments before the Tribunal on 14 and 15th November 2007. On 17 January 2008, the Tribunal unanimously issued a 34-page Final Award, which it then clarified and corrected on 27 March 2008.[4]

In the Final Award, the Tribunal first determined that Article 8.5(a)'s requirements for a price reopener had been met. It proceeded to explain that "the Buyer's end-user market is either Spain or New England depending on where the

---

3 This agreement is expected to continue until at least March 2009.

4 The corrected decision was issued in response to a request for clarification from Atlantic. Among other changes, the tribunal agreed that current prices should be used in place of lagged prices in calculating the New England component of the tribunal's new pricing scheme.

LNG is delivered." It concluded, therefore, that "since New England should be the basis for determining the value of natural gas when the Train 1 LNG is being sold in New England on a sustained basis, the Contract Price needs to include a New England Market Adjustment factor." Accordingly, the Tribunal decided to institute a two-part pricing scheme. First, it preserved the Spanish pricing formula contained in the contract but revised its base price component. Second, the Tribunal added a "New England Market Adjustment" for quarters in which more than a percentage identified in its decision (the Percentage) of the Train 1 LNG is resold for delivery to the New England Receiving Facilities. This pricing scheme was made effective from 21 April 2005, the date on which Atlantic notified GNA that it was seeking a price reopener. As a result of this revised pricing scheme, Atlantic owed GNA over $70 million for the period from 21 April 2005 through 31 December 2007.[5] The Tribunal declined to impose interest payments on the retroactive adjustment, and it rejected the parties' respective requests for attorney's fees and costs, concluding that neither one could be regarded as "the unsuccessful party." GNA now seeks to confirm this Final Award, while Atlantic has moved to vacate it.[6]

DISCUSSION

Atlantic contends that the Final Award must be vacated because the Tribunal violated the Federal Arbitration Act (FAA), 9 U.S.C. § 10(a)(3) and (4), and the Convention on the Recognition and Enforcement of Foreign Arbitral Awards (New York Convention), Art. V, when it acted in excess of its authority, acted against public policy, and violated Atlantic's due process rights. "[I]t is well-settled that the FAA does not confer subject matter jurisdiction on the federal courts even though it creates federal substantive law." *Greenberg v Bear, Stearns & Co.*, 220 F.3d 22, 25 (2d Cir. 2000). Rather, "[t]here must be an independent basis of jurisdiction before a district court may entertain petitions under the [FAA]." *Perpetual Sec., Inc. v Tang*, 290 F.3d 132, 136 (2d Cir. 2002) (citation omitted); see also Greenberg, 220 F.3d at 25. Jurisdiction over the petition in this action exists pursuant to the New York Convention, implemented by 9 U.S.C. §§ 201-08, because the Final Award involves foreign commerce and non-U.S. parties. See id. §202; *Yusuf Ahmed Alghanim & Sons, W.L.L. v Toys "R" Us, Inc.*, 126 F.3d 15, 19 (2d Cir. 1997).[7]

The New York Convention "specifies seven exclusive grounds upon which courts may refuse to recognize an award."

Encyclopaedia Universalis S.A. v Encyclopaedia Britannica, Inc., 403 F.3d 85, 90 (2d Cir. 2005) (citation omitted). But because the arbitration took place in the United States, this action is also subject to the FAA's provisions governing domestic arbitration awards. *Zeiler v Deitsch*, 500 F.3d 157, 164-65 (2d Cir. 2007). Section 10

5 Atlantic paid this deficiency in full on April 16 2008, and it has invoiced Train 1 LNG under the new contract price since the date of the Final Award.

6 GNA initially filed its petition to confirm the Final Award on February 4 2008, but it later submitted an amended petition *nunc pro tunc* after the tribunal issued its corrections. In its original petition, GNA had sought injunctive relief, which Atlantic opposed on its motion to vacate. GNA has omitted from the amended petition its earlier request for injunctive relief.

7 The parties agree that the enforcement provisions of the New York Convention apply to this confirmation proceeding.

provides the FAA's exclusive grounds for vacatur. *Hall Street Assocs., L.L.C. v Mattel, Inc.*, 128 S. Ct. 1396, 1403 (2008). Of these grounds, Atlantic relies principally on Section 10(a)(4) of the FAA, which permits vacatur "where the arbitrators exceeded their powers."[8] 9 U.S.C.§ 10(a)(4). It relies, as well, on the public policy provision of the New York Convention, Art. V(2)(b) (permitting courts to refuse recognition of an award that "would be contrary to the public policy of that country"), and on the due process provisions of the FAA, 9 U.S.C. § 10(a)(3) (providing for vacatur "where the arbitrators were guilty of misconduct . . . in refusing to hear evidence pertinent and material to the controversy; or of any other misbehavior by which the rights of any party have been prejudiced"), and the New York Convention, Art. V(1)(b) (allowing courts to refuse recognition where "[t]he party against whom the award is invoked was . . . unable to present his case").

> *"Normally, confirmation of an arbitration award is a summary proceeding that merely makes what is already a final arbitration award a judgment of the court, and the court must grant the award unless the award is vacated, modified, or corrected."* D.H. Blair & Co. v Gottdiener, *462 F.3d 95, 110 (2d Cir. 2006) (citation omitted). A court's review of an arbitration award is "severely limited" so as not unduly to frustrate the goals of arbitration, namely to settle disputes efficiently and avoid long and expensive litigation.* Willemijn Houdstermaatschappij, BV v Standard Microsystems Corp., *103 F.3d 9, 12 (2d Cir. 1997) (citation omitted). Arbitration awards are not reviewed for errors made in law or fact. Id. Moreover, "[t]he arbitrator's rationale for an award need not be explained, and the award should be confirmed if a ground for the arbitrator's decision can be inferred from the facts of the case."* D.H. Blair & Co., *462 F.3d at 110 (citation omitted). Only a barely colorable justification for the outcome reached by the arbitrators is necessary to confirm the award." Id. (citation omitted). Thus, "the showing required to avoid confirmation is very high," id. (citation omitted), and a party moving to vacate an arbitration award bears "the heavy burden of showing that the award falls within a very narrow set of circumstances delineated by statute and case law."* Duferco Int'l Steel Trading v T. Klaveness Shipping A/S, *333 F.3d 383, 388 (2d Cir. 2003).*

EXCESS OF POWERS

The FAA allows for vacatur of an arbitration award "where the arbitrators exceeded their powers." 9 U.S.C. § 10(a)(4).[9] The Second Circuit has "consistently accorded the narrowest of readings to the Arbitration Act's authorization to vacate awards pursuant to § 10(a)(4)." *Westerbeke Corp. v Daihatsu Motor Co., Ltd.*, 304 F.3d 200, 220

---

8 In the introductory pages of its brief, Atlantic also cites to Article V.1(c) and (d) of the New York Convention, apparently as additional bases for the excess of powers argument that it makes. Atlantic does not, however, specifically rely on these subsections in its legal analysis.

9 Article V(1)(c) of the New York Convention, as implemented by 9 USC § 207, similarly provides that a court may refuse to enforce an arbitration award if it "deals with a difference not contemplated by or not falling within the terms of the submission to arbitration, or it contains decisions on matters beyond the scope of the submission to arbitration". This defence "tracks in more detailed form" the excess of powers provision of the FAA, 9 USC § 10(a)(4), and should likewise "be construed narrowly". *Parsons & Whittemore Overseas Co v Societe générale de L'Industrie du Papier*, 508 F2d 969, 976 (2d Cir. 1974). "Both provisions basically allow a party to attack an award predicated upon arbitration of a subject matter not within the agreement to submit to arbitration." *Id.*

(2d Cir. 2002) (citation omitted). A court's "inquiry under § 10(a)(4) thus focuses on whether the arbitrators had the power, based on the parties' submissions or the arbitration agreement, to reach a certain issue, not whether the arbitrators correctly decided that issue." *DiRussa v Dean Witter Reynolds Inc.*, 121 F.3d 818, 824 (2d Cir. 1997). "[A]s long as the arbitrator is even arguably construing or applying the contract and acting within the scope of his authority, that a court is convinced he committed serious error does not suffice to overturn his decision." *United Paperworkers Int'l Union v Misco, Inc.*, 484 U.S. 29, 38 (1987); accord Local 1199, *Drug, Hosp. & Health Care Employees Union v Brooks Drug Co.*, 956 F.2d 22, 25 (2d Cir. 1992). Thus, while an "arbitrator may not ignore the plain language of the contract, . . . a court should not reject an award on the ground that the arbitrator misread the contract." *United Paperworkers*, 484 U.S. at 38.

Atlantic describes two ways in which the Tribunal exceeded its authority. It asserts first that the Tribunal revised the contract price despite finding that the contractual conditions precedent had not been met. Second, Atlantic contends that, having decided to alter the contract price, the Tribunal impermissibly imposed a dual price scheme. In neither instance has Atlantic carried its heavy burden of showing that the Tribunal exceeded its powers. Each of these theories is analyzed in turn.

Conditions Precedent

Although the Tribunal explicitly stated in the Final Award that "[t]he requirements for a price reopener under Article 8.5(a) have been met," Atlantic argues that the Tribunal's assertion is belied by its analysis of the parties' contentions on this issue. Specifically, Atlantic had argued that the liberalization of the Spanish natural gas market constituted an unexpected changed circumstance in Spain and thus satisfied the first precondition of Article 8.5(a). But in explaining the Final Award, the Tribunal stated that "[a]lthough the liberalized market was foreseen by both sides, the real test is whether those developments significantly disrupted the expected relationship between the Contract Price and the value of natural gas." Focusing on this statement, Atlantic argues that the Tribunal conflated the first precondition of Article 8.5(a) with the second, relying solely on a divergence between the contract price and the value of natural gas without first finding any unexpected changed circumstance in Spain that precipitated that discrepancy.

Atlantic's argument quibbles with the reasoning in the Tribunal's decision and does not suggest any abuse of power by the Tribunal. It is undisputed that the Tribunal had the power to decide whether the requirements for a price reopener had been met; indeed, the Tribunal was specifically assigned this responsibility. Atlantic has conceded this point since it was Atlantic that initiated the price reopener and arbitration and argued strenuously before the Tribunal for a new price formula. That it now finds fault with the explanation given by the Tribunal in agreeing with Atlantic is irrelevant under § 10(a)(4).[10]

Atlantic's additional arguments concerning the contractual conditions precedent – made in footnotes – that the Tribunal manifestly disregarded the law and violated public policy are similarly unavailing. Even if the doctrine of "manifest disregard of the law" could be said to have survived the Supreme Court's recent decision in *Hall*

Street Associates, 128 S. Ct. at 1403-04, and thus remain available as an avenue to attack an arbitration award, the Tribunal did not – as Atlantic contends – ignore or refuse to apply the preconditions set forth in the contract. *See Hardy v Walsh Manning Sec., L.L.C.*, 341 F.3d 126, 129 (2d Cir. 2003). To the contrary, the Final Award explicitly describes the requirements of Article 8.5(a), and it then applies them in a separate section labeled "Application of Contract Provisions to the Issues Raised in this Proceeding."

Similarly, Atlantic asserts that, by effectively merging the two conditions of Article 8.5(a), the Tribunal contravened the "fundamental and well established public policy" in the United States "that a contract be applied and enforced as written." "[C]ourts may refuse to enforce arbitral awards only in those rare cases when enforcement of the award would be directly at odds with a well defined and dominant public policy." *Saint Mary Home, Inc. v Serv. Employees Int'l Union, Dist. 1199*, 116 F.3d 41, 46 (2d Cir. 1997); see also *United Paperworkers*, 484 U.S. at 43 ("At the very least, an alleged public policy must be properly framed ... and the violation of such a policy must be clearly shown if an award is not to be enforced."). The Tribunal's decision is plainly grounded in its reading of the parties' contract and thus not at odds with any public policy identified by Atlantic.

Pricing Scheme

Atlantic next argues that the Tribunal exceeded its powers by imposing a pricing scheme that – in Atlantic's view – skewed the original bargain between the parties and effectively rewrote their contract. Specifically, the new "dual price structure," which provides one price when more than the Percentage of the Train 1 LNG is delivered to the New England Receiving Facilities, and another price otherwise, gives GNA the unbargained-for ability to determine which of two quarterly prices will apply to all shipments merely by shifting its Train 1 LNG deliveries.

This contention is also insufficient to permit vacatur of the Tribunal's decision. It is undisputed that the Tribunal was specifically charged with the duty to revise the pricing scheme once it determined that the contractual preconditions were met. The Tribunal having made that determination, Article 8.5(a) required it to reach "a fair and equitable revision" of the contract price. Neither this standard nor any other contractual provision set a structural limitation on permissible price revisions. Indeed, Atlantic's submissions to the Tribunal acknowledged the Tribunal's broad authority in this regard. In them Atlantic opined that the relevant contractual terms "do not appear to expressly limit this Tribunal's award to the imposition of a single pricing formula." Atlantic's argument concerning the dual pricing formula is better

10 Although Atlantic's attack on the tribunal's Award could not succeed even if Atlantic were able to show that the tribunal had misread the contract, it should be noted that Atlantic has not identified a flaw in the tribunal's reasoning. Article 8.5(a) sets out two preconditions for revising the contract price. The first is an unexpected change in "economic circumstances in Spain". Atlantic argues that the tribunal could not have found this first condition satisfied since its opinion notes that the parties foresaw the deregulation of the Spanish LNG market. These two findings, one implicit and the other explicit, are not necessarily inconsistent. Even if deregulation was foreseen, other changes in the market for LNG could be unexpected ones. Indeed, Atlantic itself had argued to the tribunal that the impact of US prices on the Spanish market price of LNG was unexpected and satisfied the first precondition of Article 8.5(a).

understood as a challenge to the merits of the Tribunal's decision. Such a challenge is unavailing since the Court does not review arbitration awards for legal or factual errors.

Finally, Atlantic emphasizes the parties' purportedly shared belief, expressed to the Tribunal during its proceedings, that a dual price structure would be improper. In light of this agreement between the parties, Atlantic argues, the Tribunal did not have the authority to impose a two-price formula. Even though "[p]arties to an arbitration may stipulate the issues they want determined and increase or limit the arbitrator's contractual authority by their express submission," *Hill v Staten Island Zoological Soc'y, Inc.*, 147 F.3d 209, 214 (2d Cir. 1998), the parties may not add grounds to vacate or modify an arbitration award. *Hall Street Assocs.*, 128 S. Ct. at 1405. Thus, to vacate the award Atlantic must show that the Tribunal was not acting within the scope of its authority. *United Paperworkers*, 484 U.S. at 38.

Atlantic has not shown that the parties reached any agreement that limited the Tribunal's authority to impose a dual price structure. It is true that when the Tribunal requested post-hearing briefing from the parties as to "[w]hether it is possible to have two different prices based on two different markets," both parties argued against such a scheme. GNA argued in favor of a single Spanish price for all deliveries; Atlantic contended that a single price based on the New England market should apply to all deliveries.[11]

These arguments over the wisdom of a dual pricing scheme, however, cannot be reasonably construed as an agreement to restrict the Tribunal's authority to adopt that scheme. Indeed, in opposing the Tribunal's suggestion of a two-price system, Atlantic limited its analysis to "the present facts," while accepting that under certain circumstances "it might, in theory, be possible to 'have two different prices based on two different markets.'" Thus, Atlantic foresaw that a dual scheme would be permissible, and it points to no stipulation by the parties depriving the Tribunal of the power to fashion such a price revision.

DUE PROCESS

Atlantic argues briefly that the Tribunal violated Atlantic's due process rights.[12] The FAA provides for vacatur "where the arbitrators were guilty of misconduct in refusing to postpone the hearing, upon sufficient cause shown, or in refusing to hear evidence pertinent and material to the controversy; or of any other misbehavior by which the rights of any party have been prejudiced." 9 U.S.C. § 10(a)(3).

Similarly, the New York Convention, Art. V(1)(b), permits courts to reject arbitration awards where "the party against whom the award is invoked was not given proper notice of the appointment of the arbitrator or of the arbitration proceedings or was otherwise unable to present his case." The Second Circuit has explained that these provisions protect "the fundamental requirement of due process," which is "the opportunity to be heard at a meaningful time and in a

11 Under the new scheme imposed by the tribunal, one price does apply to all deliveries irrespective of their location; the only difference is that the singular price to be applied to all deliveries depends on the quantity of deliveries made to the New England Receiving Facilities.

12 Atlantic largely abandons its due process argument in its reply brief, relegating it to a footnote.

meaningful manner." *Iran Aircraft Indus. v Avco Corp.*, 980 F.2d 141, 146 (2d Cir. 1992) (citation omitted).

Atlantic was not denied the opportunity to be heard in a timely and meaningful manner. The arbitration involved substantial amounts of briefing, as well as 12 days of hearings and two days of post-hearing argument. Atlantic's only complaint is that, because "[t]he Tribunal never disclosed any terms of the dual pricing scheme prior to issuing the Final Award, ... Atlantic was unable to present evidence or argument regarding that scheme." As noted above, however, the parties were invited to provide post-hearing briefing on the possibility of including "two different prices based on two different markets." Having requested these supplemental submissions and conducted extensive hearings, the Tribunal was under no obligation to reveal its decision to the parties and accept additional comments before issuing the Final Award. Its failure to do so in these circumstances does not constitute a violation of due process.

ATTORNEY'S FEES

Finally, GNA seeks attorney's fees for the confirmation proceeding. It does not point to any statutory or contractual authority for such legal fees, instead relying on the Court's inherent equitable powers.

> *Pursuant to its inherent equitable powers, . . . a court may award attorney's fees when the opposing counsel acts in bad faith, vexatiously, wantonly, or for oppressive reasons. As applied to suits for the confirmation and enforcement of arbitration awards, . . when a challenger refuses to abide by an arbitrator's decision without justification, attorney's fees and costs may properly be awarded.*

Int'l Chem. Workers Union (AFL-CIO), Local No. 227 v BASF Wyandotte Corp., 774 F.2d 43, 47 (2d Cir. 1985) (citation omitted).

Atlantic's motion to vacate the arbitration award does not present any argument of merit. On the other hand, Atlantic has complied with the Tribunal's decision pending the outcome of this confirmation action: It paid the retroactive deficiency due under the amended version of the Final Award on 16 April 2008, which was within the 90-day period set by the Tribunal. It has also invoiced Train 1 LNG in accordance with the new contract price since 17 January 2008, the date the Final Award was issued. In light of these facts, this Court does not find that it is appropriate to award attorney's fees.

CONCLUSION

The 4 February 2008 petition to confirm the arbitration award is granted. The 16 April 2008 motion to vacate is denied. Petitioner's request for attorney's fees and costs is denied. The Clerk of Court shall enter judgment for the petitioner and close the case.

B. EXAMPLES OF PRICE REVIEW CLAUSES IN GAS SUPPLY CONTRACTS

1. SONATRACH AND DISTRIGAS CORPORATION LNG SPA (1976)[13]

"The parties agree to meet regularly to proceed with the revision of the Contractual Sales Price defined in Article 9 above. They shall so meet for the first time during the first quarter of the year 1980 and thereafter every four (4) years.

The revision of the price shall consist in adapting it in a reasonable and fair manner to the economic circumstances then prevailing on the imported Natural Gas market and on the market for the other imported energy supplies competing with this production in the East Coast and Gulf Coast areas of the United States of America within the framework of long-term contracts. The parties shall take into account the individual characteristics of each of the above products including the quality, the continuity of deliveries, the production and transportation costs, etc..."

2. ICC CASES 9812 (AUGUST 1999) AND 13504 (JANUARY 2007)[14]

The long-term gas sales and purchase contract at the heart of both these arbitrations contained the following price review mechanism (Article 6.10 of the contract):

"(a) *If the economic circumstances in the country of the Buyer which are beyond the control of the Parties should change significantly compared to what is reflected in the prevailing price provisions under Articles 6.1-6.4 hereof, then each Party shall be entitled to an adjustment of the price provisions under Articles 6.1-6.4 hereof, reflecting such changes, in particular the value of Natural Gas in the end-user market of the buyer as such value can be obtained by a prudent and efficient gas company.*

In any case the price provisions hereunder shall allow the Buyer to economically market the Processed gas delivered hereunder in the market of the Buyer in competition with all competing sources of energy in the end-user market always assuming sound marketing practices and efficient operations on the part of the Buyer.

(b) *Either Party shall be entitled to request a review of the price provisions under Articles 6.1-6.4 hereof for the first time with effect as of 1 April 1992 or earlier if necessary in order to perform a price review six (6) months prior to start of deliveries, for the second time with effect as of 1 October 1995 and thereafter with effect as of 1 October every three (3) years after 1 October 1995. In addition each Party shall be entitled to request a review of the price provisions under Articles 6.1-6.4 hereof once within each such three-year interval with effect from the first day of the month next following the request for price review, provided that the total number of such additional requests shall be limited to three (3) for each Party during the term of this Agreement. Any request for price review shall be made in writing substantiating the reasons for it and shall be made before the date of effectiveness of such price review and shall be ineffective if received by the other Party after such date.*

Following a request for price review under this Article, the Parties shall meet to

---

13 Available at www.fossil.energy.gov. Distrigas Corporation Docket No 88-37-LNG, Exhibit E-1: Agreement for the Sale and Purchase of Liquefied Natural Gas of 13 April 1996.

14 *ICC International Court of Arbitration Bulletin*, Vol 20/2, 2009, pp69-76 and pp93-109.

examine whether or not an adjustment of the said price provisions is justified.

(c) *Each Party shall provide all necessary information to substantiate its own claim. No Party shall be required to disclose any business secrets nor to provide such information as the other Party may need to substantiate its claim.*

(d) *Failing agreement within a period of one hundred and twenty (120) days from the request for review, either Party may refer such matter to arbitration under the provisions of Article 15 hereof for decision in accordance with the criteria contained in lit. (a) above.*

(e) *If and as long as, with respect to any price review hereunder, no agreement has been reached and no arbitration award has been made and taken effect, this Agreement shall remain in full force and effect and the rights and obligations of the Parties, including, without limitations, the obligations of the Seller to sell and deliver and the obligations of the buyer to take and pay for at the applicable price Processed gas as provided for under this Agreement, shall remain applicable unchanged and unadjusted.*

(f) *If the rights under this Article 6.10 are exercised by the Buyer against the Seller they shall also be exercised against all other Associated Sellers under their [Contracts] with the Buyer as of the same date.*

If any rights under Article 6.10 lit. (b), second sentence, are exercised by any of the Associated Sellers as of a certain date, then the Seller shall not be permitted to exercise such rights as of any other date and an additional request made by one or more Associated Sellers, but not by the Seller shall be counted also against the number of additional requests allowed for the Seller.

All negotiations under this Article 6.10 shall be conducted by the Buyer and the Seller jointly with all other Associated Sellers by or against whom a price review under their [Contract] with the Buyer is requested.

3. SPA BETWEEN ATLANTIC LNG COMPANY OF TRINIDAD AND TOBAGO AND GAS NATURAL LNG (1995)[15]

The price reopener clause in Article 8.5(a) of the LNG SPA provided:

If at any time either Party considers that economic circumstances in Spain beyond the control of the Parties, while exercising due diligence, have substantially changed as compared to what it reasonably expected when entering into this Contract or, after the first Contract Price revision under this Article 8.5, at the time of the latest Contract Price revision under this Article 8.5, and the Contract Price resulting from application of the formula set forth in Article 8.1 does not reflect the value of Natural Gas in the Buyer's end-user market, then such Party may, by notifying the other Party in writing and giving with such notice information supporting its belief, request that the Parties should forthwith enter into negotiations to determine whether or not such changed circumstances exist and justify a revision of the Contract Price provisions and, if so, to seek agreement on a fair and equitable revision of the above-mentioned Contract Price provisions in accordance with the remaining provisions of this Article 8.5.

---

15 Taken from *Gas Natural Aprovisionamientos v Atlantic Lng Company of Trinidad and Tobago* (2008) WL 434425 (SDNY).

4. *ESSO EXPLORATION & PRODUCTION UK LIMITED V CITY SUPPLY BOARD* [2004] EWHC 723 (COMM)

The judgment of the High Court described the price review clause, Clause 12 of the contract for the sale and purchase of natural gas, as follows:

4. *The price itself is made up of two elements, an Energy Charge and a Delivery Point Capacity Charge. Only the terms dealing with the adjustment of the Energy Charge are relevant for present purposes. Clause 12.2 provides that the Energy Charge is to be reviewed and adjusted every 6 months by reference to four markers: (i) the price of gasoil (30%), (ii) the price of low sulphur fuel oil (30%), (iii) the price of natural gas (30%) and (iv) the rate of inflation in Ireland as reflected in the industrial wholesale price index (10%). In each case the relevant marker is the average over the 12 month period ending 3 months prior to the review date. The prices to be taken for the three commodities are in effect the spot prices for delivery North West Europe.*
5. *The Energy Charge contains two elements: an amount expressed in pence per kilowatt hour ("Po") and an amount in respect of transportation. Clause 12.6 records that the parties had fixed the initial value of Po by agreement at a level that reasonably reflected the market price at the date of the agreement obtainable for the sale of reasonably similar quantities of gas over a reasonably similar period on reasonably similar terms and conditions between parties of reasonably similar commercial and financial standing for use in a reasonably similar type of power station in the UK or Ireland.*
6. *In addition to the automatic review and adjustment provided for by clause 12.2, clause 12.6(1) allows the parties to give Price Review Notices requiring a separate review of the Energy Charge at carefully regulated intervals throughout the life of the contract. By clause 12.6(6) a Price Review Notice cannot be given by the seller unless*

   ". . . . . it is reasonably satisfied in good faith that the Energy Charge . . . . . is at the time of giving such Price Review Notice eighty five per cent (85%) or less than the Comparator."
7. *The Comparator referred to in clause 12.6(1) is defined in the opening section of clause 12.6 as follows:*

   "The market price . . . . . at the date of the relevant Price Review Notice for natural gas being supplied on the basis described above . . . . . ", that is, on the basis of the sale of reasonably similar quantities over a reasonably similar period on reasonably similar terms and conditions between parties of reasonably similar commercial and financial standing for use in a reasonably similar type of power station in the UK or Ireland.
8. *By paragraph (8) a party giving a Price Review Notice is obliged to specify in the notice itself the value of the Energy Charge which it is requesting; it is also obliged to provide the other party with a reasonably detailed explanation of how it has reached that figure and to provide it with all reasonably available published and other non-confidential information to support its position. The parties are then to negotiate with a view to agreeing an adjustment to the Energy Charge, but in default of agreement within 90 days the Price Review Notice must be withdrawn or the matter referred to arbitration to determine the Comparator and the consequent adjustment to the price.*

5. SAMPLE PRICE REVIEW CLAUSE FROM THE ENERGY CHARTER SECRETARIAT (2007)[16]

The Energy Charter Secretariat provides the following sample price review clause:

(a) If the circumstances beyond the control of the Parties chance significantly compared to the underlying assumptions in the prevailing price provisions, each Party is entitled to an adjustment of the price provisions reflecting such changes. The price provisions shall in any case allow the gas to be economically marketed based on sound marketing operation.

(b) Either Party shall be entitled to request a review of the price provisions for the first time with effect of dd/mm/yyyy and thereafter every three years.

(c) Each Party shall provide the necessary information to substantiate its claim.

(d) Following a request for a price review the Parties shall meet to examine whether an adjustment of the price provisions is justified. Failing an agreement within 120 days either Party may refer the matter to arbitration in line with the provisions on arbitration of the Contract.

(e) As long as no agreement has been reached or no arbitration award has been rendered all rights and obligations under the agreement – including the price provisions – shall remain applicable unchanged. Unless otherwise agreed or decided by the arbitral award, differences to the newly established price shall be retroactively compensated inclusive of interest on the difference calculated at a rate reflecting the conditions on the international financing market.

6. CLAUSES SUGGESTED AS TYPICAL PRICE REVIEW CLAUSES

The following clauses have been suggested as examples of typical price review clauses by practitioners:

6.1 Matthew Vinall, 2009:[17]

If a circumstance beyond the control of either party results in a significant change in the energy market of the Buyer compared to such energy market on [date], then either party may give notice for a price review.

If the parties fail to agree a revised price formula within 90 days after giving notice for a price review, the price formula shall be reviewed by arbitration.

In any such arbitration the arbitrators shall review the price formula and shall decide whether it needs to be revised to reflect, as at the review date, the relevant significant change(s) in the energy market of the Buyer which affect the value of [the product] in the end-user market of the Buyer as such value can directly or indirectly be obtained by a prudent and efficient buyer.

Any revised price formula determined by the arbitrators shall enable the Buyer to market economically [the product] delivered under this Agreement in the energy market of the Buyer in competition with other competing sources of energy in the end-user market of

---

16 Energy Charter Secretariat, *Putting a Price on Energy: International Pricing Mechanisms for Oil and Gas* (2007), 155, Box 9, at www.encharter.org/fileadmin/user_upload/document/Oil_and_Gas_Pricing_2007_ENG.pdf.

17 Matthew Vinall, *If You Start to Feel the Pinch, Will a Price Review Clause Ease Your Suffering?* (2009) 1 IELR 17–19.

18 James Baily and Paula Hodges *LNG – A Minefield For Disputes?*, Liquefied Natural Gas, Paul Griffin (2nd Ed) (2012), 244.

the Buyer, assuming always the Buyer acts as a prudent and efficient energy company."
6.2 James Baily and Paula Hodges, 2012:[18]
"Either party may request a review of the method for determining the Contract Sales Price set forth in Clause X if it has a good faith basis for believing that, for reasons outside its control, there has been a significant change in the value of imports into Y and/or regasified LNG in the Y market which is anticipated to have lasting effect.

About the authors

Martje de Vries Lentsch
Senior associate, De Brauw
Blackstone Westbroek NV
martje.devrieslentsch@debrauw.com

Martje de Vries Lentsch is a senior associate in the litigation and arbitration department of De Brauw Blackstone Westbroek in Amsterdam. She holds a degree in law and is specialised in commercial arbitration.

Ms de Vries Lentsch has been involved in and continues to work on several gas price review arbitrations, representing both buyers and sellers under long-term gas sales agreements. These agreements are governed by a variety of legal systems and provide for arbitration in various European jurisdictions. Her experience enables her to advise clients on both legal and economic issues related to price reviews.

Other commercial arbitrations that Ms de Vries Lentsch has worked on include two major arbitrations in the semiconductor industry under the International Chamber of Commerce Rules in Paris related to the interpretation of a chip manufacturing agreement and a party's exit from a joint venture.

Colm Gibson
Energy and utilities expert
colm.gibson@yahoo.com

Colm Gibson has over 20 years' experience in the energy and utility sector, mainly in the natural gas industry, in a variety of engineering, regulatory and commercial roles. He has advised various participants in a broad range of gas contract arbitrations in Northern, Central and Eastern Europe, covering around 35 billion cubic metres a year of gas in total. He is an expert on price control reviews and competition matters in the energy and utilities sectors.

He specialises in producing evidence and reports to influence external stakeholders, particularly to support companies and government authorities in price control negotiations and in assisting companies to prepare to challenge price control decisions.

He holds both MA and MEng degrees from University of Cambridge and an LLB (Hons), and is a chartered chemical engineer.

Paul Griffin
Partner, Allen & Overy
paul.griffin@allenovery.com

Paul Griffin has more than 30 years of experience as a lawyer practising in the deals and disputes of the oil and gas business around the world. Following the prevailing trends over time has led to Mr Griffin being based in Europe and in Asia, and to a broad expertise across oil, natural gas and liquefied natural gas. In recent years, natural gas and liquefied natural gas transactions have come to the fore, and the rapid changes in these markets and their pricing relationships and contract forms have led to a strong theme of natural gas and liquefied natural gas disputes and renegotiations in his recent work.

Tristram Kennedy Harper
General manager legal, Sirius Well Manufacturing Services (a Royal Dutch Shell joint venture)
T.KennedyHarper@SWMS.com

Tristram Kennedy Harper is currently general manager legal for a multinational Royal Dutch Shell Plc joint venture and is based in Beijing. He worked as a financial analyst for five years, mostly based in the Far East, after completing his MBA. He returned to the United Kingdom to retrain as a lawyer. After qualifying as a solicitor in 1995 and obtaining an LLM, Mr Kennedy Harper worked in private practice and at the British Broadcasting Corporation.

He moved to Royal Dutch Shell Plc in 2001, and has worked for Shell for the past 12 years in a variety of legal roles based in the United Kingdom, the Netherlands and China. While in The Hague, Mr Kennedy Harper worked on gas and liquefied natural gas-related projects in Africa and Europe. Upon the merger of Shell's European gas sales and marketing businesses and its relocation to London, he took responsibility for supporting both the emissions trading and European gas marketing businesses in the Shell Trading business. Mr Kennedy Harper was responsible for providing contentious and non-contentious legal support on a number of European price reviews for both gas and liquefied natural gas for the last four years.

Marnix Leijten
Partner, De Brauw Blackstone Westbroek NV
marnix.leijten@debrauw.com

Marnix Leijten chairs the arbitration department of De Brauw Blackstone Westbroek NV and works at the Amsterdam office of the firm.

Mr Leijten handles arbitration cases in a wide variety of industries, administered by the world's leading arbitration institutes and situated in many different countries. He has particular experience in advising large corporates in the electricity, oil and natural gas markets. This experience has been enhanced by his previous role as a litigator at Cravath, Swaine & Moore LLP in New York. Mr Leijten has advised on a large number of gas price review disputes over the last decade, for a variety of leading gas suppliers and buyers. In 2012/2013 Mr Leijten represented clients on over 15 gas price review disputes.

Mr Leijten has been the Dutch member of the International Chamber of Commerce International Court of Arbitration in Paris since 2006 and frequently writes and lectures on arbitration and cross-border litigation.

Mark Levy
Partner, Allen & Overy LLP
Mark.Levy@AllenOvery.com

Mark Levy is a partner in Allen & Overy's international arbitration group. He is based in the London office. He has a degree in English literature from Oxford University and has worked exclusively on international arbitration matters for over 10 years.

Mr Levy specialises in energy and commodity disputes. He has extensive experience of acting as counsel in both commercial and investment treaty arbitrations, often as lead counsel. His recent experience has been focused on the oil and gas sector, and in particular liquefied natural gas disputes.

He has acted in some of the largest recent gas price review disputes in the world, involving various markets in Europe as well as markets in Asia and the Middle East. He has also acted in pricing disputes involving commodities such as alumina.

David Mildon
Barrister, Essex Court Chambers
dmildon@essexcourt.net

David Mildon QC read economics and then law at Cambridge University. He has practised as an advocate from Essex Court Chambers, London since 1980. His practice covers a wide range of commercial litigation, international arbitration and dispute resolution. He has been involved both as advocate and as expert determiner in a number of determinations in the international energy industry. His main fields of practice include oil, gas and electricity litigation, insurance, banking, shipping and the international sale of goods and financial services. He has appeared as advocate or arbitrator in diverse locations, including Singapore, Hong Kong, Dubai, Paris, Geneva, Budapest and Antigua. He has given papers on oil, gas and electricity-related topics at international conferences, and also on shipping law issues at The London Shipping Law Centre.

Boaz Moselle
Senior managing director, FTI Consulting
boaz.moselle@fticonsulting.com

Boaz Moselle is a senior managing director in FTI Consulting's economic and financial consulting practice, based in London. He is an economist specialised in energy markets, who has worked in academia, consulting and government. He has testified in a number of international arbitrations, on issues including developments in natural gas markets and their implications for pricing in long-term gas supply contracts; quantification of damages arising from breach of contract; the impact of the financial crisis on investments in infrastructure; and the economic analysis of competition law claims.

Dr Moselle was previously a managing director at the UK energy regulator Ofgem and an assistant professor at Northwestern University. He holds a PhD in economics from Harvard University and an MA and PhD in mathematics from the Universities of Cambridge and London.

Philippe Pinsolle
Partner, Quinn Emanuel Urquhart & Sullivan LLP
ppinsolle@shearman.com

Philippe Pinsolle is a partner at Quinn Emanuel Urquhart & Sullivan LLP in Paris and specialises in international arbitration. He has been involved, as counsel or arbitrator, in more than 150 international arbitrations, both institutional and *ad hoc*, concerning activities such as investment, oil and gas, energy, telecommunications and defence. He is a member of the Paris Bar and of the Bar of England & Wales (Gray's Inn). He is the author of numerous articles and case notes on international arbitration.

Michael Polkinghorne
Partner, White & Case LLP
mpolkinghorne@whitecase.com

Michael Polkinghorne is a dual-qualified (civil and common law) lawyer, resident in Paris, where he heads the White & Case office's arbitration department and is co-head of the energy department. He has advised petroleum clients on projects in Southeast Asia, South America, the Middle East, Europe, the Commonwealth of Independent States and North Africa.

Having served as counsel and arbitrator in arbitrations conducted under most major rules, Mr Polkinghorne has significant experience in the areas of foreign direct investment and acting for and against states.

In the context of gas price reopeners, he has drafted standard-form gas sale agreements and advised both buyers and sellers in the context of negotiations, and the resolution of disputes where negotiations fail. Having advised on the Russian gas crises of 2006 and 2009, he regularly advises parties in gas price arbitrations (piped gas and liquefied natural gas), as well as acting as arbitrator.

Jonathan Stern
Chairman and senior research fellow, Oxford Institute for Energy Studies
jonathan.stern@oxfordenergy.org

Jonathan Stern is chairman and a senior research fellow at the Natural Gas Research Programme of the Oxford Institute for Energy Studies. He is also honorary professor at the Centre for Energy, Petroleum and Mineral Law and Policy, University of Dundee; visiting professor at Imperial College's Centre for Environmental Policy in London; part-time BP professor at the Moscow School of Management's Energy Centre at Skolkovo; and a fellow of the Energy Delta Institute. Since 2011 he has been the EU speaker for the EU-Russia Gas Advisory Council. He is the author of several books and many shorter works on energy and natural gas issues in the United Kingdom, Europe (western and eastern), the former Soviet Union and Asia. His most recent edited book is *The Pricing of Internationally Traded Gas*, published by Oxford University Press in 2012.

Frances van Eupen
Partner, Allen & Overy
frances.vaneupen@allenovery.com

Frances van Eupen is a partner in Allen & Overy's arbitration group, based in Hong Kong. She has advised a range of clients in arbitrations under various arbitration rules, involving jurisdictions such as Hong Kong, Singapore, the United Kingdom, the Philippines, Malaysia, Taiwan, India and China. She has extensive experience of oil and gas disputes, and is currently acting for clients in a $500 million claim against the Indian government arising under two production sharing contracts. Ms van Eupen regularly appears as an advocate at hearings and speaks at conferences on arbitration related issues in Asia. She is admitted to practise in England and Hong Kong, and is a member of the Chartered Institute of Arbitrators.

George von Mehren
Global chair, international dispute resolution, Squire Sanders
George.vonmehren@squiresanders.com

George von Mehren is the global chair of the international dispute resolution practice group at Squire Sanders. Recent editions of the American Lawyer's Arbitration Scorecard have recognised three of his victories as among the largest awards in the world during the past decade.

With more than 35 years' experience in complex adversarial proceedings, Mr von Mehren has acted as lead counsel in many major commercial and investment treaty arbitrations involving the energy, financial, gold mining, telecommunications and manufacturing industries. In 10 of those cases, claims exceeded $1 billion. He also acts as an arbitrator. He is recognised as a leading counsel in price review proceedings and other disputes involving natural gas and liquefied natural gas.

Mr von Mehren received his JD from Harvard University, his MA and BA, from Cambridge University and AB, *magna cum laude*, from Harvard University. He is a registered foreign lawyer in England and Wales and a US representative to the ICC Commission on Arbitration.

Michael Young
Partner, Allen & Overy LLP
michael.young@allenovery.com

Michael Young specialises in international arbitration and is the co-head of the global arbitration practice of Allen & Overy LLP. He has advised and represented clients in numerous arbitrations throughout the world, both *ad hoc* and under each of the major institutional rules. He sits on the International Chamber of Commerce Court of Arbitration.

Although experienced across different industry and market sectors, he has a specific focus on energy, chemicals and natural resources disputes. Those disputes have arisen worldwide, with a particular focus on the Caspian, the Middle East, Europe and Africa. He has significant experience in price review arbitrations, having acted on numerous disputes in both Europe and Asia.

He acts regularly as advocate before arbitral tribunals and experts, and sits frequently as an arbitrator himself. He has also written and spoken widely on arbitration, as well as teaching at the Faculty of Law at Sciences Po in Paris and the faculty of the University of London LLM arbitration programme in Paris.

Index